D0394219

TO HELL

ON A

FAST HORSE

TO HELL
ON A
FAST HORSE

BILLY THE KID, PAT GARRETT,

AND THE EPIC CHASE TO

JUSTICE IN THE OLD WEST

MARK LEE GARDNER

WILLIAM MORROW

An Imprint of HarperCollins*Publishers*

Grateful acknowledgment is made to the following for the use of the photographs that appear throughout the text: Collection of the author (pp. 97, 195); Robert G. McCubbin Collection (pp. 9, 14, 61, 65, 68, 73, 86, 140, 152, 157, 160, 251); Center for Southwest Research, University of New Mexico (pp. 33, 56, 59, 61, 163); Collection of the Massachusetts Commandery, Military Order of the Loyal Legion, U.S. Army Military History Institute (p. 78); University of Texas at El Paso Library, Special Collections Department (pp. 85, 95, 221, 224, 230); Pinal County Historical Museum (p. 245).

HarperCollins books may be purchased for educational, business, or sales promotional use. For information please write: Special Markets Department, HarperCollins Publishers, 10 East 53rd Street, New York, NY 10022.

FIRST EDITION

Designed by Cassandra J. Pappas

Library of Congress Cataloging-in-Publication Data

Gardner, Mark L.
    To hell on a fast horse : Billy the Kid, Pat Garrett, and the epic chase to justice in the Old West / Mark Lee Gardner.—1st ed.
        p.   cm.
Includes bibliographical references.
    ISBN: 978-0-06-136827-1
    1. Billy, the Kid. 2. Garrett, Pat F. (Pat Floyd), 1850–1908.
3. Outlaws—Southwest, New—Biography. 4. Sheriffs—Southwest,
New—Biography. 5. Frontier and pioneer life—Southwest, New.
6. Southwest, New—History—1848– 7. Southwest, New—Biography.
8. Lincoln County (N.M.)—History—19th century. I. Title.
F786.B54G368   2009
364.15'52092—dc22
[B]
                                                    2009025467

10 11 12 13 14   OV/RRD   10 9 8 7 6 5 4 3 2 1

For my daughter and son,
Christiana and Vance

Some men find an unaccountable fascination in the danger and outlawry of the frontier far beyond my understanding.

—SUSAN E. WALLACE,
wife of Governor Lew Wallace,
New Mexico Territory

I don't think history possibly can be true.

—ORSON WELLES

Contents

Ghost Stories

YOU CAN FEEL THE ghosts as you speed down the long, lonely roads of eastern New Mexico. The land is little changed, except for endless strands of wire fence and an occasional traffic sign. Out in the distance, they are there: Billy the Kid and the Regulators, Charlie Bowdre, Tom Folliard, and Pat Garrett. The days may be gone when blood flowed freely along the Pecos and Rio Bonito, but the music of the fandango, and Billy's dancing, and the lovers' kisses—all difficult to conjure—are all still there. They are in the wind, the moonlight, in the cacophony of coyotes, and in the silence before the first rays of sunlight spill over the horizon.

And there are the stories, because New Mexico is full of stories. It is through these stories that the ghosts come to haunt us. In the stories, we think we see them, understand them, even somehow know them. But they are still ghosts, and they can conceal the truth like a pirate hides his plunder.

Billy the Kid and Pat Garrett were perhaps the greatest of our Old West legends. By building on the output of previous scholars, and conducting extensive original research in archival and private collections from Texas to Arizona to Utah to Colorado, I have made the ghosts give up a few more of their secrets.

All of the dialogue in quotes on the following pages came from primary sources: contemporary newspapers, letters, oral histories, autobiographies, and the like. Nothing has been made up. Granted, some recollections were written or dictated decades after the fact, and one can legitimately question how accurately someone might remember what somebody else said forty years previous, but even so they are the recollections of eyewitnesses. And in some cases, they are all we have.

I personally explored most of the places that figure in this story: Las Vegas, Anton Chico, Fort Sumner, Puerto de Luna, Roswell, Lincoln, White Sands, White Oaks, Alameda Arroyo, Mesilla, Silver City, and on and on. In some places, crowded Santa Fe, for example, the ghosts had been obliterated by asphalt, noise, and phony adobe facades. In others, such as the stairway of the old Lincoln courthouse, Billy, Pat, Bob Olinger, and James Bell seemed to walk side by side up its creaking wooden steps.

Many of the people connected with this story did not deserve their fate, Billy and Garrett most of all. "They were like lovers, in a way—doomed," said Rudolph Wurlitzer, the screenwriter for Sam Peckinpah's classic film, *Pat Garrett and Billy the Kid*. They lived in a harsh land and time, a time that saw tremendous change while still retaining, in some instances, the cutthroat ways of its recent past. In the end, it was not as much about right versus wrong, lawman versus outlaw as it was about survival. For others to survive, Billy could not, Garrett could not.

These two men perished long ago, and that is the cold truth of history, but their ghosts are still there. Billy forever calls out to us from the darkness of the past: *"¿Quién es?"* Who is it? And like Garrett, sitting, waiting, we are unable to answer, unable to stop what happens next.

◦ 1 ◦

Facing Justice

Come and take him!
—PAT F. GARRETT

I T WAS THE DAY after Christmas, 1880, at approximately 4:00 P.M., when a mule-drawn wagon accompanied by five armed horsemen rapidly approached the outskirts of Las Vegas in the Territory of New Mexico. The leader of the men on horseback rode stoop shouldered, a natural consequence of his six-foot-four-inch frame. He was as thin as a rail, and even as bundled up as he was, he seemed to be all arms and legs. He had a dark mustache, light gray eyes, and a swarthy face that showed the years he had spent on the open range of Texas and New Mexico.

Seated in the wagon were four dirty, trail-worn men in handcuffs and shackles. They were the lanky man's prisoners, and one of them was hardly out of his teens. As the wagon bounced along, the young outlaw, his blue eyes dancing about, broke into an occasional smile or burst out in a hearty laugh, exposing two buckteeth, a feature that was unattractive in most people, but for this young man seemed to add to his charm. The boyish prisoner and the tall lawman, although complete opposites, shared a common destiny. Billy the Kid and Pat Garrett had no way of knowing it, but they were fated to be forever linked in both life and death.

The Las Vegas that spread out before them was really two towns, one old and the other new. The old town had been established on the Santa Fe Trail in 1835 along the Gallinas River (what eastern-ers would call a creek). The settlement got its name from the river's broad grassy valley: *las vegas*—"the meadows." The new town sprang up forty-four years later when the Atchison, Topeka & Santa Fe Rail-road came through a mile away on the east side of the Gallinas. In 1880, Las Vegas, the county seat of San Miguel County, numbered six thousand people, mostly Hispanos. The city's numerous hell-raisers, mostly Anglos, resided in New Town, where saloons, dance halls, and gambling establishments ran day and night.

The *Las Vegas Daily Optic* reported: "Yesterday afternoon the town was thrown into a fever of excitement by an announcement that the 'Kid' and other members of his gang of outlaws had been captured, and were nearing the city." Sheriff Garrett's party had come up the old Santa Fe Trail. Their route to the stone jailhouse on Valencia Street took them across one end of Old Town's plaza, where most people got their first glimpse of the prisoners.

Billy beamed at the crowd and spotted Dr. John H. Sutfin, owner of the Grand View Hotel. "Hello, Doc!" he called out. "Thought I jes drop in an' see how you fellers in Vegas air behavin' yerselves."

The throng of gawkers, growing by the minute, followed the wagon down the muddy street to the jail, where the prisoners and guards promptly disappeared inside. A reporter for the *Las Vegas Gazette* cor-nered the thirty-year-old Garrett for a few minutes, hoping he could get the thrilling narrative of the gang's capture. Garrett almost im-mediately passed off the excited journalist to a posse member named Manuel Brazil, saying Brazil "knew all the particulars."

Monday morning's frigid air did not stop the curious townspeople from gathering around the jail, hoping to glimpse the desperadoes: Billy the Kid, Billy Wilson, Dave Rudabaugh, and Tom Pickett, the latter being a former Las Vegas policeman. Nearly everyone knew something about Billy—even if it was only that the twenty-one-year-old had sent far too many men to their graves. His most infamous crime was the killing of Sheriff William Brady and his deputy, George Hindman, in an ambush in Lincoln during the Lincoln County War. The Kid was not the only one who fired on the sheriff and his deputies that day, but he had walked away with a murder indictment. And this murder charge was the one he feared most. In the spring of 1879, Governor Lew Wallace met with Billy in order to draw out his eyewitness testimony in another highly charged Lincoln County murder case. In exchange for this testimony, Billy was to be offered a pardon. The Kid did his part, but the pardon never came. Now Billy knew it was only a matter of time before he would face a hangman's noose.

Michael Cosgrove, the Las Vegas mail contractor, pushed through the crowd carrying four bundles under his arms. They contained new suits of clothes for the prisoners, and the Irish-born Cosgrove remarked that he wanted "to see the boys go away in style." The town's two competing newspapers, the *Gazette* and the *Optic,* both managed to get reporters into Sheriff Desiderio Romero's jail that morning, but the *Gazette*'s man got the best story. The reporter watched as a blacksmith took his hammer and cold chisel and began carefully shearing the rivets of the shackles and bracelets worn by the Kid and Billy Wilson, who were chained together. The irons had to come off before the prisoners could change their clothing. Wilson was glum and quiet, but the Kid was acting "light and chipper . . . very communicative, laughing, joking and chatting with the bystanders."

"You appear to take it easy," the *Gazette* reporter said to the Kid.

"Yes! What's the use of looking on the gloomy side of everything," Billy replied. "The laugh's on me this time."

The Kid cast his eyes around and began kicking the toes of his boots on the stone floor to warm his feet. "Is the jail in Santa Fe any better than this?" he asked. "This is a terrible place to put a fellow in."

He asked this same question of everyone who came close to him, and they all told him the Santa Fe jail was not any better. Billy then shrugged his shoulders and said he would just have to put up with what he had to. The Kid may not have liked what was happening to him, but he was thrilled at all the attention he was getting. Being a celebrity suited him just fine.

"There was a big crowd gazing at me, wasn't there," Billy said, referring to the moment when the doors were opened to let the mail contractor in. "Well," and here the Kid broke into a smile again, "perhaps some of them will think me half man now; everyone seems to think I was some kind of animal."

Not surprisingly, the *Gazette* reporter seemed to like the youthful outlaw, and he wrote the best (and most quoted) description of Billy:

> He did look human indeed, but there was nothing very mannish about him in appearance, for he looked and acted a mere boy. He is about five feet eight or nine inches tall, slightly built and lithe, weighing about 140; a frank open countenance, looking like a school boy, with the traditional silky fuzz on his upper lip; clear blue eyes, with a roguish snap about them; light hair and complexion. He is, in all, quite a handsome looking fellow, the only imperfection being two prominent teeth slightly protruding like squirrel's teeth, and he has agreeable and winning ways.

When the blacksmith popped the last rivet, and the Kid's cuffs fell to the ground, Billy stretched and rubbed his sore wrists. "I don't suppose you fellows would believe it but this is the first time I ever had bracelets on," he said. "But many another better fellow has had them too." Then, as Billy and Wilson were ushered back into their cell, the Kid said a few words about the man who had tracked him down and put him in irons. "They say, 'a fool for luck and a poor man for children'—Garrett takes them all in."

Garrett had originally planned to take the prisoners to the depot and get them on a train for Santa Fe (all except Tom Pickett, for whom he had no federal warrant), but when he and his deputies arrived at the jail shortly after breakfast, only the Kid and Wilson were led out. Sheriff Romero refused to turn over Dave Rudabaugh, who eight months earlier had shot jailer Lino Valdez while attempting to break out a friend from this very same lockup. Romero, as well as the majority of the townspeople, wanted to see Rudabaugh tried in Las Vegas for this murder.

Garrett had expected this, but he had also promised Rudabaugh he would get him safely to Santa Fe. A heated discussion ensued. Garrett reminded the sheriff that he was a deputy U.S. marshal, and his federal warrant trumped their murder charges. Garrett may have been a soft-spoken man under normal circumstances, but he had no trouble letting it be known that he was going to get his way: "[H]e was my prisoner, I was responsible for him, and intended to have him," he wrote later. Romero and his men reluctantly released Rudabaugh, but they were not through just yet.

Prisoners and guards squeezed into two or three hacks (an open wagon with three bench seats) for the short trip to the depot in New Town. Garrett's posse included Deputies Barney Mason, Frank Stewart, Jim East, Tom Emory, U.S. Marshal James W. Bell, and contractor Cosgrove. At the depot, they found the westbound train waiting on the tracks, its passengers completely unaware that the noted desperado Billy the Kid was about to join them.

Seated in the train's smoking car that day was Benjamin S. Miller, a twenty-nine-year-old native of New York State who had entered the cattle business near Medicine Lodge, Kansas. He had gone out west because he was as interested in playing cowboy and shooting wild game as he was in seeking his fortune (which he eventually found).

While recently visiting Wichita, Miller met a friend who gave him a Santa Fe railroad pass that was expiring in a few days. "Take it, and go while it lasts," his friend had urged. Miller did just that, intending to travel as far west as possible on the Santa Fe line and return within the allotted time. Because the pass was made out in his friend's name, though, Miller had to bend the truth with the conductors, but without photo IDs in that era, this was easily done, and Miller experienced not the slightest difficulty, enjoying his trip immensely—until the train stopped at Las Vegas.

Garrett and his deputies hurried their three prisoners down the track siding to the smoking car and quickly ushered them up its narrow steps. Miller and three miners, deeply absorbed in a game of cards, suddenly heard the clanking of chains entering their car. They looked up to see the lawmen and the shackled outlaws. The racket caused by the sheriff's party was quickly followed by shouts from a crowd gathered just outside the car. Many of them were well armed, and some of these men began taking up positions behind a stack of railroad ties near the tracks. Garrett addressed the passengers in a loud but steady voice:

"Any of you people who don't want to be in it, had better get out before I lock the car, as we are liable to have a hell of a fight in a few minutes."

Garrett had hardly finished speaking when Miller saw two men jump out of their seats and dash for the adjoining car, not even stopping for their valises. He then watched in amazement as the three miners he was playing cards with pulled out an assortment of weapons.

"They offered me a big six-shooter," Miller recalled, "but I declined."

One of the deputies told the uneasy stockman that the crowd outside, largely Hispanos, wanted Dave Rudabaugh, and they were sure the mob was going to lynch the outlaw as soon as they got their hands on him. Garrett was not about to let that happen, not short of a bloodbath.

Pat Garrett, circa 1881.

"It seemed as if the fight would begin any minute," Miller remembered, "and I expected to see the Mexicans fire into the car right away." Miller moved to the opposite end of the coach and crouched behind a stove.

A group of men rushed to the front of the train and confronted the locomotive's twenty-six-year-old engineer and fireman, Dan Daley.

One of them thrust a pistol in Daley's face and shouted, "My father does not want this train to pull out of here."

"And who is your father?" Daley asked.

"Sheriff Romero is my father."

When Daley let some steam escape from the engine, the young man became agitated: "I don't want to shed any blood, but if you try to pull out you will be a dead man."

Daley kept the train parked.

Somehow, as ugly as things had gotten around the train, the *Gazette*'s reporter managed to get next to the smoking car where Billy was leaning out of a window, probably on the side opposite the mob.

"I don't blame you for writing of me as you have," he said. "You had to believe others' stories; but then I don't know as anyone would believe anything good of me anyway. I wasn't the leader of any gang—I was for Billy all the time. . . . I found that there were certain men who wouldn't let me live in the country and so I was going to leave. We had all our grub in the house when they took us in, and we were going to a place about six miles away in the morning to cook it and then 'light' out. I haven't stolen any stock. I made my living by gambling but that was the only way I could live. They wouldn't let me settle down; if they had I wouldn't be here today."

Billy cursed about the chains on his wrists and ankles and let it be known that he was anxious to take part in the fight that was brewing. "If I only had my Winchester," he said, "I'd lick the whole crowd."

Benjamin Miller remembered the great contrast between the noise outside the car and the quiet inside: "Nine men with cocked rifles sturdily standing off a mob of hundreds. Those men never flinched an iota. Such bravery, even to recklessness, was new to me."

Sheriff Romero and his delegation, their pistols drawn, approached the car platform where Garrett stood and clambered up the steps. They made their blustery demand for Dave Rudabaugh, and Garrett simply replied, "Come and take him." It was not a bluff, and it must have scared Romero out of his wits.

The towering Garrett then ordered the delegation to get down off the train, and they slunk back to the crowd empty-handed.

Garrett next turned to his prisoners, telling them that he and his deputies were going to fight back if anyone tried to enter the car. More important, he told the prisoners he would arm them if a gun battle broke out. He would need their help to defend the car.

The Kid's eyes glistened at that. "All right, Pat," he said. "All I want is a six-shooter. There is no danger, though. Those fellows won't fight."

Miguel Otero then addressed the mob. A stocky fellow, he was a forwarding and commission merchant and prominent political figure in the Territory. He urged the men to let Garrett carry out his official duty. Otero also cautioned them about the consequences of delaying the U.S. mail, but it is hard to imagine that a matter as small as that had much effect on those bent on seeing "Dirty Dave" hang.

The standoff on the tracks had now stretched to about forty-five minutes when postal inspector J. Fred Morley approached Garrett.

"I have been an engineer," he told the lawman, "and if you will let me, I'll slip down through the mob, get in the cab, pull the throttle open, and we'll get out of here."

"Good, go do it," Garrett said.

Morley made his way to the locomotive, but he did more than simply pull the throttle open—he hit it *wide* open. The heavy wheels spun, grabbed hold, and the cars lurched ahead. The mob was stunned and did not move. Realizing there was nothing they could do to stop the train now, the men who were holding the locomotive's engineer and fireman released their prisoners, who quickly jumped aboard the moving train.

"By the time we got to the end of the siding," remembered Jim East, "it seemed like we were going a mile a minute, and the Mexicans stood there with their mouths open."

The *Gazette* reporter watched as Billy, still leaning out his window, waved his hat, grandly inviting the reporter to call on him in Santa Fe. He then shouted "Adios" and disappeared.

In an instant, all the tension inside the smoking car vanished. "There was plenty of whisky in the car," Miller remembered, "and a deal of it was drank."

The train stalled at the top of Glorieta Pass, just twenty-one miles from Santa Fe, where Garrett got lunch for his prisoners, and Billy amused his fellow passengers by demonstrating just how far he could bite into a piece of pie.

Miller studied the Kid intently: "His costume was quite on the Mexican order, his language much the same. His curly brown locks and handsome face would have attracted attention anywhere, and, while looking at him and listening to his conversation, it was difficult to believe that I was in the presence of such a red-handed murderer."

Before the train reached the territorial capital, Billy casually remarked to Garrett, "Those who live by the sword, die by the sword."

The train finally pulled up to the Santa Fe depot that evening, where Garrett turned over his prisoners to Deputy U.S. Marshal Charles Conklin. It had been just eight short weeks since Garrett had won the sheriff's election in Lincoln County (his term would not officially begin until January 1, 1881). In that time, despite a great expanse of territory and bitterly cold temperatures and heavy snow, his posse had tracked down the Kid and his cohorts, killing Tom Folliard and Charlie Bowdre in the process. It was a remarkable feat, accomplished by someone with absolutely no prior training as an officer of the law. But Garrett's great triumph was not capturing the Kid and his gang.

His moment had come when he faced down that lynch mob led by the San Miguel County sheriff. Garrett had grit and the power to intimidate, that was clear, and he had a sense of duty. Of utmost importance to Garrett was keeping one's word—he detested liars. That he put his life—and the lives of his men—at risk to keep the promise made to his prisoners says a lot about the man's character. There are other times in Pat Garrett's life when his sense of right and wrong can be questioned, his actions faulted, but on that tense December day in Las Vegas, Garrett's moral compass held steady on true north.

IF BILLY HAD DIFFICULTY taking in his sudden celebrity, he would have been stunned to learn that not only was he making national headlines, but his talents as a bona fide outlaw had grown to truly impressive proportions. Thanks to the telegraph, news of his capture appeared from Chicago to Boston with a delay of just twenty-four hours. The report on the front page of the *Chicago Daily Tribune* of December 29 was typical: "The notorious gang of outlaws composed of about 25 men who, under the leadership of 'Billy the Kid,' have for the past six months overrun Eastern New Mexico, murdering and committing other deeds of outlawry, was broken up last Saturday morning by the killing of two and the capturing of four others, including the leader." The *Tribune* article then recounted the thrilling details of the Las Vegas standoff.

Just days later, the *Illustrated Police News*, a weekly published in Boston, ran a genuine portrait of the "Boy Chief of New Mexico Outlaws and Cattle Thieves." The engraving was based on a tintype the Kid had made at Fort Sumner some months before. The *Police News*'s depiction of a smirking Billy in rumpled frontier garb, posed with Winchester and six-gun, was much more than a journalistic coup; it was the first appearance of what would become one of America's most iconic images.

Billy's capture and confinement became the talk of the territorial capital. On December 30, the *Santa Fe New Mexican* carried no less than four news items pertaining in some way to the Kid. Their focus that day was the Santa Fe jail, a dismal, one-story adobe building on Water Street, two blocks' distance southwest of the plaza. Well aware of Billy's reputation as an escape artist, the jail's custodians were paying careful attention to their noted prisoner. "He is shut up in a stone cell to which even the light of day is denied admittance," the *New Mexican* reported, "and only when some of the jailers or officers enter can he be seen at all." Yet Billy remained cheerful and, according to the newspaper, still hoped to pull off an escape.

The Kid received a steady stream of visitors. The Otero brothers, Page and Miguel Antonio, brought him chewing gum, candy,

Engraving of Billy the Kid from the *Illustrated Police
News*, Boston, January 8, 1881.

pies, nuts, tobacco, and cigarette papers. The Oteros had ridden on the train with Garrett and the prisoners to Santa Fe, and like many others, they had become fascinated by the outlaw. Nearly the same age as Billy, Miguel was destined to become the first Hispanic territorial governor of New Mexico and would one day publish his own book on the outlaw. Other visitors came on official business, such as the postal inspector who interviewed Billy and his fellow prisoners in early January 1881, about several stagecoach holdups. "William Bonney (alias 'The Kid') is held for murder," the inspector wrote his supervisor. "He is supposed to have killed some 11 men, but that is an exaggeration, four or five would be quite enough. He is about 21 or 23 years of age born in New York City, and a graduate of the streets."

Between entertaining his guests and the numerous gawkers, Billy devoted his energies to getting out of jail, in more ways than one. "I would like to see you for a few moments if you can spare [the] time," the Kid wrote Governor Lew Wallace. No one bothered to tell Billy that Wallace was not then in Santa Fe. No matter, when Wallace returned to the capital in early February, he made no effort to visit the jail's celebrity prisoner.

Billy had no money to pay for legal help, so he agreed to sell his renowned bay mare to lawyer Edgar Caypless. Taking possession of the horse was another matter entirely. Posse member Frank Stewart had made a big show of the Kid's mare when he came into Las Vegas with the captured outlaws in December, telling everyone how Billy had *given* the animal to him. At that time, Stewart and Garrett were the toast of the town, and when hotel proprietor W. Scott Moore presented Stewart with a beautiful factory-engraved Colt pistol valued at $60, Stewart gave the Kid's mare to Moore's wife, Mary. The mare and its transfer to Mrs. Moore made for a cheery piece in the *Las Vegas Gazette*, which said that Mary Moore "now has the satisfaction of owning one of the best, if not the best animal in the territory." Caypless filed a suit of replevin against W. Scott Moore, but the judgment he eventually won did not come until July—far too late to do Billy any good.

Billy was still hoping he could pull off an escape—that is, until the surprise jail visit of Sheriff Romulo Martínez and Deputy U.S. Marshal Tony Neis. The officers, it turns out, had offered some easy money to one of the jail's inmates to keep an eye on the other prisoners. Having been tipped off by this informant, Martínez and Neis arrived at the jail that day around suppertime. The Kid and his cohorts, Rudabaugh, Billy Wilson, and Edward Kelly, watched as the lawmen went straight to one of the beds, found it packed full with dirt and rocks, and then dragged the ticking aside to discover an impressively large hole in the floor. Had it not been for the snitch, Billy would have been a free man in one or two nights more. Instead, he got extra shackles and closer scrutiny from his guards.

On March 2, Billy again wrote to Governor Wallace. "I wish you would come down to the jail and see me. [I]t will be to your interest to come and see me. I have some letters which date back two years, and there are Parties who are very anxious to get them but I shall not dispose of them until I see you. [T]hat is if you will come imediately [*sic*]." The Kid's baiting of Wallace was met with continued silence from the Governor's Palace. "I knew what he meant," Wallace related years later. "He referred to the note he received from me [at Lincoln in 1879]. . . . He was threatening to publish it, if I refused to see him."

Two days later, Billy sent yet another letter to the governor: "I Expect you have forgotten what you promised me, this month two years ago, but I have not and I think you had ought to have come and seen me as I requested you to. I have done everything that I promised you I would, and you have done nothing that you promised me. . . . [I]t looks to me like I am getting left in the cold. I am not treated right by [U.S. Marshal] Sherman, he lets Every Stranger that comes to see me through Curiosity in to see me, but will not let a single one of my friends in, Not even an Attorney. I guess they mean to send me up without giving me any show, but they will have a nice time doing it. I am not intirely without friends."

Billy was to be transported nearly three hundred miles south to Mesilla, where he would be put on trial in a change of venue to Doña Ana County. On March 27, Billy wrote Wallace one last frantic note from the Santa Fe jail: "for the last time I ask, Will you keep your promise. I start below tomorrow send awnser [sic] by bearer." No answer came from the governor, except for the implied one the following day when the Kid and Billy Wilson were escorted onto a southbound train under armed guard. Accompanying the prisoners were the Kid's sometime-attorney, Ira Leonard, twenty-nine-year-old U.S. Deputy Marshal Neis, and the Santa Fe chief of police, Francisco "Frank" Chavez. Fearing trouble from the Territory's considerable lynch-happy element, officials tried to keep the two Billys' impending departure quiet, but word got out anyway. Upon reaching Rincon, the last station on the line, some six or seven troublemakers were waiting for them. Neis, armed with a shotgun and a six-shooter, and Chavez, cradling a rifle, hurried the Kid and Wilson off the train and toward the shelter of a nearby saloon.

"Let's take them fellows anyhow," barked one of the roughs.

"You don't get them without somebody being killed," Neis shouted back.

Once inside the saloon, Neis secured a back room where his party could wait it out until their stage was leaving the next morning for Las Cruces and Mesilla. But just outside, and making no effort to conceal their conversation, the roughs were doing their best to talk themselves into making a grab for the prisoners.

Billy became visibly shaken; Neis was clearly not as stable as Garrett in this kind of situation. Imagining that the mob's goal might actually be to *free* the Kid and Wilson, Neis yelled that he would shoot the two prisoners before allowing them to be taken from his custody. Finally, some levelheaded bystanders talked sense into the crowd, convincing them that the guards could not be overpowered short of bloodshed. The mob dispersed and their grumblings faded away. After a calm but restless night, the officers and prisoners boarded the stage the next morning unmolested.

At Las Cruces, thirty-three miles southeast of Rincon, Billy again attracted a crowd, but these townspeople were more curious than anything else. It was not every day that the Territory's most notorious criminal made an appearance on Main Street, and the certainty that he would hang before long made the Kid even more of a not-to-be-missed spectacle. One of the gawkers asked, "Which is Billy the Kid?" Before anyone in the party could answer, Billy placed his hand on Ira Leonard's shoulder, and with a straight face exclaimed, "This is the man."

Mesilla, the county seat, just three miles farther, was reached that evening, and the two Billys were shown to their new quarters. The Kid would later describe the Mesilla jail as "the worst place he had ever struck." By the time the Kid arrived, the weather had turned god-awful hot, and the flies and mosquitoes were out in full force.

THE KID WOULD NOT have to endure the Mesilla jail for long. Judge Warren Bristol would see to that. Billy was certainly familiar with Bristol, the fifty-eight-year-old judge for New Mexico's Third Judicial District, and, most important, a Jimmy Dolan sympathizer, the man whose forces Billy fought in the Lincoln County War. Bristol, a New York native, was known to occasionally bend or ignore the law, and, naturally, controversy seemed to follow him throughout his career. He could rightly be called "New Mexico's hanging judge," because by 1882, his courtroom had a record of more convictions for first-degree murder than all the other districts in the Territory combined.

The day after the Kid's arrival in Mesilla, March 30, he was escorted into Bristol's court, a cramped room within a narrow, one-story adobe on the southeast corner of Mesilla's plaza. Billy faced a federal charge first, for the murder of Andrew Roberts during a gun battle at Blazer's Mill on April 4, 1878. Bristol appointed Ira Leonard as the Kid's counsel, and the attorney entered a plea of not guilty. Because time was needed to bring defense witnesses from Lincoln County, the judge granted a delay, a holdup that did not sit well with Simeon H. Newman, editor of a fledgling Las Cruces paper that carried the creative title *Newman's Semi-Weekly*. Newman urged the court to use the interim to quickly proceed with the territorial indictments against the Kid, the murder charges for the killings of Sheriff Brady and Deputy George Hindman.

"The prisoner is a notoriously dangerous character," Newman reminded his readers, "and has on several occasions before escaped justice where escape appeared even more improbable than now, and has made his brags that he only wants to get free in order to kill three more men—one of them being Governor Wallace. Should he break jail now, there is no doubt that he would immediately proceed to execute his threat. Lincoln county, which has suffered so long from his crimes, cannot afford to see him escape; and yet every hour that he is confined in the Mesilla jail is a threat to the peace of that community. There are a hundred good citizens of Lincoln who would not sleep soundly in their beds did they know that he were at large."

As for the charges the Kid currently faced, Newman assured his readers that, "Other indictments will be found if these are not sufficient."

On April 5, the Kid, through his attorney, withdrew his plea of not guilty and entered a plea of no jurisdiction for the Roberts murder charge. Leonard, with the assistance of Mesilla lawyer Albert J. Fountain, put forward several arguments why the United States had no right to prosecute the case (Blazer's Mill was situated within the Mescalero Apache Indian reservation). The judge sided with the defense. No one, including U.S. District Attorney Sidney M. Barnes, appeared to be upset with this outcome, which cleared the way for the territorial cases. The general consensus was that Billy had no hope of getting off on that latter charge.

And Judge Bristol would continue to preside in the courtroom at the Kid's trial for the murder of Sheriff Brady. District Attorney Simon B. Newcomb would head the prosecution. Newcomb, a pleasant forty-two-year-old native of Nova Scotia and former Texas judge, was more popular with the Hispanic population of Mesilla and Las Cruces than any other lawyer in the area. Billy's jury, interestingly enough, was made up of native New Mexicans (what was called in local parlance a "Mexican jury"), a good thing if his trial was happening in Lincoln, but the Hispanos of Doña Ana County had no special relationship with Billy or any of the other gringo cowboys they saw riding around their part of the Territory.

Albert J. Fountain and John D. Bail (an attorney from Silver City) replaced Ira Leonard as the Kid's court-appointed legal representatives. Fountain had been appointed the Kid's counsel in the Brady murder case two years earlier, just before Billy rode out of Lincoln a fugitive. Although Ira Leonard may have had a closer relationship with the Kid, Fountain was the best man to defend him in Mesilla. He had had some successes there as a defense attorney (Fountain had already helped Leonard get the Kid off on the Roberts murder charge). Fountain was a handsome, respectable-looking man with a broad forehead, blue eyes, and large mustache. He liked hopeless cases and was good at swaying "Mexican juries," in part because of his Spanish language skills but also because he had married the daughter in a prominent Hispanic family. Additionally, Fountain was well familiar with the events and personalities of the Lincoln County War. In a strange connection to the case, Fountain had been blamed for inciting Brady's killers with an editorial in the *Mesilla Valley Independent* that condoned the use of "mob law" in Lincoln County—saying it was better than no law at all.

Before the trial, someone heard the Kid tell Fountain that he sure "wished somebody would come into his cell with a six-shooter." Billy may have thought he was being funny, although down deep, he must have thought of such a scenario; he was closer to a death sentence than he had ever been before.

Simeon Newman took the Kid's words seriously. "He ought to be most carefully watched," Newman wrote in his *Semi-Weekly,* "as he is liable at any time to make a break for liberty. We advise the sheriff to keep an eye on him when he takes him into court."

The Doña Ana County sheriff, James W. Southwick, did just that and more. Throughout the Brady murder trial, the Kid, his wrists kept in handcuffs, was surrounded by several armed guards. It is not hard to imagine what kind of impression these extraordinary security precautions made on the jurors.

The trial began on Wednesday, April 8, 1881, and the spectators were a mix of Hispanic and Anglo folks from around the area. They filled the long wooden seats facing Judge Bristol's bench, which consisted of a flat-topped desk on a raised platform at one end of the narrow room. The defendant, William H. Bonney, sat to one side of Bristol's desk. Court Clerk George Bowman remembered Billy as a pleasant-looking young man whose eyes seemed sullen and defiant. "It looked almost ridiculous," Bowman recalled, "all those armed men sitting around a harmless looking youth with the down still on his chin."

The Kid silently watched the court proceedings—remarkably, the first time he had ever been tried for any crime—fully aware that his fate was in the hands of the twelve strangers in the jurors' box. They knew nothing of the injustices of the Lincoln County War, of his close scrapes and firefights, of the bloody deaths of his friends, or of the broken promise of a governor. Yet they were to judge him, to decide whether he would live or die.

Most of what happened in Judge Bristol's courtroom—witness

testimony, objections from counsel, defense and prosecution arguments—is unknown. Strange for a trial that was eagerly anticipated
at the time and now ranks as one of the most famed criminal trials
in New Mexico history. At least three witnesses testified for the Territory, and there is no indication that Billy took the stand. What is
known revolves around the instructions given to the jury at the trial's
conclusion, which came on the second day. In nine long pages, Bristol
gave the jury little leeway to return with anything but a "guilty" verdict. If Billy was present and involved in any way in the Brady killing,
Bristol instructed the jurors, he should be considered "as much guilty
as though he fired the fatal shot." After deliberating for three hours,
the jury found the Kid guilty of murder in the first degree and recommended death as his punishment.

Three days later, at 5:15 P.M., Billy appeared before Judge Bristol to
receive his sentence. When asked if he had anything to say, the outlaw,
who invariably had *something* to say, spoke not a word.

Bristol then ordered that the Kid be taken to Lincoln County,
where he was to be incarcerated by Sheriff Pat Garrett until Friday,
May 13. On that unlucky day, between the hours of 9:00 A.M. and 3:00
P.M., the said William Bonney was to be "hanged by the neck until his
body be dead."

Editor Newman happily speculated that the wooden gallows would
be erected over the spot where Sheriff Brady fell.

Before Billy was transported to Lincoln, he wrote to Edgar Caypless to ask about the lawsuit over his bay mare. "Mr. A. J. Fountain
was appointed to defend me and has done the best he could for me,"
he informed Caypless. "He is willing to carry the case further if I
can raise the money to bear his expense. The mare is about all I can
depend on at present." Billy closed his letter by asking the attorney
to excuse his bad handwriting, as he was wearing his handcuffs—
his guards were not about to take any chances with their condemned
prisoner.

The Kid also talked to the local newspapers, playing to both the public and Governor Wallace. Simeon Newman promised to publish Billy's statements following the outcome of his appeal to Wallace for a pardon (or a commutation of his sentence).

"We do not believe that the Governor should or will either pardon him or commute his sentence," wrote Newman, "but we cannot refuse to a dying man the same fair play we should expect for ourselves."

When the *Mesilla News* asked Billy if he expected Wallace to pardon him, Billy said that, "Considering the active part Governor Wallace took on our side and the friendly relations that existed between him and me, and the promise he made me, I think he ought to pardon me. Don't know that he will do it. . . . Think it hard I should be the only one to suffer the extreme penalties of the law." Wallace had a much different take on the Kid's plight, and he revealed as much to a *Las Vegas Gazette* reporter later that same month:

"It looks as though he would hang, Governor," the *Gazette* man commented to Wallace.

"Yes, the chances seem good that the 13th of May would finish him."

"He appears to look to you to save his neck," the reporter said.

"Yes," the governor replied, smiling, "but I can't see how a fellow like him should expect any clemency from me."

The time for Billy's departure for Lincoln—kept secret from the public—was set for Saturday, April 16, at approximately 10:00 P.M. To throw off possible rescue attempts, officials let it slip that Billy was not leaving Mesilla before the middle of the next week. Billy Wilson was not traveling with the Kid on this trip. Wilson was granted a continuance in his counterfeiting trial and would go back to Santa Fe on a change of venue. Several months later, Wilson escaped, never to be brought to trial again. No such luck for the Kid, who was uncharacteristically doubtful about his future.

"I expect to be lynched in going to Lincoln," he told the *Mesilla*

News. And then, somewhat despairingly, he added, "Advise persons never to engage in killing."

Seven men, bristling with all manner of weapons, formed Billy's escort for the 145 miles that stretched between Mesilla and Lincoln: Deputy Sheriff David Wood, Tom Williams, Billy Mathews, John Kinney, D. M. Reade, W. A. Lockhart, and Deputy U.S. Marshal Robert Olinger. These men were being paid $2.00 a day, plus $1.50 per day board and ten cents for each mile traveled. Billy had more than a little history with a few of his guards—they had been on opposite sides in the Lincoln County troubles—but the Kid seemed to get along with most of them all right. However, if there was any trouble, either from a rescue attempt or a lynching party, the guards had made it very clear that the first shots they fired would be directed at the Kid.

Billy, handcuffed and shackled, rode in an ambulance (a covered spring wagon with seats that could be folded down to make a bed). A chain secured him to the ambulance's backseat. Three guards rode horseback, one on each side of the vehicle and one at the rear. Inside the ambulance, Kinney sat beside the Kid. On the middle bench, facing Kinney was Billy Mathews. And sitting next to Mathews, staring straight into the Kid's boyish face, was Bob Olinger, the one man with whom the Kid definitely did not get along.

Their route took them through San Augustin Pass, across the Tularosa Basin (famed for its immense, shifting dunes of white sand), over the Sacramento Mountains, and through the Mescalero Apache reservation. On April 20, they spent the night at Blazer's Mill, an old Regulator stomping ground and the scene of its infamous gun battle with Andrew Roberts. Early the next morning, with Joseph and Almer Blazer, a few idle mill workers, and his guards for an audience, Billy graphically recounted his version of the shoot-out. One of the men asked Billy why he killed Roberts, a simple question that the Kid could not find an answer for. He just shook his head, saying he did not know. Later that day, the prisoner and guards pulled into Fort Stanton. Pat Garrett was waiting there for the man he had famously brought to justice four months earlier. Then, after a short journey of nine more miles down the valley of the Rio Bonito, Garrett, Bob Olinger, and Billy arrived in the county seat of Lincoln.

Garrett now had a dilemma. Lincoln County had never had a jail that, as he later wrote, "would hold a cripple," yet he was charged with confining the Territory's slipperiest criminal for the next twenty-two days. Whether it could be done remained to be seen. Garrett was confident that he could, and that the execution would come off at the appointed time as planned. But Billy thought differently. One day, his guards allowed Mrs. Annie E. Lesnett, a friend of Billy's from Dowlin's Mill on the Ruidoso, to see their prisoner. In a sick sort of joke, Bob Olinger invited the woman to the hanging. Unfazed, Billy spoke up: "Mrs. Lesnett, they can't hang me if I'm not there, can they?"

No matter the odds, the shackles, the armed guards, Billy the Kid's old optimism was back. He somehow believed he could escape the gallows, and that belief was a very dangerous thing.

2

Trails West

His voice was as soft as a woman's, and
he rarely used it to talk of himself.
—PAT DONAN

THE CAPTURE OF THE notorious Billy the Kid put Pat Garrett's
name in newspapers throughout the Territory, even the nation.
The *Santa Fe New Mexican* proclaimed him the hero of the hour. In
addition to the reward money due him, grateful citizens passed the
hat—one Las Vegas doctor presented Garrett with $100 in gold. Yet
for all the public attention, hardly anyone really knew the lawman,
and Garrett was not much of a talker, at least when asked to talk
about himself. He seemed to have blown in off the plains and was just
suddenly there, the right man at the right place. And that was pretty
much how it happened.

Garrett was born in another place and time, in Chambers County,
Alabama, on June 5, 1850. And although he would come to sign his
name P. F. Garrett, the name given to him at birth was Patrick Floyd
Jarvis Garrett, a name that had belonged to his maternal grandfather.
Grandfather Jarvis died two years after the birth of his grandson, but

not before willing his young namesake a rifle, a saddle, and a bridle.
As young Pat would eventually learn, such basic items were crucial for
a man to survive on his own. Garrett's father, John Lumpkin Garrett,
a native of Georgia, was an ambitious Southern planter. Just three
years later, though, perhaps prompted by the death of wife Elizabeth
Ann's father, the Garretts pulled up stakes and moved to Claiborne
Parish, Louisiana. The Garrett caravan that rattled over the rough
roads to their new home included a long column of human chattel. Pat
Garrett's father was a slave owner.

In Louisiana, John Garrett purchased the cotton plantation of
John Greer, consisting of eighteen hundred acres eight miles northeast of the parish seat of Homer. Pat Garrett earned his first dollar
working in his father's plantation store. And as he got bigger, so did
the Garrett family; Pat would have seven brothers and sisters (Pat was
the second oldest and the first son).

The Garrett plantation prospered as well. The 1860 census records the value of John Garrett's real estate at $15,000, but his per-
sonal property was estimated at a whopping $40,000, which is not so
surprising considering that it included thirty-four slaves. Pat Garrett
grew up, then, in a relatively privileged world. With slaves to tend to
the household and cooking, and to cultivate and harvest the vast fields
of cotton, the Garretts probably never wanted for anything. The Civil
War changed all that.

As a large slave owner, John Garrett was exempt from Confederate military service, but he lost his overseer to the Twenty-seventh
Regiment, Louisiana Infantry. The fall of the port of New Orleans
to Union forces in April 1862 brought additional hardships, forcing
Louisiana cotton planters to transport their crops overland through
Texas to Mexico. At the close of the war, not only did Garrett lose his
slave labor force, but a portion of his cotton crop was reportedly confiscated by the occupying Federals. The debts piled up as the senior
Garrett went into a spiral, his health failing and his drinking rising in

proportion. He lost Elizabeth on March 23, 1867; she was only thirty-seven. He held on for almost a year longer, struggling to maintain both his livelihood and his large family. John Garrett died on February 5, 1868.

Pat, not yet eighteen, could only watch as court-appointed estate executors dealt with the financially ruined plantation; his father had left debts of more than $30,000. Pat's brother-in-law, Larkin R. Lay, the final estate executor, sold the lands and possessions to satisfy the creditors, and the Garrett children moved into the Lay home to be raised by their sister Margaret. Furious with Larkin, Pat struck out for Texas on January 25, 1869. He had little more than a rifle, a saddle, a bridle, and a horse.

There are a number of stories about Pat Garrett's Texas years—that he killed a black man, started and then abandoned a family, helped drive a herd of Texas cattle to Dodge City. But they remain just that, stories. Garrett first went to Dallas but soon located in Lancaster (twelve miles from Dallas), which was also the home of some old Claiborne Parish neighbors. There the strapping young fellow tried his hand at what he knew best—farming.

"I went into partnership with the owner of the land," Garrett recalled, "my share was to be one fourth of what we made and my first work was to grub the ground and clear the land. I got mighty homesick before the crop was made, but I stayed with it."

He stayed with it for about two years, until he met a cattleman from Uvalde County who was hiring cowboys, and Garrett's farming days came to an end. In 1875, Garrett started north with a trail herd bound for Kansas. After about three hundred miles, the cowboys reached the Red River at Denison, where they found thousands of head of cattle, waiting to cross the famed river, then in flood stage. Here Garrett got a close-up look at the dangers of the trail, for some punchers and their horses, as well as a number of cattle, had been lost to the deep, blood-colored waters. A few days' tough work were required to get the herds across and straightened out, after which cowboying had lost much of its romance for Garrett.

He and a buddy by the name of Luther Duke quit the herd and traded away their ponies and gear and started farming a small patch of corn and cotton. This was hardly a step up, though, and when Garrett met Willis Skelton Glenn, a twenty-six-year-old Georgia native who was about to embark in the buffalo hide business, Glenn found himself with two eager partners.

"I remember our meeting," Glenn wrote years later. "Pat was rather young looking for all of his twenty-five or twenty-six years, and he seemed the tallest, most long-legged specimen I ever saw. There was something very attractive and impressive about his personality, even on a first meeting." Garrett would remain associated with Glenn on the buffalo range for roughly the next three years, first as a business partner and later as Glenn's salaried hunter. And it is because of Willis Skelton Glenn that the details of what was, for Garrett, his most mortifying deed have been preserved. In fact, Glenn made it a mission of sorts to keep Pat Garrett's first known killing from ever being forgotten.

In the brief boom years of buffalo hunting, a good man with a rifle, and Garrett fell into this category, could down sixty or more buffalo a day, and there were hundreds of such hunters on the plains. The skinning and transporting of these hides, several hundred at a time, was hard work that required a crew of men. In camp, Garrett and the others broke the tension and monotony with an occasional practical joke, or if they were near one of the trading points, with gambling, drinking, and whoring. Still, it was not unusual for tempers to flare, even between once good friends. Sometimes, trifling disagreements escalated into deadly confrontations, just as they did with Garrett and young Joe Briscoe.

Briscoe would never have ventured onto the buffalo range had it not been for Garrett, or at least that is the story Glenn told. A native of Ireland who had lived in Louisiana before migrating to Texas, Briscoe joined the Glenn-Garrett party in the fall of 1876. After outfitting at Fort Griffin, the party headed west onto the Staked Plains. Glenn remembered that Garrett and Briscoe appeared the best of chums: "Everybody seemed to be getting on well with everybody else, and I was congratulating myself on having a harmonious outfit." Early one morning, Glenn rode off to Rath City for a replacement firing pin for one of the buffalo guns, leaving Garrett in charge. Just before breakfast the next day, Briscoe walked to a nearby pool of water with a piece of soap and began scrubbing away at his linen handkerchief. A short time later, he walked back to camp, muttering to himself, "It was no use to wash in that damn water."

Garrett overheard Briscoe and immediately chimed in.

"Anyone but a damn Irishman," he said, "would have more sense than to try to wash anything in that water."

"Yes," Briscoe replied, "you damn Americans think you are damn smart and know a damn sight."

Garrett was not about to take any sass from the young man and let fly with his fist, almost knocking Briscoe to the ground. Briscoe righted himself and took a swing at Garrett, missing, and then ran for the axe the cook used to split firewood. Realizing Briscoe's intent, Garrett lunged for a .45-caliber pistol that was used around the camp to shoot skunks and other varmints. As Briscoe came at him, fire in his eyes, Garrett turned and pulled the trigger. The two were so close together that the exploding powder from the pistol scorched Briscoe's clothing. The lead bullet punched into his left side at the waistline, then ripped across his body and exited on the opposite side just above the lower pocket of his otter skin vest. The young man collapsed at Garrett's feet.

A stunned and trembling Garrett helped the cook carry Briscoe to one of the bedrolls. When the lad complained of being cold, they quickly scrounged more blankets for him.

Then Briscoe called out to his killer: "Pat, come here, please."

Garrett walked over to Briscoe, wishing it was all a bad dream, trying somehow to make sense of what refused to make sense.

"I am dying, Pat. Won't you forgive me?"

"Yes," Garrett said, and then he returned to the campfire, tears streaming down his cheeks. Young Joe Briscoe lived only twenty minutes more.

Leaving Briscoe's body untouched, Garrett mounted a horse and trotted after Glenn in Rath City, but Glenn had taken a different route on his return to camp, and they missed each other. Garrett finally appeared the next day, muddy and wet from having been out on the prairie all night during a horrendous storm. He remorsefully told Glenn what had happened, at the same time second-guessing his actions—maybe he was too quick to fire, maybe Briscoe did not really intend to use the axe. Glenn did not have the heart to censure his partner, saying only, "It's a pretty hard thing, Pat, for a man to lose his life that way." Garrett asked what he should do, and Glenn advised him to go to Fort Griffin and turn himself in. This he did, but after a few days Garrett was back in camp. The law at Fort Griffin had little inclination to deal with the guilt-ridden buffalo hunter. There was no witness to corroborate or dispute his story (and claim of self-defense), and Joe Briscoe's body was buried miles away, marked only by an ordinary clump of mesquite. No charges were pressed and Garrett was never tried.

Winter was the main season for hunting buffalo on the Staked Plains, because the hair on the robes was longer and thicker and thus more valuable. Pat Garrett abandoned the buffalo range in the off-seasons, gambling away his earnings in places like Dodge City and St. Louis. He would, years later, recall meeting Bat Masterson in Dodge, and, also years later, Wyatt Earp would remember Garrett as among the cow town's legendary cast of gun-toting characters.

By the spring of 1878, reports were coming in from the different trading points that the once endless herds of bison were all but "played out"—approximately two hundred thousand hides had been harvested that last season alone. There were simply no more buffalo to kill. Very few hunters came away from the business with a great deal of money, especially if they, like Garrett, had developed a fondness for gambling. And the Glenn-Garrett party had experienced the extra misfortune of having lost hundreds of hides, as well as horses and supplies, in two different Comanche raids in 1877. So, early in 1878, Garrett, Glenn, and fellow skinner Nick Ross abandoned their wagons and personal possessions near a place known as Casas Amarillas (Yellow Houses) and headed west. Garrett never explained why the three chose to go to New Mexico Territory. A writer friend of Garrett's chalked it up to "a love of adventure."

IT WAS A COLD February day when Pat Garrett and his two companions first showed up at Fort Sumner on the Pecos River. The military post of Fort Sumner had been established to oversee thousands of Navajos, as well as several hundred Mescalero Apaches, confined on the Bosque Redondo reservation. Once the Navajos were allowed to return to their ancestral lands three hundred miles to the west, there was no need for a reservation or a garrisoned post.

Fort Sumner was abandoned in 1869 and its buildings sold the following year. The buyer was Lucien Bonaparte Maxwell, who paid $5,000. With more than thirty Hispanic and Indian families in tow, Maxwell moved from his old home in Cimarron to Fort Sumner. They dammed the Pecos, planted crops, and tended thousands of cattle and sheep. The fort became an instant small town, its several adobe buildings converted into family residences, a dance hall, a store, even a saloon. Lucien Maxwell died in 1875, leaving his son Peter to maintain the family empire. Instead, "Pete" Maxwell, who made his home in the substantial officers' quarters overlooking the former parade ground, oversaw its gradual decline.

Pete Maxwell and the residents of Fort Sumner were accustomed

Pete Maxwell (seated) and friend Henry Leis.

to seeing some rough characters come in off the surrounding nothing-ness, but the twenty-seven-year-old Garrett must have been among the scariest. When he arrived in February 1878, his hair was long and scraggly, and he had a scruffy beard. It was impossible on the frontier to get store-bought pants for a man six feet, four inches tall, so Pat had sewn nearly two feet of buffalo hide to the bottoms of his duck canvas trousers. His drooping, broad-brimmed hat was grimy from campfire smoke and being handled time and again by its owner's greasy hands, and his belt bristled with skinning knives and cartridges for his Sharps buffalo gun. Glenn and Ross looked nearly as rough, and all three men were hungry and broke.

Between them, they had a total of one dollar and fifty cents as they walked into Fort Sumner's store. The simple establishment served meals for fifty cents each, but Pat opted to invest all of their funds in flour and bacon, grub they could stretch out into several meals. A little later, as they sat on the bank of the Pecos enjoying their breakfast feast, they saw a cloud of dust rising in the distance. This turned out to be a herd of cattle and several riders working it.

"Go on up there and get a job," Pat prodded Ross.

The man headed over to the cow outfit but soon returned, saying the boss, Pete Maxwell, did not need any extra hands.

"Well, he's got to have help," Pat said as he got up off the ground.

Looking as wild as ever, Garrett went straight up to Maxwell and made his pitch. Maxwell declined again. Garrett told him with some conviction that he had come to work and work he would—Garrett, as Glenn later observed, "was always persistent in getting what he went after."

"What can you do, Lengthy?" asked Maxwell.

"Ride anything with hair and rope better than any man you've got here."

It was the right thing to say at the right time; Pat Garrett got his job.

Garrett and his fellow hide hunters moved into one of the fort buildings, quickly discovering Sumner's primary attraction (besides the saloon): the several good-looking Hispanic girls who also lived there. Garrett and his friends were soon sharing their modest quarters with some of these young ladies. While Garrett had probably picked up some Spanish in Texas, he received a crash course here. In Spanish, his name was pronounced "Patricio," although some preferred to call him by the nickname Juan Largo, meaning Long John.

Maxwell's sister, Paulita, remembered that everybody at Fort Sumner liked Garrett: "He was an easy-going, agreeable man, a good story-teller, and full of dry humor. He was fond of a social glass, and was a great hand to play poker and monte." Garrett also liked to cut a rug, and, by all accounts, he was good at it. The weekly *baile* (dance), held in the spacious former Quartermaster's Depot, drew attractive young ladies from the communities of Puerto de Luna, Santa Rosa, and even Anton Chico, ninety miles distant. Yet Sumner's female offerings and gay times were not enough to keep Glenn and Ross at the fort; they left before the summer was out. It was about this same time, for reasons long ago forgotten, that Garrett and Maxwell had a falling-out. The former hide hunter collected his wages but he did not pull up stakes, not this time.

Some accounts say Garrett opened a short-lived eating place with his saved cowboy wages. He is also said to have raised hogs and eventually partnered in a saloon and grocery business. In late 1879, Garrett and his friend Barney Mason opened a butcher shop. It might have been a success had they not been caught processing beef that did not belong to them. Garrett promised to pay the owners of the cattle, which he never did, and the shop went out of business after about a month. Whether or not all these ventures really took place, they do reflect a pattern in Garrett's life. A proud man, Pat Garrett was determined to get ahead, to be successful, and thus retrieve a semblance of what his family had lost in Louisiana. He was willing to try just about anything that had the promise of financial rewards and, if not a certain social status, at least respect. "Pat was a working devil," recalled his friend John Meadows. "He'd work at anything." That anything would eventually include the job of manhunter.

LIKE GARRETT, BILLY THE KID came to New Mexico in a roundabout way, although he never called himself "Billy the Kid"—a name folks started calling him in the last six months of his life. Before that, he was Billy Bonney, Kid Antrim, or just "the Kid." And not long before that, he was little Henry McCarty, the son of the widow Catherine McCarty. His string of aliases and nicknames does not say much about the origins and childhood of Billy the Kid, and the enigmatic outlaw had more than a little to do with keeping it that way.

At Fort Sumner in June 1880, Billy told census taker Lorenzo Labadie that his name was William Bonney, that he was twenty-five years old (which meant he was born in 1855), and that he had been born in Missouri, as had both of his parents. If the person who gave this information to Labadie was indeed Billy the Kid, then he was offering up a complete fabrication, a whole new identity to go along with his Bonney alias. Six months later, after Pat Garrett's much-publicized capture of Billy, the Kid told more than one person that he was born in New York City. According to Garrett's 1882 biography, the outlaw was born in that beckoning metropolis on November 23, 1859, although it is anyone's guess how that date was obtained. Birth certificates were not required in the mid-nineteenth century, and there is no family bible entry for the babe who would one day become America's most famous gunman. In January and April 1881, New Mexico newspapers reported that Billy's age was twenty-one. If his birthday did occur in November, that would make 1859 his year of birth.

The few tantalizing hints of Billy's early life must necessarily come through his mother, Catherine McCarty. She had been born in Ireland but later emigrated to the United States, perhaps while still a child but maybe as a young bride. A plucky woman, Catherine and her two boys, Henry and Joseph (born in 1863), called Indianapolis, Indiana, home for a short time in the mid- to late 1860s. She is recorded in Indianapolis city directories for 1867 and 1868 as the widow of Michael. Michael McCarty may or may not have been Billy's father. And he may have died in New York City, or he may have perished in the Civil War as a member of an Indiana regiment. As far as we know, Billy never spoke his father's name to any of his New Mexico acquaintances. In any case, the Catherine McCarty family was not much different from other families that found themselves without a husband and father immediately following the Civil War. And little Henry McCarty was probably not much different from other boys his age—hating school and living for play and mischief.

Sometime in 1865, Catherine met William H. Antrim, a veteran of the Fifty-fourth Indiana Volunteer Infantry who worked in Indianapolis as a driver and clerk for the Merchant's Union Express Company. He was twenty-three years old; she was thirty-six. Yet despite their difference in age, the two developed a relationship, perhaps platonic at first, but eventually growing into something more serious. In 1870, before the census taker made his rounds, the McCarty clan and William Antrim left Indiana and headed to Kansas. The move could have been a search for a healthier place to live, because Catherine McCarty is known to have later suffered from tuberculosis. But it could have as easily been about a move westward. Much of America's population was on the move, and there was an optimism about the West and the prospects it offered for a better life; all one needed was gumption, a piece of open land, and a little good luck. Kansas had the land.

The McCartys and Antrim settled in Wichita, a delightful culture shock for young Henry if there ever was one. Located at the junction of the Little Arkansas and Arkansas rivers, in south-central Kansas, the young town (founded in 1868 and incorporated two years later) was a true frontier crossroads. It had a strange, somewhat naked appearance—the town had been laid out on the open prairie completely absent of trees—and there was the constant and annoying sound of hammers from the construction of dozens of new houses and buildings. Lining the town's main thoroughfare were makeshift restaurants, boardinghouses, saloons, butcher shops, bakeries, clothing stores, a barbershop, a drugstore, a livery stable, and several carpenter shops.

The ten-year-old Henry McCarty saw incredible things, sights his young friends back in Indiana would have given their souls to see. On a daily basis, the pageant of the American West passed before him—a tad begrimed, to be sure. Cowboys, freighters, buffalo hunters, homesteaders, and soldiers clomped noisily up and down the town's board-walks. Indian men, women, and children, residents of Indian Territory (Oklahoma) to the south, shuffled in and out of stores as they stocked up on supplies. But the longhorn was king. Immense herds of Texas cattle forded the Arkansas here on their way to Abilene. During one three-day stretch that summer of 1870, 18,000 longhorns crossed the river, a fraction of the 200,000 to 300,000 that crossed that season.

From all appearances, Catherine and William intended to remain in the Kansas boomtown. They both invested in town lots, and Catherine started her own business on North Main Street. The *Wichita Tribune* wrote about her venture in its inaugural issue of March 15, 1871: "The City Laundry is kept by Mrs. McCarty, to whom we recommend those who wish to have their linen made clean." If the widow McCarty was suffering from tuberculosis at that time, the tedious hand washing of linens and other laundry in a damp, steamy place certainly did not help her condition. If she was not ill when she arrived in Wichita, her workplace would have made her susceptible to the disease. She then either inhaled the deadly bacteria from a coughing customer, or it came, innocently enough, through the milk of an infected cow.

Catherine and her two boys probably started out by living in the quarters over the laundry, and at nighttime they were likely treated to some occasional gunfire from the streets below—it was a woolly cow town, after all. William Antrim and widow McCarty were not yet married, and it does not appear that they were living together, although there is not enough evidence to be certain about this. On March 4, 1871, Catherine moved her family into a small frame house that William had built for her northeast of Wichita's business district. This was definitely an improvement, and it would suggest that everything was going according to plan for the McCartys that spring of 1871. But things happen, and plans change. By the end of the summer, Catherine had sold off all her Wichita property and, along with her two boys and Antrim, had left Wichita for good.

Perhaps Catherine's health prompted the hasty departure for Denver. (Billy later told his friend Frank Coe that the family moved to Denver when he was about twelve years old.) Many others stricken with consumption had traveled to Denver for its "bracing atmosphere and pure water," believing, as did their physicians, that these, along with plenty of sunshine, were the keys to their recovery. The high plains and mountains of the American West had long enjoyed a legendary reputation for healthfulness, bolstered by more than a few miracle cases. The Rocky Mountains also enjoyed a reputation for mineral riches, which could just as easily have been the overriding motivation for the McCarty-Antrim move to Colorado—William Antrim eventually became a miner obsessed with striking it rich.

Exactly how long the McCartys and Antrim remained in Denver is unknown, perhaps only a few months, because soon they were living in Santa Fe, New Mexico Territory. On March 1, 1873, William H. Antrim and Mrs. Catherine McCarty were joined in matrimony at the First Presbyterian Church of Santa Fe. Among the witnesses to the modest ceremony were Catherine's two sons, Henry and Joseph (Josie to family and friends). Significantly, the church marriage register described William and Catherine as "both of Santa Fe." No sooner had Mr. and Mrs. Antrim exchanged vows, however, than they began making arrangements to move again. William, it appears, had become seduced by the fabulous reports of mineral discoveries in the southwestern part of the Territory at a place dubbed, enticingly enough, Silver City.

Antrim was not the only one. That June, the *Santa Fe Sentinel*'s editor commented on the starry-eyed prospectors who were passing through the capital each week and expressed his wish that they would find the mines even richer than expected, so that the whole world would know New Mexico as "the great El Dorado of the West." No matter that the boomtown was 350 hard miles from Santa Fe, or that it was surrounded by rugged hills near the Continental Divide, or that it was located in the heart of Apache country. As the Spanish conquistadors, and countless other dream chasers who came after, could well attest, El Dorados never came easy. And so William Antrim whisked his family off to Silver City.

The Antrims' new home was a square-hewn log cabin on Silver City's south Main Street, near its intersection with Broadway. For whatever reason, the family no longer enjoyed the financial stability it had experienced in Wichita, and as silver ore was not piled around on the ground just waiting to be picked up, both William and Catherine had to work to put bread on the table. William found employment as a butcher and carpenter, trades that could earn as high as six to eight dollars a day. But he does not seem to have worked his jobs full-time. Naturally, he took off to prospect for his own silver mine, and, according to some accounts, to patronize the boomtown's gambling halls. Unfortunately, William Antrim was lucky at neither mining nor gambling.

Catherine took in laundry, baked pies and other treats, and even accepted boarders into their small home. Louis Abraham, a playmate of Henry and Joseph McCarty, had fond memories of the Antrim cabin. Mrs. Antrim "always welcomed the boys with a smile and a joke," he recalled. "The cookie jar was never empty to the boys. From school each afternoon we made straight for the Antrim home to play." Abraham also remembered Catherine at the weekly dances, where she kicked up her heels in a most impressive Highland fling. Such displays became less frequent, however, as her disease progressed.

Henry McCarty's friends remembered him as skinny and small, even somewhat girlish. His brother, Joseph, although younger, was actually bigger than Henry. "My sister and I went to school with Billy the Kid," recalled the sheriff's son, Harry Whitehill. "He wasn't a bad fellow." And according to Louis Abraham, Henry was "full of fun and mischief." Not surprisingly, Henry and Joseph spent as much time, if not more, in the dance halls and saloons as they did in school and at home. In fact, Silver City's first public school did not start until January 1874 and lasted less than three months. To keep the pupils out of trouble until school resumed, they were encouraged to put on some kind of theatrical entertainment to raise money for the new schoolhouse. The students decided that a blackface minstrel show was just the thing. Henry, who seems to have had a passion for music, surely reveled in the minstrel show's raucous nature and crude humor.

One of Catherine's boarders in the spring of 1874 was Marshall Ashmun Upson, known by friend and foe alike as "Ash." Born in Wolcott, Connecticut, in 1828, Ash was a gregarious newspaperman who claimed he had once tutored the children of Mormon leader Brigham Young. He appeared to be constantly on the move, finding it difficult to remain in one place for very long. He also found it difficult to remain sober for very long, and to prove it he had several battle scars, including a "badly damaged" nose. In one of those extraordinary coincidences that history often throws at us, Ash Upson eventually became Pat Garrett's best friend and the ghostwriter of Garrett's 1882 biography of Billy the Kid.

Upson boarded with Catherine and the boys for no more than three months, during which time he must have witnessed Catherine's worsening condition. In this age well before antibiotics, there was no real remedy for tuberculosis. The famed prairie or wilderness cure was largely a myth, an illusion fed by health seekers who never had TB and a few others, the lucky ones, whose disease went into remission. True consumptives were never cured, and, like Catherine Antrim, many died. Her brief obituary ran in the September 19, 1874, issue of the *Silver City Mining Life*.

Sometime before her death, Catherine extracted a pledge from Clara Louisa Truesdell, a Good Samaritan and friend who cared for her at the end. Catherine was justly concerned about her boys, remembered Clara's son, Chauncey, "and she made my mother promise to look out for them if anything should happen to her." Catherine knew she could not depend upon her husband. And sure enough, William Antrim farmed the boys out—and kept farming them out. When Henry was not in school, he made a little money working at the butcher and blacksmith shops, but he also spent more and more time at the card tables. He "was a very fine card player," remembered schoolmate Charley Stevens, "and had picked up many card sharp tricks."

Henry's first bit of trouble involved an attempted theft from a combination candy and furniture store, but his next escapade got the sheriff's attention. In April 1875, he stole several pounds of butter from a rancher by the name of Abel L. Webb. Henry sold the butter to a local merchant, and with butter bringing a dollar a pound, it was more than simple pocket change. The theft occurred shortly after Harvey H. Whitehill, a six-foot-two-inch, 240-pound former miner and Silver City town father, became the Grant County sheriff. Whitehill had no trouble connecting Henry with the stolen butter, but he let the boy go with a promise to stay out of trouble. Some twenty-seven years later, Whitehill recalled this episode and many other tidbits about young Henry McCarty for a Silver City reporter, none of it very flattering. In a colorful but highly doubtful example of nineteenth-century criminal profiling, Whitehill claimed that the young man "had one peculiar facial characteristic that to an experienced man-hunter would have marked him immediately as a bad man, and that was his dancing eyes. They never were at rest but continually shifted and roved, much like his own rebellious nature."

Even this run-in with the law failed to make much of an impression on Henry. The same could be said for a newfound friend, named George Schaefer. A stonemason by profession, Schaefer had acquired the outlaw-appropriate nickname of "Sombrero Jack," presumably because of his distinctive headgear. On Saturday night, September 4, 1875, Schaefer and a number of accomplices broke into the laundry operated by Chinese immigrants Charley Sun and Sam Chung (or Chong), making off with clothing, blankets, and two six-shooters. Days later, Mrs. Brown discovered some of the stolen property in Henry's quarters, and she wasted no time getting word to the sheriff. Whitehill arrested Henry McCarty on Thursday, September 23, and took him to the adobe jailhouse (Sombrero Jack hightailed it out of town before the sheriff could learn of his involvement). "Billy was the most surprised boy in the world when he landed in the jail," recalled Sheriff Whitehill's daughter, Josie. "But he didn't stay there long. He never did."

A day or two into Henry's confinement, he complained to Sheriff Whitehill that the jailer was picking on him and restricting him to solitary confinement, where he could get no exercise. Whitehill ordered the jailer to give Henry the freedom of the building's corridor for a short time each morning. "And right there is where we fell down," Whitehill admitted, "for the 'Kid' had a mind whose ingenuity we knew not of at that time." The sheriff continued: "He was only a boy, you must remember, scarcely over 15 years of age."

His jailers left him alone in the corridor, with no one watching or guarding him. After a half hour they returned and unlocked the heavy oaken doors to the jail. They looked everywhere but Henry was gone. Whitehill said, "I ran outside around the jail and a Mexican standing on a ridge at the rear, asked whom I was hunting. I replied in Spanish 'a prisoner.' He came out of the chimney, answered the Mexican. I ran back into the jail, looked up the big old fashioned chimney and sure enough could see where in an effort to obtain a hold his hand had clawed into the thick layer of soot which lined the sides of the flue. The chimney hole itself did not appear as large as my arm and yet the lad squeezed his frail, slender body through it and gained his liberty."

Covered from head to toe in black soot—like a reprisal of his role as the minstrel show's interlocutor—Henry fled Silver City and never came back. In Sheriff Whitehill's opinion, it was then that Henry McCarty "commenced his career of lawlessness in earnest."

CRƆ

THERE ARE TOO MANY stories about how Henry McCarty ended up in Arizona to be sure which is the real one. His schoolteacher, Mrs. Mary Chase, said that soon after his jailbreak, Henry appeared at the Knight ranch, fifteen miles southwest of Silver City, where she and her husband were living. She and Mrs. Knight loaned the boy a horse so that he could return to Silver City and turn himself in. If true, Mrs. Chase was not as smart as people thought, because Henry did not go back to Silver City. Chauncey Truesdell said his mother, honoring her pledge to Catherine Antrim, sheltered Henry after his escape and the next morning put him on a stagecoach bound for Arizona, along with her money and some food for the scrawny fugitive to eat along the way. Charley Stevens believed that Henry hid out at a sawmill up in the mountains near Silver City for a time before stealing a horse and leaving the region.

Now that he was out of Silver City, Henry McCarty was living by his wits and whatever survival skills he had picked up in and around town. It was beyond the city limits, however, that survival could be trickiest, especially in the American Southwest of the 1870s and 1880s. Traveling alone put one at greatest risk. If surprised by hostile Apaches or lawless Anglos or Hispanos, you were lucky if you only lost your horse and saddle. An ability to quickly "read" strangers was essential, a skill Henry likely honed while staring across a poker table. Most important of all, perhaps, was the language of the gun. As the saying goes, "God created man, and Colonel Colt made him equal." With a gun, a cocky teenaged boy with little to lose could kill a grown man just as quick as anybody else. Most westerners knew that; some learned it the hard way.

Much has been written about the culture of violence in the American West, but it should come as no surprise that nineteenth-century America was a violent place, or that violence was, for some, a way of life. Only a few years had passed since thousands upon thousands of

Americans had butchered themselves in a bloody Civil War. Particularly brutal was the guerrilla warfare on the Missouri-Kansas border,
with some of the participants making their way to New Mexico after
the fighting ended, as did many other Civil War veterans. America's
westward march across the continent had hardly been peaceful, nor,
for that matter, had Spain's northward march into what would become
New Mexico during Spanish colonial times. Within Henry McCarty's
lifetime, the bitter struggle between American Indians and the U.S.
government was still being played out. Despite the flowery language
of treaty makers and signers, there was no such thing as a "permanent
peace" on the frontier. Recurring outbreaks of hostilities saw Indians slaughtering setters and settlers and soldiers slaughtering Indians.
The newspapers of territorial New Mexico were seldom without some
report of a shooting, stabbing, murder, or Indian attack.

Henry may have been headed to the mining town of Clifton, just
103 miles west of Silver City, where his stepfather was then tirelessly
pursuing his El Dorado. One story has Antrim giving the boy all the
money he had on him; the other has Antrim shunning Henry: "If
that's the kind of boy you are," his stepfather is supposed to have said,
"get out." Maybe one of these stories is near the truth, maybe neither.
In any case, Henry did not remain there long. He drifted southwest,
his route taking him along the Gila River and between the rugged
Gila and Peloncillo mountain ranges.

Henry eventually ended up at Camp Grant, a military post near
the base of Arizona's massive, pine-topped Mount Graham. One of
the more prominent and picturesque ranches in this area was Henry
C. Hooker's Sierra Bonita Rancho, located some six miles southwest
of the post. Henry McCarty worked here for a time, although he was
now Henry Antrim. Then someone, somewhere, got to calling him
"Kid," and the name stuck. But the Kid lost his job at Sierra Bonita
because he was a "lightweight"; he simply lacked the stamina and
skills to measure up to the other cowhands.

Henry then worked off and on as a cook at the modest Hotel de Luna (just inside the Camp Grant military reservation), as a teamster, and as a haymaker for an army forage contractor, jobs that neither paid well nor lasted long. Helping Henry to become a nuisance—and the Kid seldom lacked assistance in such endeavors—was a former cavalryman named John R. Mackie. A native of Scotland, Mackie was ten years older than the Kid, although similar in size. The year previous, Mackie had nearly killed a man, or at least he tried to kill him, over a card game in McDowell's store and saloon. Despite being shot in the throat, the man lived, and Mackie got off on self-defense.

John Mackie and Kid Antrim discovered how easy it was to steal from the soldiers visiting the brothels and saloons in the civilian settlement adjacent to Camp Grant. "Billy and his chum Macky would steal the saddles and saddle blankets from the horses," recalled the Hotel de Luna's proprietor, Miles Wood, "and occasionally they would take the horses and hide them out until they got a chance to dispose of them." On November 17, 1876, when Henry dashed away on the horse of First Sergeant Lewis C. Hartman, the camp's commanding officer, Major Charles E. Compton, ordered Hartman and four other troopers to go after the thief. And even though the Kid had a five-day start, the cavalrymen caught up to him one hundred miles later, near the fledgling mining settlement of McMillen's Camp. They ordered the Kid off the cavalry mount, grabbed the reins, and started immediately on their back trail to Camp Grant, leaving Henry to hoof it alone.

Three months later, after three more cavalry mounts were stolen, the military was determined to put the Kid behind bars. On February 16, 1877, Sergeant Hartman stood before the recently elected justice of the peace, Miles Wood, and swore out a complaint against "Henry Antrim alias Kid" for stealing his horse the previous November. Arrested in Globe City, a silver-mining town in the foothills of the Pinal Mountains, the Kid promptly escaped. The town constable apprehended the young man a second time the next day but, being a slow learner, he somehow managed to let the Kid get loose while on their way to Camp Grant. Henry and Mackie, in an attempt to get the military off their backs, returned five horses to Camp Thomas. This may have made the army quartermaster happy, but Henry was still wanted by the law. When he and Mackie showed up for breakfast at the Hotel de Luna on March 25, Miles Wood served them up his pistol.

"I shoved the platter on the table in front of them and pulled a six-gun from under it and told them to put up their hands and then to go straight out the door," Wood remembered.

With no jail at the civilian settlement, Wood and a volunteer marched the Kid and Mackie to the post guardhouse. Just an hour or so later, Henry, ever watchful for an opportunity to get away, made a run for it. This time, however, he was chased down—and Miles Wood asked for a blacksmith. The justice of the peace stood by and watched as the smith placed shackles on Henry's ankles and pounded the rivets flat. *This would do the trick*, Wood thought, confidently. But that evening, as the setting sun cast fleeting pinks and purples on the distant mountains, Henry planned yet another escape. Sometime after dark, there was a knock at the door of the commanding officer's quarters, where the Major and Mrs. Compton were entertaining Wood and some other guests. It was the sergeant of the guard, who told his superior that Kid Antrim was gone. Captain Gilbert Smith, the Camp Grant quartermaster, was convinced that the Kid had received help from a soldier, but, as Wood later explained, Henry "was a small fellow not weighing over ninety pounds, and it was almost an impossibility to keep him imprisoned or hand-cuffed." Curiously, Henry did not flee the area completely; perhaps because, as Camp Grant cowpuncher Gus Gildea remembered, Henry always had more friends than enemies.

On Friday night, August 17, 1877, Kid Antrim stepped into George Atkins's saloon at the little Camp Grant settlement. The soldiers, cowboys, and girls inside looked toward the door and saw a strikingly different man than the scruffy stray they were used to. This Kid was all duded up, having received an advance on his wages from forage contractor H. F. "Sorghum" Smith. Henry came into town looking like a "country jake," with shoes instead of boots and a pistol stuffed in the waistband of his trousers.

Thirty-two-year-old blacksmith "Windy" Cahill noticed the Kid, too. Cahill, a native of Ireland, had joined the army in 1868 in New York. He had served nearly three years in the infantry, before receiving his discharge. Cahill maintained his ties with the army, though, working as a civilian blacksmith at Camp Grant. He was a stocky, blustering man with a gruff voice, and people called him "Windy" because "he was always blowin' about first one thing and another." In short, Windy Cahill was a bully, and the Kid was his favorite victim. "He would throw Billy to the floor, ruffle his hair, slap his face and humiliate him before the men in the saloon," recalled Gus Gildea.

On this particular August night, Windy and the Kid quickly got into it. One account states that Windy started razzing Henry about his new clothes and gun. Another claims that Windy refused to cough up the money the Kid won from him in a card game. Still another says that it all began as a friendly wrestling match. However it started, their words became heated, and Windy called Henry a pimp, and the Kid shouted back that the blacksmith was nothing but a son of a bitch. "[W]e then took hold of each other," Cahill said. The blacksmith threw the Kid to the ground, pinning his arms with his knees and then slapping the Kid's face.

"You are hurting me. Let me up!" the Kid demanded.

"I want to hurt you. That's why I got you down," Cahill said.

But Kid Antrim was, according to Pat Garrett, someone who "could not and would not stay whipped. When oversized and worsted in a fight, he sought such arms as he could buy, borrow, beg or steal." Garrett may have been overstating the case, but not by much. Wiry and fast, Henry began to work his free right hand around to his pistol. Windy saw what the Kid was trying to do and made a grab for the gun but failed. The Kid turned the pistol so its muzzle was pointing at Cahill and pushed it into the blacksmith's belly. Cahill felt the sharp poke and straightened a little, anticipating the blast from the .45, which followed with a "deafening roar." The initial stab of pain came not from the bullet but from the exploding black powder burning Cahill's flesh around the entry wound, but this being a shot to the gut, the worst was yet to come. The Kid squirmed free as Windy slumped to the floor, smoke slowly rising from his clothing. Henry rushed out the door and jumped on a well-known racing pony named Cashaw, the property of gambler Joseph Murphey. No one tried to stop him.

Windy Cahill suffered through the night and into the next day. On his deathbed, he gave a deposition naming "Henry Antrim, otherwise known as Kid" as his killer. Gus Gildea remembered seeing Joseph Murphey on that Saturday, and Murphey was much more upset about losing his favorite horse than he was about the dying Cahill. Several days later, the gambler's horse appeared courtesy of the Kid. It was also several days later that the newspapers reported that a coroner's jury had found the Kid guilty of murdering Cahill. That settled it for Kid Antrim; he would not be returning to Arizona, nor would he be riding into his old home of Silver City—murder was a hanging offense.

There was one person the Kid desperately wanted to see, and although it would take him into an area where he would be easily recognized, the Kid decided to chance it. He located his brother on the Nicolai farm, situated on the Mimbres River near Georgetown (fourteen miles northeast of Silver City). Near the end of their emotional visit, the Kid speculated that he and Joseph would probably not see each other again. As the tears welled in both young men's eyes, the Kid kissed his brother and said good-bye. Kid Antrim next visited his former teacher, Mrs. Mary Chase, now living in Georgetown. Remembering that the teacher was a good judge of horseflesh, he showed off his handsome mount and related how he had shot and killed its former owner, an Apache Indian. The Kid liked to spin a good tale, however, and if this encounter with his teacher happened at all, it is more likely that he made up the story about killing the Apache rather than admitting he had stolen the horse from some cowboy. He then told Mrs. Chase he needed money.

"My mother gave him all the cash she had in the house, voluntarily," the teacher's daughter said years later, "and Billy stayed on the rest of the day, talking with mother and telling her about his experiences. Along toward evening, he took off."

The Kid headed east across southern New Mexico, little knowing that he was riding to war.

3

War in Lincoln County

There was no law in those days. Public opinion
and the six-shooter settled most all cases.

—FRANK COE

KID ANTRIM DID NOT ride across New Mexico Territory by
himself. On October 2, 1877, he was spotted with a gang of rustlers on the old Butterfield Overland Mail route in southwestern New
Mexico's Cooke's Canyon. Once again he had made a bad choice of
associates—although as a fugitive himself, he had few options. The
leader of the outlaw band, which liked to call itself "The Boys," was
Jesse Evans. Evans was approximately six years older than the Kid,
and he stood five feet six inches tall, weighed around 140 pounds, and
had gray eyes and light hair. Pat Garrett wrote that of the two, the
Kid was slightly taller and a little heavier. Evans's early history is as
hard to pin down as Henry McCarty's. At different times, he claimed
both Missouri and Texas as his birthplace. He may have been the
Jesse Evans who was arrested with his parents in Kansas in 1871, for
passing counterfeit money. Tried before the U.S. District Court in
Topeka, this Jesse was convicted and fined $500. Because he was so

young, he received no jail time and was "most kindly admonished by the court."

Evans came to New Mexico Territory in 1872 and worked with cattle king John S. Chisum on the Pecos. That consisted primarily of stealing horses from the Mescalero Apaches and delivering them up to Chisum. It only got worse from there. By the time he and the Kid crossed paths, Evans had become one of the most hated desperadoes in southern New Mexico. Teaming up with the equally despised Mesilla Valley "rancher" John Kinney, he headed a gang of horse and cattle thieves numbering, at times, as many as thirty men. A cold-blooded killer and accomplished gunman, Evans was used to doing as he pleased with little fear of the law or anyone else. When his harshest critic, *Mesilla Valley Independent* editor Albert J. Fountain, urged the local citizenry to capture and lynch Evans and his gang, Evans threatened Fountain's life (more than once), saying he would give the editor a "free pass to hell." It was no idle threat.

The Boys, including the Kid, made their way across the *playas*, mountains, and deserts of southern New Mexico, freely taking the best delicacies, or what passed for delicacies, that each saloon or stopping place had to offer, ordering their nervous hosts to "chalk it up." At Mesilla, Kid Antrim stole a splendid little racing mare that just happened to belong to the daughter of the county sheriff. The Boys continued eastward from the Mesilla Valley, traveling over San Augustin Pass, across the White Sands, and to the village of Tularosa, which they terrorized one evening with their carousing and the firing off of their ample supply of guns. The desperadoes next crossed the Sacramento Mountains and finally ended up at the Seven Rivers settlement in the Pecos Valley, approximately 250 miles from Mesilla. By this point, the Kid was no longer with them, having separated from the main party under Evans.

Hardly more than a spot on the road, Seven Rivers consisted of a single flat-roofed adobe of several rooms, one of which contained a well-stocked store. Out back were several gravestones; close by, between low dirt banks, flowed the Pecos River. The "settlement" was actually a hodgepodge of scattered ranches and homesteads, surrounded by miles and miles of the finest grazing land in the Southwest, most notably the Chisum Range on the east side of the Pecos. Named for John S. Chisum, the range stretched from Seven Rivers north to the mouth of the Hondo, a distance of approximately sixty miles. Over the last few years, it had supported between twenty thousand and sixty thousand head of cattle, beef that went to fill government contracts at military posts and Indian reservations in New Mexico and Arizona. It had also supported some of Chisum's Seven Rivers neighbors, who were not above helping themselves to his beeves, a situation that had erupted into the short-lived Pecos War earlier in the year.

The Seven Rivers store was owned by small-time rancher Heiskell Jones, and this is where the Kid turned up by mid-October 1877, possibly horseless after a run-in with Apache Indians in the Guadalupe Mountains—at least that is the story Antrim told. He was no longer Henry Antrim or even Kid Antrim. Now he was William H. Bonney. Some have speculated that he settled on Bonney because his father was not Michael McCarty at all, and his real father was a former husband or lover of his mother's whose last name was Bonney. Regardless of what the Kid called himself, Heiskell's wife, Barbara, took the gun-toting boy in. Known affectionately up and down the Pecos as "Ma'am Jones," Barbara had a large family of her own to care for (between 1855 and 1878, she would have a total of nine boys and one daughter), yet she was famous for feeding, doctoring, and sheltering neighbors and strangers alike.

As related time and again by those who knew him, William H. Bonney had a charm or magnetism that was irresistible to the ladies; they wanted to mother him or take him for a roll in the hay. Ma'am wanted to mother him. "My mother loved him," recalled Sam Jones. "He was always courteous and deferential to her. She said he had the nicest manners of any young man in the country. She never could bear to hear anyone speak ill of him." And both Sam and Frank Jones agreed that if "Billy had been a bad boy, Mother would not have wanted him around. And she was a pretty good judge of men." Heiskell Jones freighted his own goods from Las Vegas to Seven Rivers, and the Kid went with Heiskell on one or more of these long trips. Billy also developed a close friendship with twenty-four-year-old John Jones, the eldest of the brothers. The Kid's time at the Jones place may have lasted as few as three weeks or as long as three months. However long he stayed, it was plenty of time to make the Jones family loyal Billy the Kid supporters (and Pat Garrett haters) for the rest of their lives.

By this time, the Kid had become obsessed with guns and was impressive in his handling of them. Lily Casey, no fan of Billy's, saw the Kid during this period and remembered that he "was active and graceful as a cat. At Seven Rivers he practiced continually with pistol or rifle, often riding at a run and dodging behind the side of his mount to fire, as the Apaches did. He was very proud of his ability to pick up a handkerchief or other objects from the ground while riding at a run." Lily's mother, the widow Ellen Casey, was bound for Texas with a herd of cattle and Billy hit her up for a job. But Mrs. Casey sensed, as her daughter later remarked, that Billy "was not addicted to regular work." Lily and her brother, Robert, considered the Kid little more than a bum—he did not get the job.

Sometime that fall, Billy Bonney appeared at Frank Coe's ranch on the upper Rio Ruidoso, looking for work. Coe was known to be both handy with a gun and quick to use one. But the Kid looked so young that Coe had a hard time taking him seriously. "I invited him to stop with us until he could find something to do," Frank recalled. "There wasn't much entertainment those days, except to hunt." But there *was* entertainment in watching Billy play with his shootin' irons: "He spent all his spare time cleaning his six-shooter and practicing shooting. He could take two six-shooters, loaded and cocked, one on each hand, his fore-finger between the trigger and guard, and twirl one in one direction and the other in the other direction, at the same time."

Billy soon found something to do. A short time earlier, on October 17, Jesse Evans and three of The Boys had been corralled by a posse under Lincoln County sheriff William Brady. Now they were being held in a miserable hole in the ground known as the Lincoln County jail. Completed that same month, the jail cells were in a dugout ten feet deep, its walls lined with square-hewn timber. The ceiling was made from logs chinked with mud and covered with dirt, and the only entrance was a single door. Prisoners were forced to climb down a ladder, which was then withdrawn and the door shut tight. Pat Garrett condemned the jail as "unfit for a dog-kennel." Evans and the other prisoners whiled away the time playing cards and boasting that their friends would soon come to break them out. And sure enough, by mid-November, several of The Boys, among them Billy Bonney, had a plan to rescue their leader from the Lincoln hellhole.

IF ANY SINGLE CHUNK of land embodied the American West, it was Lincoln County. The largest county in the United States at that time (nearly thirty thousand square miles), it spilled across the entire southeast section of New Mexico Territory. Stark plains rolled away to the horizon in its eastern half, bisected by slivers of water with evocative names like the Pecos and Rio Hondo. To the west, its rugged Sacramento, Capitan, and Guadalupe mountain ranges rose to nearly twelve thousand feet at their highest point. There were very few settlements, except for several ranching operations and the occasional Hispanic village or *placita*. The county's human population numbered approximately two thousand; cattle numbered in the tens of thousands. A sole military post, Fort Stanton, was located just nine miles west of the county seat, also named Lincoln, and was there to keep watch over the still-wild Mescalero Apaches.

Nestled in the Rio Bonito Valley, the town of Lincoln was like other territorial settlements. Several adobe homes and stores, their thick mud-brick walls serving as a perfect insulation against the wearying heat of summer and the biting cold of winter, were scattered for a mile on both sides of a hard-packed dirt road. In the heart of the village, on the north side of this one and only street, stood the *torreón*, a three-story tower of rock and adobe constructed by residents years before as their main defense against plundering Indians. The town saw a fairly steady stream of settlers, who came to register land transactions or conduct business with the courts, at the same time purchasing supplies, picking up mail, and hearing the latest news.

The Hispanic citizens of Lincoln, who made up the majority of the town's population, irrigated small fields on the Bonito, tended sheep flocks, and worked where they could as day laborers. Fort Stanton offered both civilian job opportunities and a market for livestock and produce. A few Lincoln families were involved in the overland freight-

Lincoln, New Mexico Territory.

ing business; Hispanos were famed *arrieros* (muleteers) dating back to Spanish colonial times. To outsiders, this place was a world both exotic and backward.

Most Anglos in the territory held strongly racist views toward Hispanos (and vice versa). Certainly, one could find affluent Hispanos in the territorial government and, more commonly, in county positions. But it was painfully clear to Hispanos what their place was expected to be. On October 10, 1875, Lincoln farmer Gregorio Balenzuela made the mistake of calling Alexander "Ham" Mills a gringo. Mills pulled out his gun and shot the man dead, after which Mills rode out of town unmolested. A year later, the New Mexico governor pardoned Mills for the murder. No wonder the Spanish-speaking Billy the Kid, who defied the gringo laws and humiliated the sheriffs and their posses, who rode like an Apache and kicked up his heels as gracefully as any vaquero, became, if not a favorite, certainly a sympathetic figure to native New Mexicans. To them, he was simply Billito or el Chivato.

IN THE EARLY-MORNING HOURS of November 17, 1877, the dark figures of more than twenty horsemen passed quietly into Lincoln. It was The Boys, including Billy, and they rode straight to the county jail. At the jail, ten men dismounted and slipped through the main door, which was curiously unlocked. The jailer was asleep inside, but he soon awoke to a gun barrel pointed at his head. It was 3:00 A.M., and the jailer watched as The Boys went to work on the trapdoor to the jail cells. The gunmen had brought heavy, rock-filled sacks, and they used these to bust through the wooden door to the dungeonlike cells below. Jesse Evans and the other gang members were waiting for them. A confederate had been able to get files and wood augurs to the prisoners, and Jesse and his pals had been busily working on their shackles in preparation for the breakout. Jesse and the others climbed up the ladder lowered to them, some with their leg braces still attached. It was still dark and tranquil when the bunch rode out of town; most of Lincoln's citizens did not get the news of the brazen escape until well after sunup.

For Evans and The Boys, it was now back to business as usual, stealing livestock and making death threats, with little to fear from the law. Not so for Billy—the law nabbed him a month later at Seven Rivers, where he was apprehended with a pair of horses that belonged to English rancher John Henry Tunstall. The Kid may have stolen the horses himself or traded with one of The Boys, but regardless, it was now his turn to spend some time in the subterranean Lincoln jail, and he did not like it one bit. He apparently requested a meeting with Tunstall, which must have gone well, because the Englishman had the Kid released and gave him a job on his Rio Feliz ranch.

Billy may have promised to testify against his friends in exchange for his freedom. The relationship between the Kid and Evans had been strained ever since Billy stole the little racing mare back in Mesilla. The mare had been Sheriff Mariano Barela's daughter's favorite, and the sheriff, Billy discovered a little too late, was a crony of Evans's. Billy also may have been ticked off that none of The Boys came to his rescue in Lincoln like he had done for them. Whatever Billy's reasons, by joining Tunstall he had officially taken sides in one of the most famous and bitter feuds in the American West, an ugly struggle for profits and economic dominance that became known as the Lincoln County War.

For years, the mercantile firm of L. G. Murphy & Co. and its successor, J. J. Dolan & Co., commonly known as "The House," had the upper hand in just about every moneymaking venture in the region. It operated for a time as the post trader at Fort Stanton and received numerous government contracts for beef, corn, flour, and other provisions. In Lincoln, The House maintained a brewery, saloon, and restaurant, as well as a large store. It also performed, on a limited basis, the services of a bank. Yet The House's unashamed greed (even though many of its business practices were not unusual for the time), its long reach into local government, and its connection to territorial power brokers in New Mexico's capital—the infamous "Santa Fe Ring"—earned it considerable ill will among the locals.

"Only those who have experienced it can realize the extent to which Murphy & Co. dominated the country and controlled its people, economy, and politics," remembered one county resident. "All Lincoln County was cowed and intimidated by them. To oppose them was to court disaster." Three men—John Henry Tunstall, Alexander A. McSween, and John S. Chisum—did oppose The House's regional supremacy, and it cost two of them their lives.

A twenty-four-year-old Englishman with plenty of gumption—and capital to go with it—John Henry Tunstall first arrived in Lincoln

John Henry Tunstall.

County in November 1876, determined to carve out his own modest empire from its vast lands. He was also a sure enough dude, complete with tailored suits (he had a penchant for Harris tweed), riding outfits, and top boots. His hair was sandy colored and wavy, though well groomed, and he sported chin whiskers and a pencil-thin mustache. In photographs, he appears as stiff and aristocratic as the man on the Prince Albert tobacco tins, but those close to the young Englishman thought he was good-looking and personable. He was a prolific letter writer, expounding at length to his father in England (his chief financial backer) on the Wild West and predicting that he would make a fortune there. His plans could just as easily have been written by a member of The House: "I propose to confine my operations to Lincoln County, but I intend to handle it in such a way as to get the half of every dollar that is made in the county by anyone, and with our means we could get things into that shape in three years, if we only used two thirds of our capital in the undertaking."

Tunstall had focused his sights on southeastern New Mexico because of a chance meeting with Lincoln attorney Alexander A. McSween at a Santa Fe hotel. McSween, a Scotsman ten years Tunstall's senior, was new to the Territory as well, having arrived with his wife, Susan, in March 1875. With a drooping mustache as thick as his Scottish brogue, McSween had initially worked as a lawyer for The House, where he got an insider's look into the firm's many business dealings. Within a few months, McSween had used this privileged information to help Tunstall buy a cattle ranch and open a mercantile store in Lincoln. The pair also established a bank; cattleman John S. Chisum served as the bank's president. Chisum had his own grievances against The House, whose loose policy when buying beef for its government contracts had served as an open invitation for rustlers to steal from Chisum's herds on the Pecos.

The carefully plotted competition from Tunstall and McSween came at a time when The House was financially on its knees (the prin-

Alexander McSween.   James "Jimmy" Dolan.

cipals were not the best businessmen). And the fact that Tunstall was
an upper-class English Protestant, while The House hothead, Jimmy
Dolan, and his partner, John Riley, were both Irish Catholic, made
this even worse. Born in County Galway, Ireland, in 1848, Dolan had
emigrated to the United States at age six. During the Civil War, he
had been a drummer boy for one of the colorful Zouave regiments
from New York State, and it was as a U.S. infantryman that he had
come to Lincoln County. He was short, just five feet, two and one-half
inches tall, and his temper was even shorter.

By early February 1878, both sides had spread vicious rumors about
the other; both had attacked each other publicly in the territorial
press; and both had spewed out a few choice personal threats. Both
had also put men on their payrolls who knew the inner workings of
a Colt six-shooter and a Winchester repeater. The House, what with
its cozy relationship with the district court, had orchestrated criminal

charges (embezzlement) and a civil suit against McSween. But Dolan's legal shenanigans achieved their finest moment on February 7, when he secured a writ of attachment against McSween. Dolan turned the writ over to Sheriff William Brady, another House tool, who happily attached any and all property of both McSween *and* Tunstall: store, lands, cattle, horses—even such personal items as portraits of Tunstall's parents.

The first blood spilled in the Lincoln County War came just eleven days later at approximately 5:30 P.M. Tunstall and four of his men, including the Kid, were on their way to Lincoln with a small herd of horses. Tunstall's party, strung out over a distance of a few hundred yards, had just crested a divide and was descending through the rugged hills above the Ruidoso Valley when they flushed a flock of wild turkeys. Two of Tunstall's men started after the dusky birds; moments later, shots rang out on their back trail. Billy and John Middleton, who had been bringing up the rear, came forward at a gallop. Behind them, riding hard, was a party of nearly twenty mounted men, members of a posse sent to gather up Tunstall's horses, except it was obvious that this posse was bent on more than simply attaching livestock. Middleton raced toward Tunstall, who had remained near the horse herd, and shouted at him to flee. Agitated and confused by the gunfire and commotion, Tunstall did nothing.

"For God's sake, follow me," Middleton pleaded before spurring his horse on.

"What, John? What, John?" was all the surprised Tunstall managed to speak.

At the first sight of the posse, the turkey chasers, Dick Brewer and Robert Widenmann, had retreated to a nearby hillside, where they planned to make a stand behind some large boulders and trees. Middleton and the Kid were close behind them. Their pursuers pulled up when they saw Tunstall by himself.

The first members of the posse who approached Tunstall were

William "Buck" Morton, who was Jimmy Dolan's stock foreman, and Tom Hill. Hill was one of The Boys who had been imprisoned with Jesse Evans in the Lincoln County jail (Evans was also a member of this posse—The Boys were Dolan men, bought and paid for). Tunstall froze when he recognized Morton and Hill, but Hill said he would not be hurt if he gave himself up. Tunstall urged his horse toward the two men. When the Englishman got close, Morton put a rifle bullet through his chest. Tunstall tumbled out of his saddle. Hill then leapt off his mount and ran up to the dying man and fired a pistol into the back of Tunstall's head. Billy and the others on the hillside heard the shots, but they could not see what had just transpired. With a stunned voice, Middleton said that Tunstall must have been killed.

In a bizarre act, the posse members carefully arranged Tunstall's body, placing one blanket beneath it and another over it. The dead man's overcoat was placed under his bloody head. Tunstall's horse, which had also been killed, was lying next to its owner. Someone in the posse lifted the horse's head and shoved Tunstall's hat under it. The posse did not bother with Billy and the others. Instead, they gathered the stock they were after and rode away. Tunstall's men waited until it was good and dark and then headed to Lincoln. They would see to Tunstall's remains later. Billy and Widenmann arrived in the county seat between ten and eleven that evening. Despite the tensions building in Lincoln for some time, the news they brought startled the town. The posse members would later claim that Tunstall had fired upon them first, but as far as the Kid and the others in the McSween camp were concerned—as well as nearly everyone else in Lincoln—Tunstall's death was nothing short of cold-blooded murder.

Tunstall's body arrived in the county seat the following day. Because the corpse had been strapped to the back of a horse for part of its final journey, the Englishman's fine clothes were torn, and his face was scratched from going through the brush and scrub oak in the mountains. Billy stared down at the corpse after it was laid out on a table in McSween's home.

"I'll get some of them before I die," he said, and then he turned away.

Billy had known Tunstall less than three months, but by all accounts, he liked him a great deal. Frank Collinson, a Texas cowpuncher who first met Billy on the Pecos in 1878, remembered years later the few words the Kid spoke about his former employer: "I heard him say that Tunstall was the only man who ever treated him as if he were freeborn and white."

It was no use going to Sheriff Brady for help—after all, the posse that killed Tunstall was acting under the sheriff's authority—but McSween was just as good at manipulating the legal system as Dolan. He marched Billy, Brewer, and Middleton over to Justice of the Peace John B. Wilson, and they swore out affidavits naming those in the posse. Warrants were issued for the accused and turned over to Atanacio Martínez, the town constable. Martínez did not especially want to confront Brady and his well-armed men, but some in the McSween crowd threatened to kill him if he did not do his duty. On Wednesday, February 20, Martínez, with "deputies" Frederick Waite (a twenty-four-year-old, part Chickasaw Tunstall man from Indian Territory), and Billy Bonney, walked to the two-story Dolan store in Lincoln to make the arrests. It did not go well. Brady refused to let the constable arrest any members of his posse, and the sheriff showed that he had the firepower advantage and arrested them.

"You little son of a bitch, give me your gun!" Brady growled at the Kid.

"Take it, you old son of a bitch!" Billy said, handing over his weapon.

Both the Kid and Waite were released after thirty hours, but they were still in jail when Tunstall's funeral took place the following afternoon. If the wind was just right, they may have heard Susan Mc-

Sheriff William Brady.

Sween's parlor organ, which had been carried outside to the burial place behind Tunstall's store. And perhaps the two comrades faintly heard the singing of hymns, all the while growing increasingly determined to have their revenge.

BY THE FIRST OF March, both sides were seething with hatred and neither would be satisfied until the other was completely ruined. Alexander McSween was so scared that Sheriff Brady would arrest him—after which he believed he would be assassinated—that he had temporarily fled his home in Lincoln, although he did not go far. Well known to never carry a gun, McSween nevertheless accepted his role as the leader in the fight against the Dolan faction, even though that fight had turned into a bloody war. Tunstall's twenty-eight-year-old ranch foreman, Dick Brewer, furious that the Englishman's killers were still at large, went to see Justice Wilson and had himself appointed a special constable. Brewer began recruiting several Tunstall men for his posse. And for the second time in less than two weeks,

Billy Bonney found himself working on the right side of the law, or so he and his companions believed. The posse called themselves the Regulators, although a more appropriate name would have been the Avengers. And they were more than ready for a fight.

The first clash came on March 6, when eleven of the Regulators came upon five riders just west of the junction of the Rio Peñasco and the Pecos. The riders, just a hundred yards away when first spotted, fled at the sight of Brewer's bunch, and the Regulators spurred their mounts to overtake them. The riders suddenly split up. Billy, pushing his horse as hard as it would go, recognized Buck Morton and Frank Baker (another member of The Boys) and took off after them. The rest of the Regulators followed. The Regulators chased the pair for several miles, ripping off almost one hundred rounds of ammunition without inflicting a single scratch. Finally, Morton's and Baker's exhausted mounts both tripped, throwing horses and riders to the ground. The two Dolan men quickly positioned themselves to make a good, long fight of it, but Brewer talked them into surrendering with the promise that they would not be harmed. This deal made Billy furious, and he ran toward Morton with the intent of killing him right at that moment. But several of the Regulators physically restrained him, Billy cursing Brewer the entire time. Posse and prisoners soon mounted up, and as they did so, a stern-faced Billy was overheard to say, "My time will come."

The Kid, of course, knew his opportunity for revenge was being taken away from him. Everyone knew what Sheriff Brady would do—or rather not do—with these men once they were handed over in Lincoln. There was not much Brewer could do, either. He was the leader of the Regulators, but he was also a duly appointed peace officer, and he had given his word.

On their way back to Lincoln, the Regulators made stops with their prisoners at John Chisum's South Spring ranch and the tiny settlement of Roswell. At Roswell, Buck Morton handed a letter to postmaster Ash Upson, Billy's old Silver City acquaintance. Addressed to a relative in Virginia, the letter said that Morton had heard some of the Regulators say that he and Baker would be killed sometime before they reached Lincoln. *Some* of the Regulators, not all.

Shortly after the prisoners were captured, William McCloskey, a former Tunstall employee, had joined the Regulators, and he was a friend of Morton's. While at Roswell, McCloskey loudly announced that he would not let anything happen to Morton and Baker. But instead of protecting the men, all he did was make the Regulators even more suspicious of him than they already were. McCloskey had been part of the posse that had run down Tunstall, although he had not had anything to do with the Englishman's murder.

About twenty miles out of Roswell, in Agua Negra Canyon, Frank MacNab, a loyal Regulator, casually rode up behind McCloskey, whipped out his revolver, and pointed the muzzle at McCloskey's head.

"You are the son of a bitch that's got to die before harm can come to these fellows, are you?" McNab shouted.

He jerked the gun's trigger as he spoke and blew McCloskey out of his saddle.

When Morton and Baker saw what had happened, they violently spurred their broken-down horses and desperately tried to get away before they met the same fate as McCloskey. It was no use. The Regulators opened up on the fleeing pair, finally cutting them down after a dash of four hundred yards. Baker had been hit five times, Morton nine. Billy got off his horse and walked up to Morton's body. He stooped down and turned Morton's head so that he could see the man's face. He stared at it for a moment, likely taking satisfaction in his revenge, and then walked away. All three bodies were left to bloat and turn in the New Mexico sun. They were eventually buried by some sheepherders.

"Of course, you know," Billy later remarked to his friend George Coe, "I never meant to let them birds reach Lincoln alive."

EARLY ON THE MORNING of April 1, Sheriff William Brady stopped in at Wortley's Hotel for breakfast. Like Jimmy Dolan and John Riley, his friends who operated The House, the forty-eight-year-old lawman was a native of Ireland. He had served for fifteen years in both the regular army and the New Mexico Volunteers, and most of that time was spent fighting Indians. After he left the army, Brady was elected to a two-year term as sheriff of Lincoln County in 1869 and again in 1876. He knew most everyone in the massive county—he was the federal census taker in 1870—and most everyone in the county knew the five-foot-eight-inch, blue-eyed sheriff. There was no question that Brady was influenced by Dolan and Riley, and on this particular day, the sheriff must have been certain that his friends had the upper hand in their feud with lawyer McSween.

Looking east down Lincoln's main and only street.

For one thing, New Mexico governor Samuel B. Axtell, a dim-witted, pompous man who was practically a puppet of the Santa Fe Ring, had made a brief visit to Lincoln a month earlier and issued a highly unorthodox proclamation that voided John B. Wilson's appointment as justice of the peace. This was devastating for the Regulators because it meant that Dick Brewer was no longer a special constable, and the warrants he carried were not worth the paper they were written on. And worse, he and his posse were just a bunch of outlaws. Their leader, Alexander McSween, was no better off. The Scotsman had been promised safety at nearby Fort Stanton if he turned himself in (thereby avoiding incarceration in the local dungeon), but promises in Lincoln County had not been worth much of late.

McSween was expected to arrive in Lincoln that April morning, and when Sheriff Brady stepped out of Wortley's after finishing his breakfast, he carried not only a warrant in his pocket but also a pair of handcuffs.

Brady walked across the street to the Dolan store, where he was joined by four armed deputies, and at about 9:30 A.M., the party started east down Lincoln's main street. It would be Brady's last look at the town of Lincoln. As the lawmen passed the Tunstall store, a burst of gunshots split the air. From behind the wall of Tunstall's corral, at least six Regulators, including Billy Bonney, had let loose with their rifles. Brady and Deputy George Hindman fell at the first fire; the rest quickly scattered for cover behind anything they could find. In the calm that followed the first fusillade, a slow moaning could be heard coming from the street. Brady, obviously a primary target, was covered with blood—he had been pierced by several bullets. Hindman was alive but he was badly wounded, and he kept calling out for water. Saloon keeper Ike Stockton bravely stepped out into the street to help Hindman, but as Stockton lifted up the poor man, another rifle shot ended the deputy's life.

Billy and Jim French raced out of the corral and over to Brady's outstretched body. Presumably they were going to take the fallen law-man's weapons, as well as the despised legal documents he carried. But as soon as the Kid and French were in plain view, Billy Mathews, one of Brady's deputies who had found a hiding place across the street, opened fire. With bullets kicking up dust around them, Billy and French scampered back to the corral, but not before a bullet seared French in his leg. Soon all the Regulators except French, who was in a great deal of pain, mounted their horses and rode out of town. Brady's surviving deputies managed a few shots as the killers fled, but they were smart enough not to pursue them.

The Regulators were confident they had not only torpedoed Bra-dy's plan to arrest McSween but also gotten revenge on the sheriff, whom they held responsible for Tunstall's murder, and Hindman, who had been part of the infamous sheriff's posse. And despite Gov-ernor Axtell's proclamation placing them outside the law, the Regula-tors saw no reason to stop pursuing the men who murdered Tunstall. But no matter how much the Regulators believed they were right, the assassination of a county sheriff caused the people of the Territory to turn against them and their cause. Such a heinous deed could not go ignored or unpunished.

ANDREW L. ROBERTS THOUGHT it was time to get out of Lincoln County. As a member of the posse that murdered Tunstall, he fig-ured the Regulators wanted to find him. And considering their bloody record, he had good reason to fear the worst if he fell into their hands. Sometime during the latter part of March, he spotted Billy and Regu-lator Charlie Bowdre near the village of San Patricio. Roberts, con-vinced that the pair was after him, grabbed his rifle and opened fire. The long-range gun battle was brief and no one was wounded, but Billy and Bowdre recognized their attacker, and Roberts knew it.

So Roberts sold his small ranch and prepared to move on to some place less dangerous. The only thing keeping Roberts in the area was money. He was expecting to receive payment for his land through the mail, and he had traveled to the small settlement of Blazer's Mill on Tularosa Creek and waited for the letter to arrive. The letter never came, but the Regulators did. They arrived at Blazer's Mill at about 11:00 A.M. on April 4, demanding that Dr. Joseph Blazer feed them a hearty meal.

Roberts was not there when the posse pulled up because he had been warned that they were in the area, and he had ridden off, leaving instructions to have his mail forwarded. Then Roberts made a terrible mistake. On his way out of the valley, he spotted the Regulators, fifteen in number, heading east toward the settlement. He also saw the mail carrier traveling in the same direction. Thinking that the mail wagon might have the letter he was waiting for, he cautiously retraced his steps to Blazer's Mill. When he came in sight of the mill, it appeared that Brewer's men had not stopped but passed through the settlement. What Roberts could not see, though, were the Regulators' horses in Blazer's corral. Roberts calmly rode up to the main house, a large two-story adobe that included a store and office, and dismounted near an old stump, making sure to remove his holster and cartridge belts, which he draped over his saddle horn. Roberts knew old man Blazer did not like weapons in the house.

As Roberts walked up to the main entrance on the south side of the building, one of the Regulators stepped out the door and gave Roberts the surprise of his life. "Here's Roberts," he shouted back to his buddies, after which he sprang back inside the building. Roberts turned and ran to his mount, at the same time yelling to Blazer's son, Almer, and two other boys nearby to get the hell out of there. Roberts jerked his Winchester repeating carbine out of its scabbard and headed for the building's southwest corner. He then backed along the house's west wall, carbine at the ready. The Regulators poured out of the building, guns drawn. John Middleton was the first to run out past the corner. He took a bullet in the lung. Roberts swiftly worked the carbine's lever action; his next shot hit Charlie Bowdre in the midsection. Had it not been for a simple belt buckle, Bowdre would have been a dead man. At this point, the Regulators figured out that it was not the best idea to go beyond the building's corner.

The Regulators stuck their guns out around the corner and blasted away in the direction of Roberts, who had hunkered back into the door frame of Blazer's office. Another shot from Roberts took off George Coe's right trigger finger. Roberts was clearly getting the best of Brewer's men, but Billy had noticed Roberts's pistol hanging from his saddle, and he knew the type of carbine Roberts carried and how many cartridges it held. When Billy figured that Roberts had exhausted all his ammo, he slipped around the corner and ran toward the office door. The Kid fired before he had a clean shot, and his bullet passed through the facing of the door frame. But even so, the bullet pierced Roberts's stomach just left of the navel and exited above his right hip. Roberts, who had not seen Billy until it was too late, punched the muzzle of his carbine violently into the Kid's belly, nearly knocking the Kid over. Before Billy had a chance to recover, Roberts burst into Blazer's office; the Kid turned and raced back for the corner of the building.

Bleeding and in great pain, Roberts discovered a Springfield rifle in .45-70 caliber that belonged to Dr. Blazer, as well as a belt of cartridges. He yanked the mattress off a couch in the room and threw it in front of the door. He then got down on the mattress in a prone position and aimed the Springfield out through the doorway and waited for his next target. Roberts was an old buffalo hunter; it was said he had worked with Buffalo Bill Cody in the late 1860s supplying bison meat to railroad crews in western Kansas. Dr. Blazer's Springfield was a special "Officer's Model," equipped with a tang peep sight for precision shooting at long distances—and Roberts knew how to handle such a weapon.

Keeping out of Roberts's sight, Dick Brewer and one of his men

Richard "Dick" Brewer, leader of the
Regulators.

made their way from the big house to the sawmill. Brewer crawled
out into the mill's log yard, from where he had a clear view of the
office door from 125 yards away. When Brewer thought he saw some
movement in the doorway, he took a shot. The bullet hit the office's
back wall with a thud, and that immediately got Roberts's attention.
Roberts looked out toward the log yard, but he patiently held his fire.
After a short, tense few moments, he saw a hat slowly rising above one
of the logs. When he guessed there was enough hat above the log, he
squeezed the Springfield's trigger. A loud crack and an explosion of
white smoke came from the office door. In the log yard, Dick Brewer
tumbled backward. He was dead.

When Billy got word that Brewer had been killed, he exploded with anger, yelling at Dr. Blazer to put Roberts out of the house. Blazer refused. The Kid then told the old man he would kill him if he did not do what he was told, but Blazer said Roberts would do the same thing if he attempted to force him out of the office. Billy called Blazer a damned old fool and threatened to burn his house down, but Blazer, unshakable as ever, responded that there was nothing he could do to stop that.

Demoralized, disgusted, and shot all to hell, the Regulators stormed off to the corral, got on their horses, and rode away, leaving the Blazers to deal with Brewer's body and the wounded Roberts. Roberts died the next day, and he and Brewer were buried side by side on a hill overlooking the settlement. Frank Coe later said that Andrew Roberts was probably the bravest man he ever met.

FOR THE REGULATORS, THE next ninety days were a blur of shooting scrapes, *bailes,* and hard riding. On April 18, a grand jury indicted Billy and three of his fellow Regulators for the murder of Sheriff Brady, and Billy was again named, along with five other Regulators, for the killing of Roberts. The House forces received their fair share of attention from the grand jury as well. Jesse Evans and, as accessories, Jimmy Dolan and Billy Mathews were among those indicted for the murder of John Henry Tunstall. Alexander McSween, on the other hand, achieved a minor victory when the grand jury exonerated him of the criminal charge of embezzlement, at the same time commenting that it regretted "that a spirit of persecution has been shown in this matter."

Despite the indictments, the Regulators remained just as determined to hunt down Tunstall's killers. McSween, acting upon the authority of Tunstall's father in England, posted a $5,000 reward for the apprehension and conviction of the culprits. The Scotsman sounded a lot like Billy when he wrote Tunstall's sister that "There will be no peace here until his murderers have paid the debt."

No peace was right. Gun battles between the two factions broke out wherever they met (or, rather, caught up to each other)—in the streets of Lincoln, at San Patricio in the Ruidoso Valley, and even at Chisum's South Spring ranch on the Pecos. Frank MacNab, who had replaced Dick Brewer as the Regulators' captain, was killed in an ambush on April 29. Two weeks later, the Regulators shot and killed Manuel Segovia, known as "the Indian," in a raid on a Dolan cow camp (Segovia had been a member of the posse that murdered Tunstall). The feud consumed everyone and everything in the region, and it was virtually impossible for anyone to remain neutral. The Dolan men forced settlers to feed and shelter them, or worse—to join their posses—and the Regulators did the same. Jimmy Dolan brought in even more gunmen from the Seven Rivers country and the Mesilla Valley.

The final showdown came in mid-July in the county seat, in what would be called the "Big Killing." McSween had been dodging the Dolan crowd for weeks when he received news that appeared to be a dramatic turn for the better: William Rynerson, the district attorney and a fierce Dolan supporter, and Governor Axtell were to be removed from office. Weary of roughing it, McSween was determined to return to Lincoln with a strong show of force, nearly sixty men in all. Riding with him, of course, was eighteen-year-old Billy Bonney, who had demonstrated that not only could he handle a gun and ride as well as any man in Lincoln County, but he also had grit—and, even better, he shot to kill. The plan was that McSween would go to his home, the Regulators would secure key buildings in town, and they would wait. Whatever happened, McSween decided, nothing could make him leave his home again—not alive, that is.

Just after dark on July 14, a Sunday, McSween and his followers rode into Lincoln. The night's full moon had not yet spilled its light into the canyon, which meant the riders could take up their positions without being detected. The structures being secured were the Ike Ellis store and dwelling, the José Montaño store, and the McSween house, all thick adobe buildings. Sheriff George W. Peppin, Lincoln County's most recent sheriff and, naturally, a Dolan man, was staying at Wortley's Hotel, as was Jimmy Dolan. Most of the sheriff's men were out hunting the Regulators; the dozen or so he had in town were divided between Wortley's and the old *torreón*.

News of McSween's arrival with his large force came soon after dawn. One of Reverend Taylor Ealy's pupils burst into the Ealy residence in the old Tunstall store: "There will be no school today," the boy said excitedly, "as both parties are in town." Sheriff Peppin sent a rider to find the rest of his posse and tell them to hurry back to Lincoln.

Billy was in the McSween house along with fourteen other gunmen, as well as McSween and his wife, Susan; Susan's sister Elizabeth Shield and her five children; and, ironically enough, a health seeker by the name of Harvey Morris. The flat-roofed adobe house was built in the shape of a "U" and contained as many as nine rooms; the opening of the U faced the Bonito River. Billy and the other combatants began to prepare for a long siege, placing heavy adobe bricks in the windows and carving gun ports in the walls. Later that day, a loudmouthed deputy named Jack Long was sent to serve warrants on the Kid and others at the McSween place. Four months earlier, an inebriated Long had told the Reverend Ealy that he wished a whore had come to Lincoln instead of the minister and that he had once helped hang a preacher in Arizona. Long's typical bluster did not go far with the boys at McSween's, though. A volley of gunfire sent him heading backward.

By that evening, the rest of the Dolan faction was back in town, approximately forty men in all, including Jesse Evans—free on bail from the Tunstall murder charge—and Mesilla Valley hoodlum John

Kinney. The two sides began shooting and yelling, and this continued sporadically into the next day and night. Fresh water was a problem for the defenders in both the McSween house and the Montaño store, and communication was nearly impossible between the three groups of McSween fighters. But at the same time, Sheriff Peppin was unable to get any real advantage. Nothing other than a cannonball was going to penetrate those solid adobe walls—and that is exactly what the sheriff had in mind. In a note to Fort Stanton's post commander, Lieutenant Colonel Nathan A. M. Dudley, Peppin requested the "loan" of a mountain howitzer to aid him in persuading the McSween men to surrender. Peppin, who held a commission as a deputy U.S. marshal, asked Dudley to do this "in favor of the law." The law, however, was the new Posse Comitatus Act, passed on June 16, 1878, and it specifically prevented the use of U.S. soldiers as law enforcement.

Dudley sent his regrets to the sheriff via a courier, and that should have ended the matter. But as the courier was riding into Lincoln, he was fired upon, allegedly by men in the McSween home. Dudley ordered an investigation, which again resulted in some of his men coming under fire. Then, on the evening of July 18, Jimmy Dolan made a trip to the fort to see Dudley. The fifty-two-year-old lieutenant colonel, known as "Gold Lace Dudley" because of his penchant for accessorizing his uniforms, was a career army man with not much of a career. He was arrogant, noisy, vindictive, a heavy drinker, and, not surprisingly, generally unpopular with his fellow officers. And he clearly favored one side over the other in the Lincoln County War. Earlier in the year, he had been defended in a court martial by Thomas Benton Catron, the U.S. attorney for New Mexico, who also happened to be one of the wealthiest men in the Territory and a central figure in the Santa Fe Ring. A longtime Murphy-Dolan backer, Catron now controlled The House's assets, having foreclosed on J. J. Dolan & Co. back in April.

According to a witness who claimed to have overheard the conver-

Lieutenant Colonel Nathan A. M. Dudley.

sation between Dudley and Dolan, the post commander told Dolan to
go back to Lincoln and keep the McSween party at bay and he would
be there by noon the next day. Later that same evening, Dudley consulted with his officers about sending troops into town. Their sole purpose, he said, would be to protect the women and children and any
noncombatants caught in the cross fire. The officers knew better than
to disagree with their commanding officer, and they unanimously
concurred with his plan.

The next day, at approximately 11:00 A.M., the sound of drums
was heard to the west of Lincoln, the *rat-a-tat-tat* growing louder as a
military column came into sight. Dudley rode in the lead, followed by
four officers, eleven buffalo soldiers (black cavalrymen), and twenty-
four white infantrymen. The soldiers wore their full-dress uniforms—
nothing less would do for Gold Lace Dudley. Far overshadowing the
spiffy appearance of Dudley's command, however, were the twelve-
pound mountain howitzer and Gatling gun they had with them. The
McSween forces dared not fire on the soldiers, and as the column
moved past the McSween home, Dolan's gunmen followed along,
taking up better positions around the Scotsman's house.

McSween and his men had definitely not prepared for troopers
with artillery. Dudley established his camp across from the Montaño
store and ordered his howitzer aimed at the building's front door. This
was too much for the defenders inside, and they prepared themselves
to flee the building. They covered their heads with blankets to hide
their identities and burst out of the store, running east down the street
to join their compadres in the Ellis store. When the artillery was faced
in that direction, a similar scene ensued, the escaping Regulators
firing parting shots at Sheriff Peppin's men who were pursuing them.
Within a matter of minutes, McSween lost two-thirds of his fighters.

McSween wrote a hasty note to Dudley, which was carried out of
the house by his ten-year-old niece: "Would you have the kindness to
let me know why soldiers surround my house? Before blowing up my

property I would like to know the reason." Dudley responded flippantly through his adjutant: "I am directed by the commanding officer to inform you that no soldiers have surrounded your house, and that he desires to hold no correspondence with you; if you desire to blow up your house, the commanding officer does not object providing it does not injure any U.S. soldiers." Susan McSween left the house next and pleaded separately with Sheriff Peppin and Dudley. Both men were hostile to her, especially Dudley. Susan returned to her husband's side. If there was ever any doubt as to whose side Dudley was on, there was none now.

Sheriff Peppin now turned his full attention on the Scotsman's home. If McSween and his remaining men would not surrender, then he would burn them out. At about 2:00 P.M., one of Peppin's men started a fire at the summer kitchen that was situated in the house's northwest corner. Heavy gunfire prevented the Regulators from extinguishing the flames, but because the house was adobe, the fire burned very slowly, room by room. Coughing and gasping from the smoke, their eyes stinging, the men did what they could to fight the blaze from the inside. There was no water, of course, but by pulling up floorboards and moving furniture, they robbed the flames of fuel. The ceiling, with its wooden *vigas* and *latias,* was where the fire had taken hold, however, and there was little that could be done there. But if they could slow the fire enough, it would be dusk before the defenders would be forced to evacuate the home; some of them might get away. Peppin's men would be anxiously waiting for that moment as well, but it was far better to sell one's soul with guns ablazin' than to be consumed alive by the flames.

At about 5:30 P.M., Susan and her sister and the five children were allowed to flee the house. The Ealys, next door in the Tunstall store, were also allowed to leave safely. Once these noncombatants were out of the way, the shooting picked up again. The heat was intense, and the leaping flames cast a bright light upon the hills overlooking the town. Forced by the fire into the final room in the house, the northeast kitchen, it was time for bold and decisive action. Alexander McSween was not a fighter, never had been. Now, overcome with a sense of doom and failure as his home burned down around him, he sat, comatose, with his head down. Billy, though, was exactly the opposite, jumping around the room like a caged cat. He shook McSween and ordered him to get up.

"Boys, I have lost my reason," McSween cried.

"Mack, now we must run for our lives," the Kid told him, "it is the only chance for our lives!"

McSween listened as his men went over the escape plan. Five of the defenders, including Billy, would burst out of the house first, drawing the fire of Peppin's men, after which McSween and the rest were to make their dash for safety. Although the flames illuminated the ground a good distance from the home, the first group got a good jump on the sheriff's posse before being spotted. Billy saw three of Dudley's soldiers blasting away at him, or so he later claimed. Morris, the unfortunate health seeker, collapsed in front of the Kid, but he was the only casualty in the first group, the remainder making it safely across the Bonito and into the night. Had McSween and the others followed close on the Kid's heels, they might have had a chance too, but they did not. The Kid's party, then, only served to alert the sheriff's men to the breakout.

When McSween and the rest of his followers did abandon the burning house, they were immediately hit by a deadly spray of bullets that kicked up the dirt around them. They headed for shelter in the backyard. They may not have been in danger of burning alive, but they were still trapped. After a tense several minutes, McSween called out that he wished to surrender. Deputy Robert Beckwith and three other men walked out into the open and approached the Scotsman. When Beckwith came within a few steps, McSween suddenly blurted out that he would never surrender. Gunfire erupted on both sides. Beckwith fell dead and McSween toppled over on top of him, his body pierced by five bullets. Three others in the McSween group, all Hispanos, also fell in the firefight. One, a young Yginio Salazar, was severely wounded and unconscious but Peppin's men took him for dead. When he came to, Salazar wisely remained motionless until it was safe to drag himself to a friend's house.

THE KID'S MAD DASH through the gauntlet of Dolan gunmen had been his greatest feat to date, but with the death of Alexander McSween, the Lincoln County War was all but over. Yet there were still hard times ahead, especially for the war's veterans. Lincoln County continued to be a violent place, and the bitter feelings between the two factions remained as healthy as ever. For many, the future offered little more than a return to routine, dirt-poor lives of punching cows and scratching out crops, but for those like the Kid, whose names appeared on arrest warrants from the district court, there were very few options. The war had molded Billy, tested him, but it had also reinforced a lifestyle of doing and taking what one pleased, regardless of the law. For Billy, it was but a short step from being a desperate and defiant young man to being a full-fledged desperado.

4

A New Sheriff

Advise persons never to engage in killing.
—BILLY THE KID

As THE LINCOLN COUNTY WAR raged, Pat Garrett stayed over a hundred miles away at Fort Sumner. Garrett knew some of the Lincoln County warriors from the buffalo range, but he had no history with Dolan, McSween, John Chisum, or any of them. The fight did not involve him, nor was it any of his business. Within a year of the Big Killing, the shrill whistle of a locomotive had been heard at Las Vegas for the first time, and more and more Anglos were flooding into New Mexico. Garrett was part of that change, and he would play a prominent role in even bigger changes to come, yet he respected the old ways of his adopted home, and Fort Sumner's native New Mexicans respected him. A few did more than just respect him.

The girls of Fort Sumner thought the rawboned former buffalo hunter was quite a romantic devil. Sallie Chisum, the Pecos cattle king's niece, remembered that Garrett walked "with a certain swinging grace that suggested power and sureness. Despite his crooked mouth and crooked smile, which made his whole face seem crooked, he was a remarkably handsome man." Juanita Martínez may have missed his crooked smile, but she certainly noticed his towering height. Juanita was a sparkling young woman, remembered Paulita Maxwell, "who had the charm of gaiety and light-heartedness." Everyone adored her, and at the frequent Fort Sumner *bailes,* she had a great many admirers. The admirer she fell in love with, though, was Garrett.

Sometime in the fall of 1879, Pat and Juanita exchanged wedding vows. Their wedding was a huge affair, as were all weddings in the small community of Fort Sumner. It was traditional for the *musicos* to play *La Marcha de los Novios* ("The March of the Newlyweds") after the nuptials. Oddly enough, a favorite melody for this march was "Marching Through Georgia." If the *musicos* did play this tune, Pat Garrett, a born and raised southerner, must have gritted his teeth as he joined the new Mrs. Garrett in the grand march. As more dances followed, one after the other, the single girls of Fort Sumner, some carefully chaperoned by their mothers, sat around the edge of the long room on benches or chairs, their brightly colored dresses especially selected for this gala evening. When a girl accepted an invitation to dance, her partner would place his hat in her seat, thus holding her place. And when that particular waltz or polka was finished, the gentleman escorted his partner back to her seat and retrieved his hat, and so on throughout the evening.

Among the folks at the Garrett wedding were some young men who, during the last year, had become regular fixtures around Fort Sumner. Garrett knew them because they were customers at his off-and-on saloon and store operations. And their informal leader went by the name of William H. Bonney, although most knew him as the Kid, or Billito. The Kid spent a lot of time gambling—especially three-card monte—and he loved dancing.

Billy was "a lady's Man," recalled his friend Frank Coe, "the Mex girls were crazy about him. . . . He was a fine dancer, could go all their gates [gaits] and was one of them." The Kid had a favorite dance tune, and without fail, at some point during the evening, he would tell the fiddlers, "Don't forget the *gallina.*" By *gallina,* the *musicos* knew he wanted to hear "Turkey in the Straw." They knew this because even though *gallina* means "hen" or "chicken," native New Mexicans used *gallina* for the wild turkey. Like Garrett, Billy had mastered New Mexican Spanish.

Hanging close to Billy that evening were his pals, and former Regulators, Tom Folliard and Charlie Bowdre. Born in Uvalde County, Texas, in about 1861, Folliard lost both of his parents to smallpox when he was very young, and as a teenager, he stood over six feet and weighed close to two hundred pounds. He had worked for a short time for a Seven Rivers cattleman before stumbling upon the Frank Coe place on the Ruidoso. When Coe decided to try the lad out as a farmhand, Folliard hitched Coe's draft team to a right-handed plow and proceeded to plow around the field *left-handed.* The Kid took an immediate liking to Folliard and decided he could make a passable gun hand out of him. With practice, Folliard got as fancy with a six-shooter as the Kid. He was very close to Billy in

Tom Folliard.

personality, good-natured and fun-loving, always singing or humming a song to himself.

"He was the Kid's inseparable companion," recalled Frank Coe, "and always went along and held his horses. He held his horses when the Kid would pay his attentions to some Mexican girl. It mattered not whether he was gone thirty minutes or half the night, Tom was there when he came out."

Charlie Bowdre had a ranch on the Ruidoso not far from the Coes and Doc Scurlock, another prominent Regulator. He was born in Georgia, but he had been raised in DeSoto County, Mississippi, the son of a wealthy plantation owner. Bowdre had been in trouble with the law well before the Lincoln County War. One of his worst episodes occurred in August 1877, when he and two companions terrorized

Charlie and Manuela Bowdre, 1880.

the town of Lincoln in a drunken rampage. One resident referred to Bowdre as a "would be desperado." On the other hand, George Coe thought that Bowdre and Bonney were the Regulators' best fighters.

"They were both cool and cautious," Coe recalled, "and did not know what fear was."

Bowdre was eleven years older than Billy and had another distinction: he was the best dressed of the lot, having a fondness for fancy vests.

The fourteen months since the Big Killing in Lincoln had been mostly hell for the Kid and his compadres. On August 5, 1878, Billy, Folliard, and Bowdre, along with seventeen other Regulators, swooped down on the Mescalero Apache Indian Agency. Their sole purpose was to steal a few of the Indians' horses. When someone saw what they were doing and the shooting broke out, agency clerk Morris Bernstein was killed. Even though Billy did not have anything to do with ending the clerk's life, he was one of four men indicted for Bernstein's murder. George Coe had also been indicted for the killing, and later that same month, he and cousin Frank decided it was time to get away from Lincoln County. Billy pleaded with the Coes to stay, but the cousins were tired of living like outlaws, and they wanted out.

"Well, boys, you may all do exactly as you please," the Kid told them. "As for me, I propose to stay right here in this country, steal myself a living, and plant every one of the mob who murdered Tunstall if they don't get the drop on me first."

In September 1878, after numerous complaints from the Territory's citizens, and a highly critical report from a Department of Justice special investigator, Governor Samuel B. Axtell was finally removed from office. He was replaced by Major General Lew Wallace, an aspiring novelist who had been a member of the military commission that tried the conspirators in President Lincoln's assassination. In November, Governor Wallace granted amnesty for those who participated in the Lincoln County War. Unfortunately, this amnesty did not include any who had already been indicted on criminal charges, and that included Billy and some other Regulators. But Wallace was no friend of the Dolan crowd, either, and he quickly decided that Gold Lace Dudley was one of Lincoln County's biggest problems.

In mid-February 1879, Billy tried to make peace with Jesse Evans and the rest of the Dolan faction, and the two sides met in Lincoln on the eighteenth. Billy brought along Folliard, Doc Scurlock, George Bowers, and José Salazar. Facing them were Jesse Evans, Jimmy Dolan, Billy Mathews, Edgar Waltz, and Billy Campbell. After a tense and shaky start, the two sides came up with several conditions for a truce—one of them being that neither side would testify against the other in court. The penalty for breaking any of the conditions was death. Once everything was settled and agreed upon, the drinking commenced. About 10:00 P.M., the men spilled out onto Lincoln's main street, singing and shooting their guns into the air. It was then that lawyer Huston I. Chapman, who had just arrived from Las Vegas, made the mistake of thinking he could walk through the rowdy bunch. The one-armed Chapman had been hired by Susan McSween to bring Dudley to justice for his role in the killing of her husband, which made Chapman an enemy of the Dolan crowd.

A drunken Billy Campbell accosted Chapman and asked where he was going. Chapman, his face bandaged due to an attack of neuralgia, told the boys to mind their own affairs. It was the wrong answer; Campbell ordered the lawyer to talk differently—or else.

"You cannot scare me, boys," the feisty Chapman said while lifting a bandage from his face to get a better look at the ruffians. "I know you and it's no use. You have tried that before."

"Then," Campbell replied, "I'll settle you."

And with that, Campbell fired his pistol into Chapman's breast. As the attorney fell, Jimmy Dolan decided that he would double the deed, aimed his Winchester and fired a round into the poor man's body. As Chapman's clothing smoldered from a small fire ignited by the pistol's powder flash, a joyous Campbell let slip that he had promised Dudley he would kill the troublesome attorney. The Kid and the others did not know what to do. John Henry Tunstall had been shot down exactly one year earlier, and ever since that horrible day, many people in Lincoln County had been killed, and now another man was dead.

Chapman's murder outraged Wallace, who realized that he had to take serious action. In early March 1879, the governor traveled to Lincoln and got Dudley removed from command at Fort Stanton. He then set about going after Chapman's murderers, and he believed the guilty parties included the Kid and Folliard, as well as Dolan and his cronies. During these efforts, the governor received a curious letter from W. H. Bonney:

> Dear Sir: I have heard that You will give one thousand $ dollars for
> my body which as I can understand it means alive as a Witness. I
> know it is as a witness against those that Murdered Mr. Chapman.
> if it was so that I could appear at Court I could give the desired
> information, but I have indictments against me for things that
> happened in the late Lincoln County War and am afraid to give up
> because my Enemies would Kill me. . . . I was present When Mr.
> Chapman was Murdered and know who did it and if it were not
> for those indictments I would have made it clear before now. . . .
> I have no Wish to fight any more indeed I have not raised an arm
> since Your proclamation. as to my Character I refer to any of the
> Citizens, for the majority of them are my Friends and have been
> helping me all they could. I am called Kid Antrim but Antrim is
> my stepfathers name.

Bonney's letter led to a secret meeting between him and the governor, and the Kid agreed to testify before the grand jury about Chapman's murder in exchange for a full pardon. The Kid's cooperation was no easy thing because he knew that Dolan and Jesse Evans, both indicted for Chapman's murder, would be anxious to put a bullet in his back. Wallace had no such risk. On the contrary, there was the good possibility that the Territory's newspapers would laud the governor for prosecuting Chapman's killers. Unfortunately for both the Kid and the governor, it did not work out that way. As Governor Wallace famously wrote some time later, "Every calculation based on experience elsewhere fails in New Mexico."

Billy held up his part of the bargain. He testified openly at both the grand jury proceedings and the subsequent military court of inquiry for Gold Lace Dudley (Dudley was exonerated of any wrongdoing). But he never got the pardon the governor promised, and District Attorney William Rynerson made it clear that he was not going along with any deal the governor made.

"He is bent on going after the Kid," Wallace's confidant, Ira Leonard, wrote the governor on April 20. "He proposes to destroy his evidence and influence and is bent on pushing him to the wall." Fed up with waiting on Wallace to make good on his pledge, the Kid and Folliard, who had also submitted to arrest, quietly slipped out of town on June 17 and headed for Fort Sumner. Billy's chance to go straight—if such a thing was truly possible—was gone.

Sumner became the Kid's safe haven and base of operations. Charlie Bowdre found part-time employment as foreman of the Thomas Yerby ranch in an isolated area known as Las Cañaditas (Little Canyons), ten or so miles northeast of Sumner. Tom Folliard signed on with Yerby as well. Doc Scurlock followed the lead of the Coes and abandoned New Mexico for Texas, and never saw the Kid again. No matter, Billy never lacked for friends, and Fort Sumner offered plenty of girls, lots of dancing, some gambling and horse racing, and a whole lot of other people's cattle and horses out on the open range that could be sold to more than a few unquestioning buyers. Even better, there was not a lawman in the Territory who was brave enough to go after the Kid and his confederates—not just yet.

PAT GARRETT KNEW THAT some of the men at his wedding *baile* were wanted by the law—everyone did. Most men in New Mexico Territory had a past—and some of them were hardened killers. That, too, was not unusual for the time and place, nor was it any cause for alarm. It was a time for celebration, and the attention was on Garrett and his bride. But as the guests watched the newlyweds dance, Juanita suddenly collapsed in what was described as some kind of fit or attack. She was quickly carried to a bed in a nearby room, where she died the next day. No one knew what happened to her. Her final resting place remains undiscovered, and she left no photographs, and no children. All that survived was a scar on Pat Garrett's psyche and a faint memory in the minds of a few Fort Sumner old-timers.

More than most, it seems, Garrett and the Kid had experienced the tragic loss of loved ones. There was a good deal that the two had in common, actually: certain leadership qualities, for one, and their well-known fondness for the *baile*, horse racing, and gambling. Both were men you would want on your side in a fight. Garrett and the Kid were not good friends at Fort Sumner—but they were not enemies either. They saw each other frequently enough, and they had a healthy respect for each other, certainly each other's ability to take care of himself. Garrett was usually serious and the Kid was usually boisterous, and they each had a reputation as a better-than-average shot with a six-gun; they were considered the two best shooters at Fort Sumner. On a slow day, and there were more than a few of those there on the Pecos, the Kid and Garrett might take part in an impromptu shooting match. Billy was ambidextrous, and people said he could shoot a pistol with one hand just as well as the other, although he favored the right hand whenever he got into a "jackpot." According to Paulita Maxwell, Billy was better than Garrett with the revolver. She remembered a time when a terror-stricken jackrabbit on a Fort

Sumner lane somehow managed to dodge every bullet Garrett fired at him. The Kid whipped out his revolver and pancaked the rabbit with his first shot. Maybe this happened, maybe not.

Others considered Garrett the better shot, possibly even the best man with a revolver in the entire Southwest. And Garrett did not rate Billy's shooting nearly as high as many who were acquainted with the Kid. When asked if Billy was a good shot, Garrett admitted that he was, but he added that the Kid was "no better than the majority of men who are constantly handling and using six-shooters. He shot well, though, and he shot well under all circumstances, whether in danger or not." That last was the key, of course. As Garrett remarked years later, "A man with nerve behind a gun is worth twenty-five who are after him." There is no question that Billy Bonney had nerve; Joe Grant discovered that in January 1880.

Grant had shown up at Fort Sumner, presumably from Texas, with no job and apparently no interest in finding one—never a good sign. But somehow he had enough means to keep himself in liquor for several days. He had immediately buddied up with the Kid and his associates, who were also hanging around and not working. At some point, Grant got it into his head that he would be quite the hombre if he took out the Kid. Some claim he came to Fort Sumner with that purpose, but Grant's scheme, which he let slip one day, could also have been the whiskey talking. In any event, Grant's blustering got back to Billy, who remained friendly with the Texan but kept his eyes on the man.

On January 10, a Saturday, Billy and two friends rode up on a small herd of cattle that James Chisum (brother of John) and three of his cowhands were moving southward. The cattle had been stolen from the Chisum range—almost certainly by the Kid—and Chisum was taking them back. With a straight face, Billy asked to inspect the herd, as if he might actually find an animal that had not been given Chisum's Jinglebob brand. After Billy had his look, he invited Chisum and his men to have a drink at Bob Hargrove's saloon in Fort Sumner, less than a mile away.

Joe Grant was in the saloon when Billy, Chisum, and the others got there, and Grant was well inebriated already. As Jack Finan, one of Chisum's men, walked past the drunken Texan, Grant yanked Finan's pearl-handled revolver from its holster and replaced it with his own. Billy immediately stepped over to Grant and said, "That's a beauty, Joe," and then reached out and took the pistol from Grant. Billy examined the six-shooter's cylinder and noticed that three of the six chambers were empty. He carefully rotated the cylinder so that when the gun was cocked and the trigger pulled, the gun's hammer would fall on an empty chamber. The Kid then casually handed the pistol back to Grant.

"Pard, I'll kill a man quicker'n you will for the whisky," Grant said to Billy.

"What do you want to kill anybody for?" Billy said. "Put up your pistol and let's drink."

Pistol still in hand, Grant stepped behind the bar and used the gun's barrel to smash the glasses and decanters on the counter. Everyone watched nervously as Grant pointed the pistol wildly around the saloon. Billy pulled his six-shooter. "Let me help you break up housekeeping, pard," he said, and gleefully joined Grant in finishing off the saloon's glassware.

Then Grant saw James Chisum across the room and mistook him for John Chisum. And, for some unknown reason, Grant had a strong grudge against the Pecos cattle baron.

"I want to kill John Chisum, anyhow, the damned old son of a bitch," Grant said.

"You've got the wrong pig by the ear, Joe," Billy said, "that's not John Chisum."

"That's a lie," Grant screamed. "I know better!"

Quick as a flash, Grant pointed his pistol at Billy and pulled the trigger. There was a click, then the sound of Grant cursing as he again cocked the gun's hammer. But that was immediately followed by the loud blast of Billy's six-shooter as he sent a lead ball into Joe Grant's head. Grant collapsed behind the blood-splattered bar. A moment later, someone asked the Kid if he was sure Grant was dead. Billy nodded his head confidently.

"No fear," he said. "The corpse is there, sure, ready for the undertaker."

The following day, Billy, Tom Folliard, Charlie Bowdre, and a Charlie Thomas went to pick up their mail at the post office in Sunnyside, approximately five miles above Fort Sumner. Bowdre casually told the postmaster, Milnor Rudolph, that another man had "turned up his toes" at Sumner. That got Rudolph's attention, and he asked the name of the deceased. Bowdre said it was Joe Grant, and he had been shot by the Kid. Rudolph then looked at Billy and asked him why he killed Grant.

"His gun wouldn't fire," Billy coolly explained, "and mine would."

Four days after Billy sent the local undertaker a gift of Joe Grant, Pat Garrett stood before the parish priest at Anton Chico, a village ninety miles northwest of Fort Sumner, and married Polinaria Gutiérrez, the daughter of José Dolores and Feliciana Gutiérrez. Garrett's period of mourning had been brief, but this was not unusual in a land where time was the last thing one could count on. Polinaria's first name was actually Apolinaria, although her friends and family called her "La Negra" or simply "Negra," presumably because of her dark complexion. Garrett towered over the petite girl, who may have been as young as sixteen. And although Garrett was basically a nonbeliever, Polinaria was a devout Catholic, and that meant the rites had to be performed by a priest. This may have seemed even more important because Garrett's first marriage had been performed without a priest, and that had not worked out so well.

Pat and Apolinaria Garrett, circa 1880.

NEARLY THIRTY YEARS OLD and married, Pat Garrett was tired of struggling to make a living at Fort Sumner—and tired of the criminals who seemed to have the place under their control. He wanted something better. So, too, did Pecos Valley cattleman and entrepreneur Captain Joseph C. Lea. Lea was a former Missouri guerrilla who had fought alongside the likes of Cole Younger and Frank James under Quantrill and Jo Shelby during the Civil War. Pardoned by President Andrew Johnson in 1865, Lea had tried his hand at farming and livestock trading before coming to New Mexico Territory in 1875. Early in 1878, Lea had moved his family to Roswell, where he soon purchased the town's two adobe buildings, a store and a hotel. Later that same year, he was elected a Lincoln County commissioner, a good indication of the favorable first impression he had made on the region's ranchers and settlers. What Lea wanted was to see an end to the thieving and violence in the Pecos Valley so that farming and livestock raising, not to mention little Roswell itself, could prosper. That meant getting rid of Billy the Kid and his cohorts. That meant, ultimately, the end of an era.

For this to happen, he knew that Lincoln County needed a new sheriff, one who understood the risks but was willing to see the job to its conclusion. Lea, who was every bit as tall as Garrett, became convinced that Garrett was the man for this job. He persuaded Garrett to pick up and move to the Roswell area (Fort Sumner was just outside of Lincoln County) and run for election as sheriff that fall. By early June, Garrett and Polinaria were settled into their new home, and the census taker recorded Garrett's occupation as farmer.

William Bonney was noted in that census. He shared an adobe dwelling at Fort Sumner with his friends Charlie and Manuela Bowdre (it was rumored that he and Charlie shared more than the house). The census taker wrote down that Charlie and Billy both "work in cattle," which, like most things about Billy, was true yet not true. Sometime that same year, a traveling photographer arrived at Fort Sumner. With tintype portraits going for only a few cents apiece, a professional photographer could draw settlers from miles around. Billy decided to have his picture taken, if only to have a few tintypes to present to the girls he was sweet on. Although Paulita Maxwell insisted that Billy

Billy the Kid, from the tintype made at Fort Sumner.

was a neat and tasteful dresser around Fort Sumner, Billy is rather odd-looking in this tintype, wearing rumpled, trail-worn clothes: a loose sweater, unbuttoned vest, a showy bib-front shirt embroidered with a large anchor across the chest, a bandanna knotted clumsily about the neck, and a narrow-brimmed felt hat with a large dent in the crown.

Billy was never without a weapon, and in the photograph he is grasping the muzzle of a Model 1873 Winchester carbine, with its butt resting on the floor. Around his waist is a cartridge belt and holster with the curved butt of a six-shooter sticking out. These were the tools of the Kid's trade—and what he needed to survive. Billy apparently paid for four tintypes, which would have been made simultaneously with a camera that featured four individual lenses mounted on the front. After developing the tin plate with its four identical images, the photographer would simply snip it into four parts and mount the portraits in thin paper mattes. The single surviving photograph of Billy the Kid in all his glory is anything but a flattering portrait—his mouth is partially open, exposing his buckteeth, and his eyelids appear to be drooping, snake-eyed. Nearly everyone remembered Billy as attractive, extremely likable, and full of life. It is as if he was just too big—or too elusive—to be captured in a tintype that would fit in the palm of one's hand.

At the time that this photograph was taken, Billy had become the most prominent member of a very successful gang of livestock thieves that operated back and forth between the rowdy cow town of Tascosa, Texas, southwest to the mining boomtown of White Oaks, New Mexico, a distance of some three hundred miles. With markets on both sides of the state line, and several large ranches with not nearly enough cowhands to be everywhere at once, it was easy enough to round up a few head of cattle, alter the brands, write up a fake bill of sale, and be gone down the trail before the owner knew what hit him. And with beef bringing between $15 and $25 per head (the gang got

$10 for their stolen beef), a loss of fifty head of cattle was a painful hit to the account books. The cattlemen of this area knew who Billy was and were desperate that he and his cohorts be captured or run out of the country.

Unless a horse or cow was padlocked in a barn stall, not a one of them between Tascosa and White Oaks was safe. The Mescalero Apache reservation south of Fort Stanton was one of the gang's favorite targets, because the Mescaleros were exceptional horsemen and had fine horse herds. The Mescaleros called Billy and his fellow horse thieves the "broad hat people."

"At Fort Stanton Billy the Kid was making a raid on the Indians all the time for their horses," recalled Percy Big Mouth. "We made a big brush corral at Fort Stanton right near the fort . . . to protect us against Billy the Kid. One night they came over, tore all the brush down and got all our horses. The soldiers would go after Billy."

But the soldiers never got Billy, no one did. On the evening of August 9, 1879, Sheriff George Kimbrell with a military escort numbering one officer and fifteen men trapped the Kid in a cabin six miles from Lincoln. Even though they greatly outnumbered the outlaw, neither the sheriff nor the soldiers were interested in busting into the cabin and shooting it out with Billy the Kid. Kimbrell chose to wait until daylight and negotiate a surrender. But that was far too much time to give the Kid. Demonstrating that he still retained the slim figure and athleticism of his Silver City days, Billy clawed up the chimney and slipped away in the darkness, leaving his weapons—and the posse—far behind.

By the fall of 1880, the gang of rustlers included several ne'er-do-wells who had not been close to Billy during the Lincoln County War. Among them were Dave Rudabaugh, Tom Pickett, and Billy Wilson. The twenty-six-year-old Dave Rudabaugh had a handsome, though weather-beaten, face and a black mustache. His blue eyes and winning smile made him look like a decent guy, but he was an accomplished train and stage robber, a hired gun, and a murderer. A year earlier, Rudabaugh had killed a Las Vegas jailer while attempting to break a friend out of jail; he had been on the run ever since. Many considered Rudabaugh a far worse character than the Kid, and some people said that even Billy was afraid of him.

Thomas Pickett was twenty-four years old, the son of a well-to-do Wise County, Texas, rancher who had been a Texas Ranger, a justice of the peace, and a Texas state legislator. Young Tom joined the Texas Rangers in 1876, but his troubles started almost immediately when he was charged with several counts of stealing cattle. He eventually ended up in New Mexico, where in 1879 he worked as a policeman in Old Town Las Vegas. In mid-May 1880, when he found out that someone wanted to send a bullet or two into his brain, Tom hastily resigned from the Las Vegas force and traveled to White Oaks, where he became the assistant city marshal and a bartender in Patterson's saloon. A close shooting scrape a month later—so close that a bullet creased his cheek—convinced him to move on again. Pickett drifted to Fort Sumner, where he hired on under Charlie Bowdre at the Yerby ranch.

William "Billy" Wilson, two years younger, slightly stouter, and far quieter than the Kid, was born in Ohio. Before coming to New Mexico, he had navigated the hell-raisers and prostitutes of Dodge City, Kansas, where he likely ran into Dave Rudabaugh. He carried the two most popular firearms in the American West, a Winchester Model 1873 carbine and a Colt Single Action Army revolver. Both weapons were chambered in .44 caliber and, thus, fired the same ammunition.

Wilson put the gang on the U.S. Treasury Department's radar when he began freely passing $100 counterfeit notes in Lincoln. Secret Service "Special Operative" Azariah Wild arrived at Fort Stanton on October 1, direct from New Orleans, determined to have Wilson, and anyone else connected with the counterfeiting ring, arrested. Once in

New Mexico, however, the forty-two-year-old Wild got a crash course on Lincoln County and how big a challenge he faced. It did not take Wild long to become a supporter of Pat Garrett.

Joseph C. Lea had started the campaign to elect Garrett to be sheriff, but it only kept rolling with the support of other key power brokers in Lincoln County. These included Fort Stanton post traders Will Dowlin and John C. DeLaney, Lincoln merchant Joseph La Rue, and La Rue's clerk, the infamous Jimmy Dolan. Garrett's supporters succeeded in forcing his name on the ballot in place of the incumbent, Sheriff Kimbrell. Kimbrell, who was known to drink and play cards with those for whom he possessed arrest warrants, decided to run anyway.

Among those campaigning for Pat Garrett was nineteen-year-old George Curry, then working on the Block ranch, a sheep operation twenty-five miles from Fort Stanton in the Capitan Mountains. On Monday evening, November 1, 1880, a young stranger appeared at the ranch about suppertime, and, as was customary, Curry invited him to a place at the table. The stranger, slight of build, was dressed as a puncher and spoke fluent Spanish. Curry observed that the Hispanic ranch hands knew the young man, but the stranger never offered his name, and, as was also customary, Curry did not ask. As they continued to talk after supper, Garrett's name came up.

"Do you know Garrett?" the stranger asked.

"No, I don't, but from all I hear he is a splendid man," Curry answered.

"Do you think he will be elected?"

"I don't know," Curry said, "but I'm sure he will carry this precinct. I have a gallon of whiskey on hand, and I think that will help carry it."

"You are a good cook and a good fellow," the stranger said before riding away, "but if you think Pat Garrett is going to carry this precinct for sheriff, you are a damned poor politician."

After the stranger was gone, Felipe Miranda, the sheep boss, told Curry that the man he had been talking to was William H. Bonney. And Bonney was right. Las Tablas was the home of Billy's good friend Yginio Salazar, and the next morning, Kimbrell carried the precinct.

Fortunately for Garrett and his backers, the Las Tablas outcome was not repeated in the other precincts. Garrett, who generally spoke in a low tone and rarely talked of himself, had not been the best campaigner for public office, but the people who supported him were interested in action, not words. Garrett handily won the election, receiving 320 votes to Kimbrell's 179. The day after the election, Acting Governor W. G. Ritch (Wallace was away from Santa Fe at the time) penned a proclamation calling for the people of the Territory to recognize November 25 as a day of Thanksgiving and Praise.

"Peace now prevails within our borders," Ritch proclaimed. "On every hand, among the humble and weak, as well as among the bold and powerful and wealthy, are found causes to remember with thankfulness the goodness which crowns the year."

This was easy to say from the Governor's Palace in Santa Fe, but there was still a whole lot of hell going on in Lincoln County.

5

Outlaws and Lawmen

There is only one way to deal with outlaws: Offer
rewards for them dead or alive, the former preferred.
—*THE DENVER TIMES*

FRANK PAGE HAD COME from Arkansas to New Mexico Territory for his health—he was a consumptive—and got a job working as a bookkeeper for Alexander Grzelachowski, a merchant in Puerto de Luna. Grzelachowski was a former Catholic priest known to the locals as Padre Polaco. About the second week of November 1880, the Kid and Billy Wilson stepped into Grzelachowski's large mercantile. The store clerk had seen these outlaws approaching and abruptly left the store without saying anything to Page. The puny bookkeeper, whose affliction had whittled his body weight down to about a hundred pounds, went out to meet the two men. After making some minor purchases, the outlaws suddenly spotted three shiny Colt double-action "Lightning" revolvers the store had gotten in just recently. Unlike a single-action revolver, which required the shooter to manually cock the gun's hammer, a double-action revolver cocked the hammer and fired the pistol with a single pull of the trigger. It was quick and deadly. The Lightning was also fairly light, weighing in at about one and a half pounds. Page handed over the .38-caliber six-shooters to the Kid and Wilson to examine.

As the two outlaws dry fired the pistols and spun their cylinders, the bookkeeper left them to wait on a woman who had just come into the store. The Kid and Wilson promptly shoved the pistols into their belts and quietly slipped outside. When Page returned to the counter, he was outraged to see that the pistols were gone. He quickly figured out where the two men were staying, and he barged into their room. He saw the pistols lying on the bed and began scolding the two as he gathered up the handguns. He told them they "were fine men to take advantage of a poor invalid," and that he would not stand for it. Page watched the Kid's face turn red—he was not used to being spoken to this way—and he observed the Kid's hand move toward the .45 six-shooter in his belt. Suddenly, Wilson said something to the Kid in Spanish. Page later learned that Wilson said, "Don't kill him." Billy's dark mood instantly disappeared, and he and Wilson walked with the bookkeeper back to the store, all the while telling him that they had been playing a prank on him when they took the pistols.

But Billy was still intent on getting one of the Lightnings and he told Page that one of the local saloon owners owed him $50 and that he would sign an order on the man for the amount of the pistol and a box of cartridges. This was a common way of doing business at the time when cash was not readily accessible—if the parties trusted each other. By now, Page should have known better, but he went along with this. He had the Kid sign the order, which came to $34.90, and Billy took one of the pistols with him. A day or two later news arrived that some horses had been stolen from Grzelachowski's ranch, twenty miles east of town, and people were saying that the Kid and Wilson were the thieves. Page apparently never laid eyes on the Kid again, but every time he opened the store's books, he was reminded of his encounter with Billy the Kid because the order on the saloon owner was never paid: the man said Billy owed *him* the $50.

NOT ONLY WERE BILLY and the gang stealing cattle and horses, but they had also been robbing the U.S. mail, a handy source of cash money. Because there was no money order office at Fort Stanton, the soldiers there sent cash back home in registered letters. All the gang had to do, then, was hold up a stagecoach and dig through the mail to find the registered envelopes. Near Fort Sumner on the night of October 16, the gang stopped the outbound stagecoach and relieved it of its mail sacks. A female passenger recognized Billy Bonney as one of the thieves—they robbed her, too.

On the night of November 20, Billy and the gang rode into White Oaks. Billy needed to fence some of Padre Polaco's horses, and he also wanted to see lawyer Ira Leonard, who was then living there. The Kid knew that Leonard was a conduit to Governor Wallace, and he had written Leonard the previous month offering his services, saying he was tired of "dodging the officers." In other words, Billy was willing to squeal—again. But Leonard was not there, and there would be no more deals with the outlaw. Instead, the gang went on a robbing spree in White Oaks, stealing rifles, blankets, overcoats, and some mules. They galloped out of town before most people knew what had happened.

Although the Kid and his cohorts usually had Lincoln County's residents quaking in their boots, some of White Oaks's citizens were not about to put up with the gang's thievery. When Deputy Sheriff Bill Hudgens learned that the gang was hanging out at Blake's Sawmill, a few miles outside of White Oaks, he quickly put together a posse to go after them. Hudgens, a twenty-nine-year-old saloon operator, had grown up in the same Louisiana parish as Pat Garrett, and he had built the first house in the mining camp just the year previous. The

posse that left White Oaks on November 22 was made up of nine de-
termined citizens and included former Texas Ranger James W. Bell.
After hunting for just a few hours, they found a deserted camp and a
trail left in the snow that they believed was from Billy and his cohorts.
As Hudgens's posse followed the trail, they came upon two men who
were connected with the gang. The men were on their way back to
White Oaks after delivering news and provisions to the outlaw camp.
Hudgens arrested the men and then continued the search.

At a place known as Coyote Springs, the posse was suddenly hit by
a spray of gunfire by the outlaws who had heard them approaching
their camp, the bark of Billy's new Colt Lightning undoubtedly adding
to the chaos. But the posse recovered quickly, and as men cursed and
bullets flew through the air, several horses on both sides were killed.
Billy's mount was shot out from under him. When it became a little
too hot for the outlaws, they fled in different directions. Hudgens's
men inspected the camp and found Billy's dead horse, along with his
fine saddle, and a number of provisions strewn about the ground.
Hudgens apparently decided they had done enough for one day and
led the posse back to White Oaks. The Kid and Billy Wilson, both
on foot, headed for a stage stop and store north of White Oaks on the
Las Cruces–Las Vegas stage route. Somewhere along the way, they
reunited with Dave Rudabaugh.

Jim Greathouse, a former Texas buffalo hunter, and Fred W. Kuch
ran the store, as well as a ranch at the same location. In addition
to peddling a few dry goods and providing grub to stagecoach passengers, they were eager buyers of stolen stock, and their reputations
were at about the same level as the Kid's. They were also well known
to be chummy with the outlaw band. When some freighters arrived
in White Oaks with the news that they had spotted the Kid at the
Greathouse-Kuch roadhouse, another posse immediately left town to
hunt down the outlaws.

This hastily organized second posse consisted of thirteen men under the leadership of Constable Thomas B. Longworth. Several of them were veterans of the first posse, such as Hudgens and James W. Bell. Blacksmith Jimmy Carlyle, twenty-six years old and a popular fellow in White Oaks, had been in the first posse but was eager to be in the second because the gang had his mules. And he wanted the personal satisfaction of helping to make the arrests or, if need be, shooting the rustlers dead.

The posse arrived at the Greathouse-Kuch establishment early on the morning of November 27, a Saturday. Sleeping soundly inside were Greathouse, Kuch, the Kid, Wilson, Rudabaugh, and a German cook named Joe Steck. The posse quietly surrounded the house, created makeshift breastworks, and waited in the snow for the sun to come up. Steck was the first to come outside (the Kid was not an early riser—long nights of women, dancing, and gambling will do that), and quickly he was staring into the wrong ends of two rifles. Strangely enough, Steck did not know the identities of the men staying there that night. The cook had apparently acquired the healthy habit of not asking too many questions. When the posse members prodded him about Billy the Kid and the others, Steck confidently said he did not know anything. At first, the lawmen thought Steck was playing dumb, but after they described the characters they were after, Steck confirmed that three men in the house matched those descriptions. Hudgens scribbled a note to the Kid demanding that he and his two companions surrender—escape was impossible, Hudgens wrote. Steck was sent inside to deliver the note.

The Kid read Hudgens's letter out loud to the gang, and they burst out laughing. They sent Steck back with a note of their own. "You can only take me a corpse," the Kid had written—which would have been perfectly acceptable to the posse. The negotiations continued back and forth until Hudgens proposed a face-to-face talk with Billy Wilson. He swore that if Wilson declined to surrender, he would let Wilson go back in the house. Wilson declined, of course, but he, the

Kid, and Rudabaugh requested that Jimmy Carlyle be sent inside the house to talk about the situation—Wilson is said to have known Carlyle when they were youths in Ohio.

Hudgens thought this a very bad idea, but Greathouse, who had come outside with Steck, offered himself as a hostage to guarantee Carlyle's safety. The deputy sheriff still objected, but Carlyle was determined to talk to the outlaws. He took off his gun belt and walked across the open ground to the house and was let in.

Carlyle may have been well liked, but he was also a fool. His presence in the house did little more than entertain the outlaws. There was plenty of whiskey in the store, and Carlyle joined in far too many rounds. Eventually, an inebriated Carlyle insisted on leaving, while the outlaws demanded that he stay. At the same time, the posse was getting impatient; Carlyle had been in the house for hours. They sent in another note that said if Carlyle was not released within five minutes, they would kill Greathouse. This surely sobered the blacksmith. But what happened next sent Carlyle into a panic. One of the men in the posse fired a single shot, and Carlyle immediately assumed that Greathouse was dead. This frightened him so much that he jumped up and ran for a window, crashing through the panes and tumbling onto the ground outside. Carlyle was bleeding, but he got up and scrambled for the breastworks. Billy let loose with his Colt Lightning, firing two shots at the fleeing man. Rudabaugh and Wilson each fired once. Carlyle collapsed just ten feet from the window. He was dead.

The lawmen opened up with everything they had. Kuch and Steck, who were caught outside the house when Carlyle was killed, ran for the breastworks—until they realized the posse was shooting at *them*. It was only after several dozen shots that they realized their mistake and stopped firing. The murder of Carlyle demoralized everyone. And the posse had not been whiling away their time in a warm dwelling with plenty of whiskey to take the edge off. It was damn cold, and there was no food or water. Hudgens called his men back from their positions around the house; they would go find shelter and wait for reinforcements. The posse saddled up and rode off, leaving Carlyle's crumpled body on the ground.

Billy must have grinned smugly as he watched them leave. Once it was dark outside, he, Wilson, and Rudabaugh trudged through the snow to a friend's ranch before setting out for Anton Chico, where they were met by Jim Greathouse, who had been released by the posse shortly after Carlyle was killed. Greathouse gave the outlaws horses to ride, and they headed to the Yerby ranch (northeast of Fort Sumner) and met up with Tom Folliard, Charlie Bowdre, and Tom Pickett. The Kid may have had an entertaining tale to tell his pals, but Carlyle's cold-blooded murder was met with public outrage. Many of those who had remained sympathetic to Billy, who thought he had gotten a raw deal in the Lincoln County War, now were disgusted, if not horrified, by his actions. Maybe the Kid was just a heinous killer after all.

AS A HARSH WINTER settled in over New Mexico Territory, Special Operative Azariah Wild methodically planned for a surprise raid on Fort Sumner. He had a long list of the outlaws he wanted to capture, and the Kid and Billy Wilson were at the top. At the same time, the cattlemen of the large ranches in the Texas Panhandle organized a force of cowpunchers to ride into the Territory and help root out Billy and the gang of rustlers and recover what stolen stock they could find. And even though Pat Garrett would not begin his term until January 1, 1881, he was not going to wait two months or even two days to fulfill his promise to bring law and order to southeast New Mexico. Sheriff Kimbrell appointed Garrett a deputy sheriff and then politely got out of the way. Garrett was also invested with the powers of a deputy U.S. marshal. Wild had recommended Garrett to U.S. Marshal John Sherman in Santa Fe, but Sherman ignored the request. However, when Wild received by mail two commissions for another man he had recommended, he simply scratched out the name on one of the commissions and wrote in: Patrick F. Garrett.

Wild noted triumphantly that, "I have now had men commissioned as Deputy U.S. Marshals who will execute warrants of arrests or die in the attempt."

On November 20, 1880, Garrett arrived in Lincoln to meet with Wild about their plans for the Sumner raid. Garrett had his friend Barney Mason with him. Twenty-six years old and a native Virginian, Bernard "Barney" Mason had spent some time in Texas before settling in New Mexico, where, like Garrett, he had worked for Pete Maxwell. Mason did not have much of a reputation as a gunman, but he had been in a strange sort of gunfight in a Fort Sumner store. On December 29, 1879, with no apparent warning, a thirty-four-year-old drifter named John Farris fired three errant shots at an unarmed and very surprised Mason, who quickly ran out of the building. Mason was not gone long, though. He went to get his revolver and returned to shoot Farris twice in the chest. He was never charged in the killing and the episode was quickly forgotten.

Mason knew the Kid, Billy Wilson, and the rest of Fort Sumner's outlaw element and got on with them well. Wilson even boarded with Mason and his wife, Juana, when the gang was in Fort Sumner. Yet Mason had come to offer Garrett his help in bringing in the rustlers. The Kid, as well as some of Fort Sumner's residents, later viewed Mason as a turncoat. Mason, however, had to make a choice: either his friend Garrett or the gang. He chose Garrett. Wild hired Mason as an "informer" at two dollars a day plus expenses.

Mason told Wild he had seen Wilson with counterfeit bills, and that he had been propositioned by Dan Dedrick (one of the counterfeiting ringleaders on Wild's list) about taking a large amount of counterfeit money to Mexico and purchasing a bunch of cattle for Dedrick. Mason also said that the Kid and Wilson had left Fort Sumner on November 15 with sixty head of stolen horses and that they planned to return to the Pecos in two to three weeks. Mason thought the outlaws could be easily arrested at his house when they returned.

At the end of their meeting with Wild, Garrett started back for Roswell to organize his posse while Mason headed for White Oaks for a few days of snooping. The posse would be led by Garrett and a fellow deputy U.S. marshal, Bob Olinger (another Wild pick), and would be made up of Garrett's Roswell neighbors. Wild arrived in Roswell by stagecoach on November 24, and Mason got there three days later. On Monday, November 29, Wild sent a rider with a message for Frank Stewart, the leader of the Texas Panhandle posse, which was reported to be at Puerto de Luna. Wild wanted Stewart to know what Garrett and Olinger planned to do. He wanted to use the various posses to catch both the counterfeiters and cattle thieves. Later that same day, Garrett asked his neighbors to meet him in Roswell after dark. Everything was ready for a bold raid on the outlaws.

At approximately 9:00 P.M., Garrett and Olinger led their twenty-man posse out of town. Their first stop would be Bosque Grande and Dan Dedrick's ranch, some thirty miles to the north. Garrett had been told that the Kid, Wilson, and any others with them were traveling on foot, and he suspected that they would go to Dedrick's to get horses. The posse reached the Dedrick place at daybreak, but the Kid and Wilson were not there. Garrett did surprise and capture two men who had recently escaped from the Las Vegas jail. Taking along their two prisoners, the posse pushed on to Fort Sumner, where they hoped to finally corral the Kid and gang, but that was another disappointment. The place was dead quiet; not a single man they were hunting was then in the town. Here Garrett received a letter from Captain Lea, which told him for the first time what had happened at the Greathouse-Kuch place—the murder of Jimmy Carlyle and the Kid's escape.

Garrett found a Fort Sumner resident who he believed could confirm if the Kid had been around or not. The man assured Garrett that

Billy had not yet returned but that Charlie Bowdre, Tom Folliard, and Tom Pickett were at the Yerby ranch near Las Cañaditas. Garrett allowed his men a short time for breakfast and then they started for the Yerby place. Garrett had a federal warrant for Bowdre in connection with the Bernstein killing at the Mescalero Agency. Maybe, he thought, he could salvage something of this raid yet.

The last thing Garrett wanted to do was alert the men at Yerby's ranch to his approach, so over the next few miles he kept the posse off the main trail and stopped regularly on various high points to use his field glasses to scan the country. When they were eight miles from their destination, Garrett spotted a single horseman in the distance, riding toward Yerby's. The rider was Tom Folliard, and Garrett quickly put together a plan to intercept the Kid's best buddy. He knew of a pass through the hills where they had the best chance of surprising and capturing Folliard. What Garrett did not remember about the pass—actually, more of a ravine—was the overgrown weeds and brush, as well as loose rock, which made for extremely tough going. When Garrett and two of his men finally rode out of the ravine and onto the hard road, they were within three hundred yards of Folliard, and they scared the hell out of him. Folliard put the spurs to his mount and flailed away at the horse with his quirt. He then worked the lever of his Winchester like a jackhammer, firing back behind him at his three pursuers (the rest of the posse was still struggling in the ravine). Putting their horses into a hard gallop, Garrett and his men returned the fire, wounding Folliard's horse in the thigh. But the ravine had taken its toll on Garrett's horses, and, more significantly, Folliard's horse was damn fast; outlaws generally try to steal the best horses. All Garrett could do was watch as Folliard quickly pulled away.

Folliard reached the Yerby place well ahead of the posse and warned the other members of the gang. They were long gone by the time Garrett and four of his men came in view of the ranch, but he thought there was a slight chance that the fugitives might be holed up in the ranch house waiting to fight it out with the posse. With his blood still pumping from the chase, Garrett proposed that the five of them split up and charge the house from different directions. His men, not as gung ho as their leader, urged the sheriff-elect to wait until the rest of the posse came up. When the full posse did advance on the ranch house, they only encountered Bowdre's fetching wife, the twenty-five-year-old Manuela, and a Hispanic servant woman. Both women tried their best to pretend they were surprised and terrorized.

When he returned to Fort Sumner, Garrett decided to take a stab at Los Portales, sixty-five miles southeast of Fort Sumner. A conspicuous rock formation rising fifteen feet above the surrounding plains, Los Portales was on a cattle trail running from Fort Sumner to the Texas Panhandle, a path the Kid liked to use for moving stolen stock. Its overhanging limestone ledge is believed to have been the inspiration for the formation's name, because it resembled several porches, *portales* in Spanish. Two springs bubbled up from beneath the ledge, and a good-sized cave in the rocks provided adequate shelter from the elements. The Billy the Kid who was "always looking into the future" envisioned a stage line running by Los Portales one day, and when that day came, he hoped to operate a station there. The Billy the Kid of the present thought the remote springs were an excellent place to gather stolen horses and cattle and alter their brands.

At the very least, Garrett believed he could recover some sixty cattle the Kid was thought to be hiding at Los Portales. When the posse arrived, though, they located only two cows and calves and a yearling. Inside the cave, the posse found some musty flour, a little salt, and a pile of blankets. Garrett later learned that the Kid had moved the stolen stock to a location fifteen miles away. Los Portales, then, was another bust for Garrett and his posse. On their return journey, they stopped at a ranch co-owned by Thomas Wilcox and Manuel Brazil, twelve miles east of Fort Sumner. Billy and the gang also liked to hang out at the Wilcox-Brazil headquarters, even though the owners found this rather exasperating. The posse had dinner in the ranch house, and over the meal Wilcox told Garrett that Charlie Bowdre was anxious to meet with the lawman. Bowdre wanted to make some kind of deal with the authorities. Garrett left instructions for Bowdre to meet him at 2:00 P.M. the following day, December 9, where the road forked, two miles east of Fort Sumner. Bowdre, Garrett cautioned, should come unarmed.

Bowdre showed up, but he was not unarmed. Garrett saw the six-shooter on Bowdre's hip and launched into the man: "Look here, you've betrayed my confidence." The sheriff-elect maintained a stern tone throughout the exchange and showed Bowdre a letter from Captain Joseph C. Lea that promised Bowdre that if he gave up his old ways and dumped his thieving friends, an effort would be made to get him released on bail, after which he would have a chance to "redeem himself." Bowdre was not completely happy with these terms, nor did he believe Lea or Garrett would come through for him. Still, he assured Garrett he would sever his relationship with the Kid and the others. Of course, Bowdre quickly added, he would have to feed the boys when they were at his ranch, but he would try not to shelter them. Garrett ended the meeting with a final warning: "I told him if he did not quit them or surrender, he would be pretty sure to get captured or killed, as we were after the gang and would sleep on their trail until we took them in, dead or alive." For Charlie Bowdre, those last words of Garrett proved tragically prophetic.

MANY OF THE HORSES ridden by Garrett's men had become sick (not surprising considering the hard miles of snow and ice they had covered), so Garrett disbanded his posse at Fort Sumner, sending all but Barney Mason back to Roswell under the charge of Bob Olinger. Garrett still had his two Las Vegas prisoners to deal with at Fort Sumner, however. He had written the sheriff at Las Vegas about the prisoners upon his first arrival at Sumner a little over a week earlier but received no reply, so he decided to get the prisoners there himself. It would be good to get into a real town and have a decent bath. Garrett hired a man with a wagon to haul the two wanted men.

Garrett's small party started for Las Vegas on December 10. On the road, he received word that a sheriff's posse sent from Las Vegas to retrieve the prisoners was then at Puerto de Luna, and Garrett left the main road to find them. He met the "posse" eight miles from the village, and it had picked up a good number of recruits there, so that it now numbered more than twenty wannabe heroes. Garrett was not impressed, describing the posse's approach later as resembling a "whirlwind of lunatics," the men boasting and puffing and causing their horses to prance and race about. One of the prisoners, John J. Webb, began giving serious thought to what this posse might do to him and his companion after Garrett and his men left. Arriving at Puerto de Luna, Webb offered Garrett $10 to stay with him until they reached Las Vegas. Garrett told Webb to put his money away; he would accompany the prisoners to Las Vegas.

As the prisoners were escorted to the blacksmith shop to get fitted with irons, Garrett walked into Padre Polaco's store, sat down on the counter, and helped himself to a hard cracker. That's when two village toughs, who had followed Garrett into the mercantile, decided to test the lawman. Juan Maes, twenty-seven years old, stepped up to Garrett and threw up his hands, saying, "Here I am, take me."

"I don't want you, man," a dumbfounded Garrett exclaimed.

Maes turned and walked away, but it was far from over, for next Marino Leiva, the village's "big bully" and a known thief, approached Garrett.

"No cabrón like Pat Garrett can take me," Leiva said.

"I don't want anything with you; I have no warrant to arrest you," Garrett told him.

Failing to get a rise out of Garrett, the twenty-five-year-old Leiva then walked out to the store's porch, all the while running his mouth about Pat Garrett and bragging about himself. Garrett, unable to enjoy his cracker in peace, got up off the counter and followed Leiva outside.

"Go 'way from here," Garrett ordered, and as he spoke, he gave Leiva a hard push, so hard it knocked the man to the ground.

Leiva sprang back up, drawing his six-shooter as he did so. When Garrett saw Leiva go for his pistol, the lawman drew his as well. Leiva got off two quick shots, both missing their mark. Garrett accidentally fired his six-shooter prematurely, the bullet kicking up the dirt at Leiva's feet. But his second shot, rapidly following the first, struck the bully in the left shoulder, the slug passing completely through his body. Leiva turned and ran for his horse, firing back as he fled. Barney Mason, who had been outside the store, drew his pistol and chased after Leiva, getting off several shots before Leiva reached his or someone else's horse and galloped away.

Garrett went back into the store, followed soon after by Mason. Garrett placed his Winchester within easy reach and continued eating his cracker. If anybody wanted to pester him again, he would be more than willing to accommodate. Soon, one of the deputies, Francisco Romero, walked in and told Garrett he was under arrest for shooting at Leiva. He ordered the sheriff-elect to turn over his weapons. An exasperated Garrett made it clear to Romero that while he had no intention of evading the law, there was no way he was going to turn over his arms, especially after one man from the town had just tried to kill him. Mason then picked up his own rifle.

"Shall I cut the son-of-a-bitch in two, Pat?" Mason barked.

Garrett told him to calm down; there was no need to shoot the deputy. At this point, Padre Polaco, a good friend of Garrett's, began to talk some sense into Deputy Romero, who left the store. The next morning, Garrett visited the local *alcalde* (justice of the peace) about the arrest, and after a few questions, the alcalde told Garrett he was free to go. Garrett was more than happy to oblige, departing Puerto de Luna that day with Mason, the posse, and their prisoners for Las Vegas.

They soon met up with yet five or six more possemen sent from Las Vegas. This last bunch, under the charge of the sheriff's brother, Dolores Romero, also failed to impress Garrett, but there was nothing he could do about it. As they neared Anton Chico, Garrett received word that Frank Stewart and his Panhandle posse were in the town. He sent Mason to deliver a message for Stewart to meet him in Las Vegas. This caused the Las Vegas deputies to put up a fuss, because they thought of Mason as a member of the Kid's gang (not an entirely wrongheaded assumption). Garrett waved Mason on and told the deputies that if they wanted to arrest the man, they could do it in Las Vegas.

When Garrett and Stewart met, they had a long confab about the Kid. Stewart's plan was to look for stolen cattle and the gang in the White Oaks area. If unsuccessful there, he would cross over the mountains and follow the Rio Hondo east to Roswell and then ride up the Pecos Valley to Fort Sumner. Garrett considered that a waste of time. Not only that, Garret informed Stewart, he would be allowing the Kid an opportunity to escape to a safe refuge, likely out of the Territory. Garrett knew, probably from information obtained by Barney Mason when he went to deliver Garrett's message to Stewart, that the Kid had recently been in Anton Chico. Garrett's posse had just scoured the Kid's stomping grounds of Fort Sumner, Las Cañaditas, and Los Portales, and come up empty-handed. But Garrett was confident the Kid had now moved back into the Fort Sumner area.

Garrett wanted to sneak into Sumner again, but he and Barney Mason could not bring the gang in alone. He needed men—Stewart's men. By this time, the news of Governor Wallace's reward proclamation had reached Las Vegas, and Garrett offered Stewart a share of the reward money if Stewart and his men would join him on an expedition to Fort Sumner. Stewart agreed to run Garrett's plan by his men (all except the offer of the reward money), but they would have to ride hard to overtake them, for they had likely already decamped for White Oaks.

The Texas posse, composed primarily of cowboys from the large LS and LIT outfits, was camped just a few miles from Anton Chico when Garrett, Mason, and Stewart caught up with it. Over breakfast, with Garrett watching, Stewart addressed his men. Although one of the posse's goals was to apprehend the rustlers, the cattlemen who had supplied the cowboys and paid the expenses preferred that recovering livestock be the posse's first order of business, with rounding up notorious outlaws coming in second. Stewart began, then, by bending the truth a little, saying there was a bunch of steers near Fort Sumner he wanted to round up and take in. The boys did not buy a word of it. They knew Fort Sumner was Kid country, and it was obvious why Garrett was in their camp and what he was after—the sheriff-elect and deputy U.S. marshal was, first and foremost, a manhunter. So Garrett told it to them straight. He was going after the Kid and his gang, and there was a good chance there would be some fighting before they were through. He wanted only volunteers; no one would be forced to go against their will.

"Do what you please, boys," Stewart chimed in, "but there is no time to talk. Those who are going with me, get ready at once. I want no man who hesitates."

Six men got up off the ground and began to saddle their horses.

6

The Kid Hunted

If it hadn't been for the dead horse in the
doorway, I wouldn't be here.
—BILLY THE KID

BILLY BONNEY KNEW THAT Pat Garrett, unlike the sheriffs he
had dealt with in the past, could be as hardheaded as a snapping turtle; he would not let go, and he would not quit until the job
was finished. And as more and more men went after Billy and his pals,
it was getting harder and harder to dodge them—there were only so
many roads, so many camps, so many places to hide. The Kid was
getting whipped in the territorial press, too. In an editorial of December 3, 1880, the *Las Vegas Gazette* portrayed the outlaws as a despicable
bunch of hardened criminals. And the paper said there were forty or
fifty of them. This was a gross exaggeration, of course, but that is what
the Kid inspired. And as far as the *Gazette* was concerned, Bonney was
the worst of the lot.

"The gang is under the leadership of 'Billy the Kid,' a desperate
cuss, who is eligible for the post of captain of any crowd, no matter
how mean and lawless," the paper wrote.

This was the first time he had been referred to in print as "Billy the Kid," three simple words that rolled off the tongue and into immortality.

The *Gazette* was doing more than reporting on the outlaws; it was serving notice to the community: "Shall we suffer this horde of outcasts and the scum of society, who are outlawed by a multitude of crimes, to continue their way on the very border of our county? We believe our citizens of San Miguel County to be order loving people, and call upon them to unite in forever wiping out this band to the east of us."

Billy read the newspapers whenever he could get his hands on them. He read the *Gazette* editorial soon after its publication, and he attempted some damage control by writing a four-page letter to Governor Wallace, dated Fort Sumner, December 12. "I noticed in the *Las Vegas Gazette*," Billy wrote, "a piece which stated that, Billy 'the' Kid, the name by which I am known in the Country was the Captain of a Band of Outlaws who hold Forth at the Portales. There is no such Organization in Existence. So the Gentleman must have drawn very heavily on his Imagination."

Billy went on to explain the recent events at Coyote Springs and the Greathouse-Kuch station. Jimmy Carlyle, he claimed, was shot and killed by the possemen, who believed it was the Kid escaping out the window. Billy also insisted that he had been living at Fort Sumner since he left Lincoln, making a living there as a gambler. His troubles, the Kid told Wallace, were all caused by John S. Chisum. Billy held a considerable grudge against the cattleman because he had never paid the money he allegedly promised the Kid for fighting on the McSween side during the war. Now, Billy firmly believed that Chisum was the mastermind behind Pat Garrett's campaign to track him down.

Billy assured the governor that "so far as for my being at the head of a band [of outlaws] there is nothing of it."

Billy's carefully composed letter was a waste of ink and paper. On

December 13, Wallace signed a proclamation offering a reward of "five hundred dollars ($500.-) for the apprehension and arrest of said William Bonney alias 'The Kid' and for his delivery to the Sheriff of Lincoln County at the county seat of said county." The *Las Vegas Gazette* complained that the $500 reward was too small:

> It is no jackrabbit hunt that Garrett and his band, Frank Stewart and his Panhandle boys and the White Oaks rangers are engaged in, but a determined campaign against lawless fellows who have nothing to fear, as the remainder of their lives will be passed behind bars, to pay the penalty of their crimes if they are ever caught. What should be done by the people of this and neighboring counties is to raise a purse of $5,000 to be paid the men engaged in this campaign providing they drive the desperadoes from our border.

JUST BEFORE DAYLIGHT ON December 18, Garrett led his posse into Fort Sumner. In addition to the six men from the Texas Panhandle posse, he had also picked up four men from Puerto de Luna. With Barney Mason and Frank Stewart, that gave him twelve gunmen. The Kid and gang were not then in the town, but it was believed that they were not far off. Garrett obtained quarters for his exhausted men and told them to get some rest (they had been in the saddle for close to fifteen hours). No sooner had the men gotten settled, though, than Barney Mason busted in and told Garrett that the Kid's gang was camped in an abandoned building nearby. The possemen jumped up, grabbed their guns, and cautiously proceeded to the adobe Mason pointed out. Peering through the wavy glass windowpanes, they saw a small fire in the fireplace—and the silhouette of a man in front of it. Garrett whispered to his men not to take any chances; they should shoot to kill as soon as they got inside. With that, he kicked in the door and rushed in, followed by several members of the posse.

"My God, don't shoot, boys!" screamed the man in front of the fireplace. Fortunately, Garrett and the boys held their fire, for the trembling man turned out to be the mail carrier from Las Vegas. The excitement over for the time being, Garrett led the men back to their quarters, where they finally got some much-needed sleep.

Later that morning, Garrett took Mason with him to see what he could find out about the gang's whereabouts. He told the posse to stay in their quarters; he did not want word to get out about their presence in Sumner. The Kid had many sympathizers who would be eager to alert the outlaw to any danger. And sure enough, one of the first individuals Garrett and Mason ran into was Yginio Garcia, a friend of Billy's. Garrett at first ordered Garcia not to leave the plaza, but as the lawman was certain that Garcia knew nothing about his posse, he decided it would be advantageous to give Billy the impression that he only had Mason with him. He let Garcia go, who claimed he had urgent business at home, but, as Garrett had suspected, Garcia got a message to Billy about his encounter with the two manhunters.

Garrett and his men kept to themselves the rest of that day and night. The next morning, December 19, Garrett spotted Juan Gallegos, the sixteen-year-old stepson of Thomas Wilcox, loafing about the plaza. Garrett had a strong hunch that the young man had been sent there as a spy for the Kid. He was right. The boy readily admitted that the gang was at the Wilcox-Brazil ranch, east of town. Gallegos's father and Manuel Brazil were in no way sympathetic to the outlaws, but they had no choice but to put up with them. Garrett easily persuaded young Gallegos to help him lay a trap for the gang.

Garrett next located Kid confederate José Valdez and forced him to write a note to Billy saying that Garrett and the few men with him had departed Fort Sumner for Roswell; all was clear. Garrett then wrote a note of his own to Wilcox and Brazil asking for their cooperation. Garrett handed the two notes to Gallegos, warning him that whatever he did, not to get them mixed up.

The Kid had been anxiously waiting for Gallegos, and when the young man handed him Valdez's note, the outlaw scanned it and then read it to his pals. They gleefully voiced their contempt for the great Pat Garrett who had seemingly abandoned the chase to go home. The boys then proceeded to boast among themselves about how they had intended to go into Fort Sumner and shoot it out with the sheriff-elect but now that he had run off, they had a good mind to follow him and finish the business once and for all. As the outlaws continued to deride Garrett and anyone else who would oppose them, Gallegos discreetly slipped Garrett's note to his stepfather.

Back at Fort Sumner, Garrett got his men ready to give the gang a warm reception. He was confident the gang would be in Fort Sumner that night. There were just too many amusements for them to stay away—women, gambling, and liquor made for a powerful triumvirate. Garrett knew that Bowdre's wife, Manuela, was now living in a room in the old Indian Hospital building. The hospital formed the northeast corner of the complex of buildings that made up Fort Sumner, and the road coming from the Wilcox-Brazil place passed just behind it. Garrett figured that the gang would make the hospital building their first stop, so he placed a guard outside and stationed the rest of his posse inside. Also inside with the posse were a few Hispanic residents whom Garrett was holding in custody for fear that they would attempt to get word to the gang.

At about 8:00 P.M., Garrett, Mason, and posse members Tom Emory and Bob Williams were deep into a game of poker. They had spread a blanket on the floor and were using that as their gambling table. Another posse member, Jim East, was in a corner rolled up in his blanket trying to get some sleep before it was his turn at guard duty. Garrett was not expecting the gang until later in the evening, not for another two hours, at the earliest. Just then, posseman Lon Chambers popped his head in.

"Pat, someone is coming!"

"Get your guns, boys," Garrett said as he stood up from the floor. "None but the men we want are riding this time of night."

Garrett, Chambers, and another man stationed themselves on the east porch while Mason and the others took up their positions at the rear west wing, which gave them clear shots in case Billy and the gang rode straight to the plaza without stopping. With the snow cover helping to illuminate the night, Garrett clearly saw the riders Chambers had spotted just moments before. And Billy Bonney could just as easily make out the Indian Hospital and other Sumner buildings, the occasional lantern or candle appearing as warm, flickering orbs in the windows. Billy rode in front with Tom Folliard, but as the gang neared the hospital building, Billy sensed that something was not quite right. That bump of caution had saved his skin before, and he did not hesitate to react to it now. Billy was always looking out for Billy all the time, and he did not bother to pass along his suspicions to his pals. Instead, he said he had just been struck by a sudden craving for a chew of some good tobacco, and Billy Wilson, who was bringing up the rear, had the best tobacco. The Kid gently pulled on his reins and let the others go ahead of him.

By this time, Pat Garrett was standing close up against the adobe wall, where he was well hidden by the shadow of the porch and some harnesses suspended from above. His heartbeat quickened slightly as the riders veered off the main road and headed directly toward him. He recognized Folliard, who was riding in the lead with Tom Pickett. "That's them," Garrett whispered to his companions.

Folliard rode on up to the building and halted, the head of his horse just under the porch's roof. At that moment, Garrett yelled out to the outlaws to throw up their hands. Instead of obeying this command from the darkness, Folliard reached for his six-gun. When Garrett and Chambers saw this, they both jerked the triggers of their Winchester rifles and streaks of fire lit up the air. Folliard's horse wheeled and took off in a run, its rider crying out in agony—"You never heard a man scream the way he did," Garrett said later.

Pickett, terrified and yelling at the top of his lungs, spurred his horse to get away, but Garrett drew down on him and fired. Unfortunately the muzzle flash from Chambers's rifle spoiled his aim, and Pickett was able to escape unscathed.

An instant after Garrett fired on Folliard, Barney Mason and the rest of the posse spotted Billy, Rudabaugh, Bowdre, and Wilson and began blasting away at them. Rudabaugh's horse took a hit in its guts, but the outlaws were able to gallop away safely, Billy having perfectly positioned himself in the rear of the group. Mason and the others then ran around to Garrett's side of the building just in time to see a lone horseman coming slowly toward them across the snow. It was Folliard, who had turned his horse around after racing some 150 yards from the hospital building.

"Don't shoot, Garrett," Folliard pleaded. "I'm killed."

"Take your medicine, old boy," an excited Barney Mason shouted as he walked toward Folliard, "take your medicine."

Garrett cautioned his friend that Folliard was not yet dead; the young outlaw could still pull a trigger, and he might very well want revenge. Garrett then called to Folliard to throw up his hands. He was not about to give the outlaw a chance to kill him. Folliard feebly replied that he was dying and could not even raise his hands. Powerless even to dismount on his own, Folliard begged to be helped off his horse so that he could lie down. A few of Garrett's men, their guns drawn, stepped up to Folliard and gently pulled him off his mount and carried him inside, placing him on Jim East's blanket. By candlelight, they examined his body and found that Garrett's first bullet had punched through his chest just below his heart. Another slug had cut across the front of Folliard's coat. When they removed his pistol, they found that it was at full cock. Folliard was just about to draw his weapon and had just cocked the hammer when Garrett's first shot struck—the pistol had never left its holster.

Garrett did what he could to make Folliard comfortable. The

posse members returned to their poker game. But as Folliard's pain got worse, he begged Garrett to kill him. If Garrett was his friend, Folliard told the lawman, he would put him out of his misery. "I told him I was no friend to men of his kind, who sought to murder me because I tried to do my duty," Garrett wrote later. Then, when Mason came into the room, the outlaw became panicked. Garrett surmised that Folliard feared Mason would be more than happy to end his misery. "Don't shoot anymore, for God's sake," Folliard cried. "I'm already killed!" Mason again cruelly told Folliard to take his medicine, to which Folliard replied, "It's the best medicine I ever took."

Folliard requested that his grandmother back in Texas be informed of his death. "Oh my God, is it possible I must die?" he asked no one in particular. Then the outlaw began to curse.

"God damn you, Garrett; I hope to meet you in hell," Folliard said.

"I would not talk that way, Tom," Garrett said. "You are going to die in a few minutes."

"The sooner the better. I will be out of pain."

Folliard, groaning now, asked for water. Jim East brought him a drink, and after struggling to take a small sip, Folliard lay back onto his blanket, shuddered, and died. He had lived forty-five minutes after taking Garrett's bullet.

AFTER GARRETT'S SURPRISE AT Fort Sumner, Billy, Rudabaugh, Bowdre, and Wilson rode their horses like hell to the Wilcox-Brazil ranch, twelve miles away. Just as they arrived, Rudabaugh's horse collapsed and died from its wounds. Rudabaugh lost no time securing another mount, and after the fugitives quickly grabbed some grub from the ranch house, the four rode off into the nearby hills. Afraid that Garrett might be on their back trail, they spent the following day with their binoculars, carefully glassing the Wilcox-Brazil place and surrounding country from a safe distance. Failing to see any sign of Garrett, they returned to the ranch in the evening.

As Billy and the others rode up to the ranch house, they were surprised to see Tom Pickett crawl out of a haystack. Pickett, who was separated from the gang at Fort Sumner and scared out of his socks, had spurred and whipped his horse nonstop for twenty-five miles, until the poor animal, its tongue extended and a lathery sweat dripping from its body, tumbled to the ground and died. Pickett then walked more than twelve miles back to the Wilcox-Brazil place, where he hid himself in the haystack, praying his pals would show up soon—at least sooner than Garrett. As Pickett brushed himself off, he started going on about how he was sure he had nailed the man who had ordered them to throw up their hands back at Fort Sumner (Pickett never got off a shot). For the rest of the evening, the gang took turns guarding the place.

The outlaws initially suspected that Wilcox and Brazil were in on Garrett's ambush scheme, but the ranchers finally convinced them otherwise. Tired and demoralized, they tried to figure out what to do next. Leery of making a move until they knew Garrett's whereabouts, they decided to send another spy to Fort Sumner. They drafted Manuel Brazil for the job, and he left the ranch the next day. Brazil, of course, went straight to Garrett upon his arrival in Sumner. The outlaw bunch was all at his ranch, he told the lawman, and feeling rather dejected. Garrett then conspired with Brazil, telling the rancher to carry the news to the boys that he was at Sumner with only Barney Mason and three Hispanos, and that though he wanted to go back to Roswell, he was worried about leaving the safety of the plaza after having made the gang so mad by killing Tom Folliard.

As Brazil prepared to leave the next morning, December 22, Garrett went over the plans with the rancher. If the gang was still at his ranch, Brazil was to remain there. But, if the outlaws were either not there, or if they left a short time later, Brazil was to ride back to

Sumner and report to Garrett. If Garrett did not hear from Brazil by 2:00 A.M., Garrett would assume the gang was still holed up at the ranch, and he and his posse would start out from Fort Sumner.

At midnight, Brazil rode back into Fort Sumner, his beard crusted over with icicles. The gang had left his place after supper, he reported. Garrett immediately ordered his men to mount up; they were going after the outlaws. The night was clear and bone cold, the type of cold that causes the snow to make a tight crunch sound with each step. Garrett sent Brazil on ahead (in case the gang had returned) while he and the posse pushed on to the Wilcox-Brazil place. Three miles from their destination, Garrett and his men met Brazil. The Kid and gang had not returned, he said, but he could easily show the posse the trail the outlaws had left behind. With four inches of snow on the ground and the moon high in the sky, Garrett had no trouble following the tracks Brazil pointed out to him. The tracks led east, and Garrett instantly knew where he would find the outlaws. About three miles beyond the Wilcox-Brazil ranch, at a place known as Stinking Spring, there was a small, one-room rock and adobe house that stood by itself on the edge of a wide arroyo. The dwelling had been built years before by a Hispanic sheepherder, but now it was abandoned. Garrett was convinced he would find the gang camped there for the night.

Well familiar with the country he was now leading his posse over, Garrett halted his men a half mile from Stinking Spring and cautioned them that silence was critical for them to trap Billy and the others. Then, when within four hundred yards of the rock house, Garrett divided his posse into two groups. By this point, it was 3:00 A.M. Leaving posse member Juan Roybal to hold the horses, Garrett circled around the side of the house with half his men and dropped into an arroyo, which allowed his party to creep up to within seventy-five yards of the front of the structure. Frank Stewart and the rest of the posse took up positions within two hundred yards of the building.

The house, which was only twelve feet wide and thirty feet long, had a single narrow entrance and no door. Plainly visible in the moonlight, Garrett counted three horses tied up outside. Two horses, he reasoned, were sharing the small space with the gang. There were no sounds inside, and Garrett assumed that the outlaws were asleep with no idea what was waiting for them out in the cold.

Excited to finally have the Kid within his grasp, and sensing the kill, Garrett sent Stewart a message suggesting that they quietly slip in on the sleeping men, guns drawn, and then hold the outlaws until daylight. Posseman Lee Hall was all for the idea, but Frank Stewart was against such a bravado move. He would rather sit out in the freezing cold than run the risk of getting into a gunfight inside that small space. So, lying flat on their blankets in the snow, they waited for the dawn, which was more than three hours away—posse member Charlie Rudolph suffered frostbite to his feet before the whole thing was over. After what surely seemed an eternity to Garrett and the others, they finally saw the predawn glow rising in the east.

Billy had let it be known more than once that he would never be taken alive, and Garrett was perfectly willing to forgo any efforts to obtain his surrender. A dead Billy the Kid would be much less to worry about than a live one. Garrett had already told his men that if he saw the Kid, he was going to kill him. Garrett believed that once the Kid was gone, the rest of the gang would simply give up. The sheriff-elect had a good description of what the Kid was wearing, which included a distinctive sombrero. Garrett told his men that the signal to begin firing was when he raised his rifle to his shoulder.

Although it was not yet daybreak, it was light enough now for Garrett to easily make out the frigid faces of his men. They stared at the dark entrance to the house, trying to detect anything inside when, suddenly, a man appeared in the doorway holding a feedbag. There was the sombrero—he looked to be the Kid—he had to be the Kid. Garrett raised his rifle and drew a steady bead on the man. Seven shots broke the winter silence like claps of thunder, followed instantly by the loud slap of lead bullets slamming into flesh and bone. The man spun back into the building. The next thing the posse heard was Billy Wilson yelling that they had mortally wounded Charlie Bowdre and he wanted to come out. Garrett had sent the wrong man on his final journey.

All of Bowdre's pals were wide awake now, and they realized how desperate their situation was. Billy looked at his friend, who was white as a ghost, deep-red blood soaking his clothing, and he heard someone outside shout that it was okay for Bowdre to come out—with his hands up. The Kid grabbed hold of Bowdre and tugged on his gunbelt until the holster was positioned just below Bowdre's navel.

"They have murdered you, Charlie," Billy said to his pal, "but you can get revenge. Kill some of the sons of bitches before you die."

Bowdre stumbled out of the doorway, with his hands in the air. He took several steps toward the posse, looking across each man until he recognized Garrett. As he approached the lawman, Bowdre pointed back to the house. He tried to speak, but it was a struggle because blood was gurgling up with every breath: "I wish—I wish—I wish . . . ," he said. Then, as Garrett grabbed him, Bowdre whispered, "I'm dying!" A remorseful Garrett carefully laid Bowdre down on some blankets, and in the time it took the six-foot-four lawman to straighten back up, Charlie Bowdre was dead.

All eyes turned back to the rock house. Able to reach the tethers of the horses tied outside, the outlaws were trying to bring one of the horses in through the door. Billy's plan was to mount up and make a mad dash out the narrow entrance—this was just the kind of hairbreadth escape the Kid was famous for. Garrett knew exactly what they were trying to do, and his first thought was to shoot the first horse's lead rope in two, but it was swaying too much from the outlaws jerking at it. Ultimately he concluded that it was easier to kill the damn horse, and as the animal's head and shoulders passed into the doorway, Garrett sent a bullet into its chest. The horse collapsed in its tracks, blocking the entrance and making it difficult to get another horse in or out, especially one with a rider on its back. To be sure, Garrett and his men shot the lead ropes of the other two horses, and they slowly walked away, their noses nuzzling the snow in search of grass.

At first, Billy was not sure who had them surrounded, because Manuel Brazil had fed them a good amount of false information. It came to them soon enough, however. Garrett hailed the Kid and asked him how he was "fixed in there."

"Pretty well," the Kid answered, "but we have no wood to get breakfast."

"Come out and get some," Garrett said. "Be a little sociable."

"Can't do it, Pat. Business is too confining. No time to run around."

Garrett could not resist throwing some of Billy's big talk back at him. (Brazil had told Garrett how the Kid had been eager to go after the lawman after the rancher informed him it was only Garrett, Mason, and three Hispanos back at Fort Sumner.)

"Didn't you fellows forget a part of your program yesterday?" Garrett asked. "You know you were to come in on us at Fort Sumner, from some other direction, give us a square fight, set us afoot, and drive us down the Pecos."

The Kid had no response. Garrett then told the outlaws the obvious: they were surrounded, there was no chance to get away, and they might as well come out and surrender. Garrett got a response this time—the Kid told him to go to hell.

Not long after that, the posse heard the sounds of digging and picking. The outlaws were using their knives and firearms to make gun ports in the walls of the house. Garrett directed Jim East and Tom Emory to shoot at the area of the wall where the sounds were coming from, and the digging stopped. As the hours passed, the posse periodically fired a shot or two into the doorway, just as a friendly reminder to the outlaws that they were still there.

At some point that morning, Garrett decided to get his men some breakfast. He took half the posse with him to the Wilcox-Brazil place, leaving the others to watch the house. When Manuel Brazil anxiously asked Garrett the news, the sheriff-elect was still kicking himself about Charlie Bowdre.

"I told him the news was bad," Garrett wrote later, "that we had killed the very man we did not want to kill."

What Brazil said next, however, caused Garrett to rethink Bowdre: "I don't see why you should be sorry for having killed him. After you had the interview with him the other day, and was doing your best to get him out of his troubles, he said to me, as we were riding home, 'I wish you would get that damned long-legged son of a bitch out to meet me once more. I would just kill him and end all this trouble!' Now, how sorry are you?"

After breakfast, Garrett asked Wilcox to take one of his wagons and haul out to Stinking Spring some provisions, firewood, and forage for the horses. The Kid, Garrett knew, was stubborn enough to hold out in the rock house for a long time, all the while working his brain to come up with some kind of escape plan. The posse might as well be comfortable. When Garrett returned to the spring, Frank Stewart took the rest of the posse back for their turn at the breakfast table.

The hours passed with not a sound from the outlaws. At approximately 3:00 P.M., movement in the doorway of the house excited the posse, but it was only the two horses that had been inside with the outlaws, one of which was the Kid's noted bay mare, beautiful and fast. Having abandoned a mounted getaway, the outlaws were turning the horses loose. The horses hopped over the dead beast in the doorway and were taken in by the posse. An hour later, the wagon arrived with the provisions.

Garrett had the men build a big fire and told them to get a meal going. Soon, the smell of flame-roasted beef drifted in the direction of the rock house, and the outlaws, who had not eaten or had a drop of water all day, received a strong whiff—the gang quickly began to weaken. The Kid tried to convince Rudabaugh, Wilson, and Pickett to hold out longer, at least until dark, but they voted to surrender. Billy, disgusted, called them a bunch of cowards, but his rants did not change their minds. Dave Rudabaugh tied a dirty rag to the end of a Winchester and shoved it up through the old chimney and yelled out that they wanted to surrender.

Garrett told them to come on out with their hands up, but only Rudabaugh walked out the door. He walked up to Garrett and said the whole bunch would surrender if Garrett promised to protect them. Garrett gave his word and Rudabaugh went back inside. After an anxious few minutes, a scruffy-looking foursome, their hands up, stepped across the dead horse and through the doorway. Billy was the last to walk out. This was the first time that most of the men in the posse had laid eyes on the notorious rustler. Garrett, still just a deputy sheriff, was about to fulfill his promise to the people of Lincoln County to bring the notorious outlaw to justice.

"Kill the son of a bitch," Barney Mason shouted, pointing his gun at the Kid. "He is slippery and may get away."

But East and Lee Hall had heard Garrett's surrender terms and threatened to kill Mason if he fired a shot. Mason lowered his weapon. Garrett's reaction to this incident is not recorded, but he surely recognized that his friend was acting out of fear of what the Kid might do to him if he ever got the chance.

The Kid never really got over the humiliating surrender at Stinking Spring. "If it hadn't been for the dead horse in the doorway I wouldn't be here," he later told a Las Vegas newspaper reporter. "I would have ridden out on my bay mare and taken my chances of escaping. But I couldn't ride out over that, for she would have jumped back, and I would have got it in the head."

ONCE THE GANG WAS disarmed and fed, they were taken to the Wilcox-Brazil place. Garrett then sent Brazil, Mason, and Rudolph back for Bowdre's body. Both the posse and the prisoners spent the night at the ranch headquarters, where the possemen took turns watching the prisoners, two guards at a time. Garrett's orders were that if any of the prisoners tried anything, they were to be shot. After breakfast the next morning, the entire entourage—including Bowdre's corpse—departed for the Pecos, arriving at Fort Sumner before noon. It was Christmas Eve. As Garrett's party neared the Indian Hospital, Manuela Bowdre ran out in the snow to confront them.

She frantically looked for her husband with the other prisoners, and then she saw one of Garrett's men riding her husband's horse. The men driving the wagon with Bowdre's body did not want to deal with the visibly angry woman and drove on past her. As Manuela screamed and cussed at Garrett, the two men stopped the wagon, took hold of Bowdre's body, and carried it into his widow's quarters and laid it out on a table. When Garrett finally got an opportunity to speak, he told Manuela to go to the store and pick out a suit of clothes for her husband. He would pay for it, and he would pay to have the man buried as well.

The prisoners were taken to the blacksmith shop to be fitted with irons, but, because of a lack of materials or time, only Billy and Rudabaugh were shackled and chained. Wilson and Pickett, obviously deemed the two least dangerous members of the gang, went without irons for the time being. The Kid and Rudabaugh were then led across the plaza to a long, two-story structure that had once served as officers' quarters but now housed the Maxwell family. Garrett had been approached by Deluvina Maxwell, the Maxwell's Navajo servant, with a message from Mrs. Luz Beaubien Maxwell. Would Garrett permit the Kid to be brought to their residence so that her daughter, sixteen-year-old Paulita, could tell the Kid good-bye? The nice-looking sister of Pete Maxwell was not the only Fort Sumner female Billy had wooed in recent months, but she had become his favorite, and the young lady was equally taken with him. Garrett acquiesced, but he told Jim East and Lee Hall, the two guards, to keep a close watch on the Kid.

Before the prisoners and their escort reached the Maxwell place, the shackle on Rudabaugh's ankle somehow broke loose. "That is a bad sign," Billy said. "I will die and Dave will go free." He was not joking—the Kid, it seems, had a superstitious streak. After the prisoners entered the house, Mrs. Maxwell politely asked the guards if they would release Billy so that Paulita and the Kid could say their good-byes privately in another room. East and Hall said no—they had worked too hard to catch the outlaw, and it would take more than these women's transparent machinations to get him away from them now.

"The lovers embraced," East wrote later, "and she gave Billy one of those soul kisses the novelists tell us about."

After a few respectful moments, the guards pulled Paulita and the Kid apart and then escorted the prisoners to Garrett, who was ready to leave for Las Vegas.

With the fighting over and what was left of the gang well in charge, Garrett and Stewart no longer needed the entire posse. It was decided that Barney Mason, Jim East, and Tom Emory would accompany them; the rest of the men were dismissed. The prisoners were loaded into a two-mule wagon loaned by Brazil, who also served as the vehicle's driver, and with the slapping of the reins and a couple of sucking clicks from Brazil's clenched jaw, the entire cavalcade departed Fort Sumner, the Kid and Rudabaugh laughing and chatting as if they were on a Sunday stroll. In fact, over the next few days, Garrett learned a lot about Billy Bonney. Tom Pickett, on the other hand, seemed worried, and Billy Wilson was withdrawn and dejected. The wagon made for slow going in the snow, but by about 8:00 P.M., Garrett's party had reached John Gerhardt's ranch, twenty-five miles up the Pecos, and stopped for the night. Twelve hours later, the men were back on the road, arriving at Padre Polaco's Puerto de Luna store at 2:00 P.M. It was Christmas day, and the jolly Padre Polaco served Garrett, his men, and the prisoners a hearty meal.

The Christmas dinner was served in shifts, and Jim East was the first to guard the prisoners. East and the prisoners were sequestered in a long adobe room in the store building. Its single door was locked, and Garrett had the key in his pocket. East sat on a woodpile near the door, facing the prisoners, who were gathered around the fireplace at the opposite end of the room. After a bit of small talk, the Kid asked East if he had anything to smoke. The guard replied that he did, to which the Kid responded that he had some rolling papers. East got ready to throw the tobacco to the Kid, but the outlaw offered to come over and get it, and with that, he and Rudabaugh started for the guard's end of the room. They were halfway across the open space when East shouted to them:

"Hold on, Billy, if you come any farther I am going to shoot you."

The prisoners kept coming; East leveled his gun at them.

"Hold on, Billy, if you make another step I'll shoot you."

The prisoners hesitated.

"You are the most suspicious damned man I ever saw," Billy said, feigning disgust, and then he and Rudabaugh turned around and walked to the fireplace.

East pitched the tobacco over to the Kid, but he picked it up and tossed it right back; Billy did not want East's damn tobacco.

Garrett was able to get Wilson and Pickett fitted with irons at Puerto de Luna, and later that afternoon, the party started again for Las Vegas. They traveled all through the night and rode into the San Miguel County seat about 4:00 P.M. on December 26. Not in their wildest dreams could these trail-worn westerners have imagined the excitement and extreme curiosity their arrival generated. It was as if the circus had come to town with horses prancing, elephants trumpeting, and clowns frolicking. Indeed, with Garrett as the taciturn lion tamer and Billy the Kid as the caged-beast-that-cannot-be-tamed, it had all the makings of the greatest show on earth—or a tragedy for the ages.

7

Facing Death Boldly

Billy never talked much of the past; he was always
looking into the future.
—FRANK COE

IT HAD NOT BEEN easy, but Pat Garrett kept his promise to the
outlaws. Despite a well-armed lynch mob at the train station in Las
Vegas, he had gotten Billy, Wilson, and Rudabaugh safely to Santa Fe.
Once he turned the prisoners over to Deputy U.S. Marshal Charles
Conklin, however, he believed his job was done. Garrett did not travel
to Mesilla to witness the Kid's trial for Sheriff Brady's murder. He
had plenty to keep himself busy as the new sheriff of Lincoln County,
which he officially became on January 1, 1881. During the humdrum
workdays of serving writs, collecting taxes, and completing annoying
paperwork, he may have wondered if he would ever see the Kid again.
When the Kid's trial ended in a guilty verdict, there was no more
wondering. Judge Bristol ordered that Billy be transported to Lincoln,
where he was to be placed in Sheriff Garrett's care until May 13, on
which date the sheriff was to conduct a public hanging. Garrett had

never hanged a man, but a bigger concern was how to hold the Kid until the execution date.

Garrett took custody of Billy on April 21. The sheriff confined the county's prisoners in makeshift quarters on the second floor of the two-story adobe courthouse (formerly the Murphy-Dolan store) on the west end of Lincoln. Billy would be incarcerated on that floor as well, but in a room all to himself. Well aware of the building's shortcomings as a jail, Garrett assigned two guards to watch the Kid: Bob Olinger and friend James W. Bell.

Olinger was born Ameredith Robert B. Olinger in Delphi, Indiana, in 1850. Ten years later, the Olinger family was scratching out a living on a farm in Linn County, Kansas. After a sojourn in Indian Territory (Oklahoma), Bob followed his older brother John Wallace to the Seven Rivers country of southeastern New Mexico in 1877, where they seem to have divided their time equally between chasing cattle and men, particularly the Regulators. In October 1880, Olinger was commissioned a deputy U.S. marshal for Lincoln County and spent several weeks with Deputy Marshal Pat Garrett hunting counterfeiters and rustlers, especially the Kid's bunch. On April 10, 1881, Sheriff Southwick appointed Olinger a deputy sheriff for Doña Ana County with the special task of delivering the Kid to Garrett in Lincoln.

Only three photographs survive of Bob Olinger. Now spotted and yellowed with age, the photos reveal a sizable man, someone the *Las Vegas Daily Optic* described as "the tall sycamore of Seven Rivers." Perched upon his head, making him appear even taller than his six feet two inches, was a wide-brimmed hat, and like most men of the time, Olinger wore a vest and coat. Around his collar he liked to sport a colorful bandanna, neatly tied, its long ends dangling down the front of his chest. From his vest swung a watch chain and fob. He had a rather expressionless face (not uncommon in nineteenth-century portraits), and his modest mustache failed to make him look distinguished

Jimmy Dolan and Bob Olinger.

in any way. Some photographs are able to hint at a subject's character or personality—these do not. But in the case of Bob Olinger, there is no lack of opinion regarding the man's character.

Olinger had acquired a reputation as a bully, at least among his enemies, of which there were many. Texas Ranger James Gillett, on a visit to Roswell, was told in no uncertain terms that Bob Olinger was the meanest man in New Mexico. Gus Gildea wrote that Olinger "hated anyone who he could not bluff. I knew him well and considered him a coward." The most damning assessment, however, came from Pat Garrett, who said that Olinger "was born a murderer at heart. I never slept out with him that I did not watch him."

"Of course," Garrett added, "you will understand that we had to use for deputies such material as we could get."

It was Olinger's killing of John Jones on August 29, 1879—a chilling murder according to most accounts—that created bad blood between him and the Kid. Billy had a warm relationship with the Jones family, and even though he and the Joneses had been on opposite sides during the Lincoln County War, they remained good friends. "Don't let any of your boys bother Bob Olinger," Billy told a grieving Heiskell and Ma'am Jones in the front yard of their Seven Rivers home. "I will get him." Olinger knew about Billy's grudge, but he put little stock in the Kid's reputation, dismissing the outlaw as nothing but a cur. "There existed a reciprocal hatred between these two," Pat Garrett wrote later, "and neither attempted to disguise or conceal his antipathy from the other."

Unlike Olinger, James W. Bell was well liked by most everyone. Bell had served in the White Oaks posses, and he had helped Garrett transport the Kid, Wilson, and Rudabaugh from Las Vegas to Santa Fe back in December. Only twenty-seven years old and a native of Georgia, he had tried his luck at gold mining in White Oaks until his appointment as a deputy U.S. marshal, an often dangerous job but one with a more reliable income. "Mr. Bell is a very cool and daring man," observed a newspaper correspondent. "The citizens of White Oaks have full confidence in him and believe that he will conscientiously discharge his duties at any cost."

As Billy's guards, both Bell and Olinger served in the capacity of deputy sheriffs under Garrett, although their duties also included tending to the other prisoners in the courthouse, then numbering five men. Billy's room, located in the northeast corner of the courthouse, featured two double-hung windows, one facing north and the other east, giving the Kid a nice view of Lincoln's dusty main street and its lackluster comings and goings. Across the street to the northeast, and set back from the road, was the single-story adobe hotel owned by Sam Wortley. All the county prisoners were taken to the hotel for their meals; Billy's meals were prepared at the hotel restaurant and brought to him.

The Kid wore leg shackles and handcuffs at all times—well, sort of. Both cuffs were actually locked on one wrist. This was convenient at mealtime and for visiting the outhouse, but it also allowed the Kid dangerous flexibility, a situation that would not have been tolerated at the Mesilla jail. Located between Billy's room and the second floor's main north-south hallway, was Garrett's office, which made it easy for the sheriff to visit with his prisoner. Billy gave Garrett all kinds of excuses for each crime or killing he had been connected with, except for the killing of White Oaks blacksmith Jimmy Carlyle.

"That was the most detestable crime ever charged against you," Garrett said one day to Billy.

"There's more about that than people know of," the Kid answered defensively but did not bother to elaborate.

Garrett could see that Billy liked Deputy Bell, who showed no ill will toward the Kid, even though Bell had been a friend of Carlyle. Olinger, on the other hand, like any other bully, enjoyed taunting the Kid at any opportunity and making his prisoner aware of the power he held.

"He used to work me up until I could hardly contain myself," Billy told a friend.

Like many before them, Olinger and Bell underestimated their young prisoner. In a pinch, William H. Bonney could be as ruthless and cold-blooded as any outlaw and thug who plagued New Mexico Territory. When life and death hung in the balance—Billy's, that is—that was the time to be most cautious around the Kid. Everyone knew he was a killer. Everyone had heard about his flair for escaping tight spots. If you could read, all you had to do was to pick up one of the Territory's newspapers to see that Billy had been talking of escape ever since his confinement at Santa Fe. But Billy's real and deadly talent was fooling people. Time and again, they misjudged the diminutive outlaw's abilities and resolve. Billy joked and smiled, but his quick mind was always sizing up the situation, looking for a sign of weakness, a slight mental error, something that would give him an edge.

Foolishly, Olinger and Bell brushed aside several pointed warnings, from Sheriff Garrett and others, to be extremely careful around the Kid. Even back in Mesilla, a man had noticed Olinger's indifference and tried to talk some sense into him:

> You have guarded many prisoners, and faced danger many a time in
> apprehending them, and you think that you are invincible and can
> get away with anything. But I tell you, as good a man as you are, that
> if that man is shown the slightest chance on earth, if he is allowed the
> use of one hand, or if he is not watched every moment from now until
> the moment he is executed, he will effect some plan by which he will
> murder the whole of you before you have time to even suspect that he
> has any such intention.

Bob Olinger, his arrogance in peak form, smiled at the man, saying there was as much chance of the Kid escaping as there was of the Kid going to heaven.

More than once, Garrett's deputies demonstrated an unfathomable lack of good judgment around the Kid. On April 26, Olinger stupidly left his pistol loose on a table in front of Billy. Someone quickly snatched up the gun, no doubt imagining that they had prevented a bloody melee. But something must not have been quite right about the situation, or the Kid would have made a grab for Olinger's pistol. No, Billy was biding his time, all the while allowing, if not encouraging, the guards their lackadaisical attitude toward him. Olinger boasted to one Lincoln man that it did not matter whether the Kid wore his irons or not—there was no way he could get away. Olinger even laughingly told Garrett he could turn Billy loose and herd him like a goat.

ONE OF GARRETT'S IMPORTANT duties as county sheriff was to collect taxes and business license fees, an arduous and time-consuming job in a county as large as Lincoln. So on April 28, a Thursday, Garrett was collecting the taxes in White Oaks. Back in Lincoln, Bell and Olinger went about their daily routines, which, for Olinger, meant goading the Kid. That morning he made sure Billy was watching as he loaded his shotgun, a Whitney double-barrel 10 gauge. It was a fairly unusual weapon in that it had two trigger guards and three triggers under the receiver. The forward trigger was a release that opened the breechloader for access to the gun's two chambers. Olinger carefully slid in two shotshells, each loaded with 18 buckshot, then snapped the barrels back in place. As he did this, he looked at the Kid and said, "The man that gets one of those loads will feel it."

"I expect he will," Billy calmly said, "but be careful, Bob, or you might shoot yourself accidentally."

At approximately 6:00 P.M., suppertime, Olinger took all the prisoners except the Kid across the street to Wortley's for their evening meal. As soon as Billy could no longer hear the voices of Olinger and his prisoners, he asked Bell to take him to the privy, which was out behind the courthouse. It was a necessary chore that Bell and Olinger undoubtedly performed several times a day, not just with Billy but with the other prisoners as well. But with Garrett out of the equation and Olinger out of sight, the Kid figured his odds were as good as they were going to get.

After finishing at the privy, the Kid and Bell reentered the building and started up the staircase to the second floor, Billy moving slowly because of the shackles on his ankles, Bell coming up behind. At the top of the staircase, the Kid suddenly whirled around and struck Bell a violent blow to his head, perhaps two, with the arm that held his handcuffs. Wincing from the pain, and with blood spurting from an ugly wound (one report stated that the blow was so severe it broke Bell's skull), the deputy still managed to put up a good fight. He and Billy tumbled to the floor, the Kid struggling with Bell for his pistol. In the scuffle Billy somehow managed to wrestle away the six-shooter, and the deputy decided to flee his attacker. He broke loose from the Kid and scrambled down the staircase. Billy, flat on his stomach in a pool of Bell's blood, raised the pistol. He may have called out for Bell to stop, and then he pulled the trigger. Some townspeople claimed they heard three shots come from the courthouse, but only one bullet struck Bell. And that one was a fluke, ricocheting off the adobe wall of the staircase before entering Bell's right side and ripping completely through his body. It was not Billy's best shooting, but it did the trick. Bell, on his feet through pure adrenaline, made it to the bottom of the stairs and stumbled out the southwest door, where he collapsed into the arms of Gottfried Gauss, a part-time county employee. Bell died without saying a word.

The Kid jumped up and went just a few feet down the upstairs hall to his right and broke into the armory. He quickly made an assessment of the weapons and ammunition, grabbed Olinger's shotgun and other firearms, and then hurriedly shuffled down the hall to the front of the building. He turned into Garrett's office and passed through to his own quarters, where he looked out the north and east windows for any activity on the street below, particularly any evidence that Bob Olinger had heard the shots too. Billy rightly guessed that he had.

At Wortley's, Olinger bolted up from his table and said, more to himself than anyone else, "They are having a fight over there."

He rushed out of the hotel and across the street to the courthouse. Because the only access to the second floor was from a room in the rear of the building, Olinger headed directly for the courthouse's northeast corner, where a gate opened to a path along the east side of the structure to the horse corral behind. Billy had no trouble seeing big Bob Olinger coming. As Olinger stepped through the gate, the

Kid, poised at the open east window, pulled back the hammers to both barrels of the Whitney until they clicked at full cock. At the same time, Gauss appeared at the corral gate.

"Bob, the Kid has killed Bell!" Gauss shouted.

Gauss had no sooner finished uttering these words than the Kid spoke down to Olinger: "Hello, old boy." Olinger knew that voice, and in the fraction of time it took him to glance up, a sick feeling must have pulsed through his mind. Billy fired on him with both barrels, a stream of white smoke belching out from the muzzles and hanging briefly in the air before drifting away with the breeze. The Sycamore of Seven Rivers died instantly, 36 heavy buckshot piercing his head and chest.

For the next hour, a surreal scene played out in Lincoln. From the second floor of the courthouse, Billy had complete control over the people in the west part of town. He ordered Gauss, who liked the Kid, to throw him up something he could use to break his leg shackles; Gauss tossed up a small prospector's pick. Billy then sent the old man to the corral to saddle up a horse. The Kid also enlisted a trembling eleven-year-old Severo Gallegos, who had been playing marbles with two friends in the street when Olinger was killed. Oddly, the boys had not heard the shots fired at Bell, but they had seen Olinger rushing to the courthouse and witnessed his grisly death.

"Severo, don't you run," Billy said. "Come and help Gauss catch the horse."

The Kid moved out onto the courthouse's second-story front porch, which gave him a commanding view of Lincoln's main street, but he frequently ducked back into the building to look out its different windows, presumably to check on Gauss and to make sure no one was trying to surprise him. When a witless or perhaps terrified Bob Brookshire stepped out of the Wortley and started to head down the street away from the courthouse, Billy leveled his Winchester at him.

"Go back, young fellow, go back," the Kid shouted. "I don't want to hurt you, but I am fighting for my life. I don't want anybody to leave that house."

From the porch, Billy spoke off and on to a group across the street at the hotel. One witness later wrote: "He told the people that he did not want to kill Bell but, as he ran, he had to. He declared he was 'standing pat' against the world; and, while he did not wish to kill anybody, if anybody interfered with his attempt to escape he would kill him."

Only two men admitted later that they had been tempted to stop the Kid: John Lilly, the thirty-year-old restaurant operator at Wortley's, and Joseph La Rue, a fifty-year-old Lincoln dry goods merchant. Lilly grabbed his gun and was about to fire on the Kid but was stopped by two acquaintances, who were probably worried what would happen to Lilly if he missed. La Rue got down his weapon, intent on being a hero as well—until his wife saw what he was up to and put a stop to it.

Some people looked on in fear, a few in secret admiration (the Kid was not without his sympathizers in Lincoln), but they were all transfixed by the Kid's macabre antics on the porch. Billy "danced about the balcony, laughed and shouted as though he had not a care on earth," Garrett wrote later. When Billy decided it was time to leave town, he slammed Olinger's Whitney on the porch railing, breaking the gun into two pieces at the wrist. He flung the pieces at Olinger's body.

"There is your gun, God damn you!" he shouted at the guard's gruesome stretched-out corpse. "You won't follow me with it any longer."

He then slipped his cuffs over his wrist and hurled them at Bell's body, still lying at the back of the building.

"Here, God damn you! Take them," Billy yelled. "I guess you won't put them on me again."

He then cursed and threatened his enemies and vowed that although he did not believe he had been bad before, from now on folks would truly see what it was to be a "bad man."

As the last rays of daylight began to fade from the Rio Bonito Valley, Billy walked down to the courthouse's first floor and out to the front of the building, where Gauss had, with some difficulty, led the troublesome mount, a pony belonging to William Burt, deputy probate clerk. Billy had been able to break apart only one of the ankle bracelets, so the cumbersome shackles remained attached to one leg. The shackles undoubtedly spooked the already flighty horse, or perhaps it smelled death on the Kid, because as Billy tried to mount, the horse jumped sideways and broke loose. Billy ordered the animal retrieved, and after taking a moment to settle the pony, he climbed back into the saddle and rode to the west, shouting to no one in particular, "Tell Billy Burt I will send his horse back to him."

He went only a few hundred yards when he abruptly stopped at the home of a Hispanic resident next to the road and bought a rope. The escaping outlaw, well accustomed to taking whatever he wanted, actually bothered to pay for the rope. That is fairly remarkable, but it also shows the kind of character that endeared him to New Mexico's native population.

After he had completed this transaction, Billy the Kid disappeared into the twilight.

"When he rode off he went on a walk," wrote an eyewitness, "and every act, from beginning to end, seemed to have been planned and executed with the coolest deliberation."

BILLY BONNEY KNEW THAT the only way he could keep ahead of the law was to rely on friends. A few miles west of Lincoln, he turned north, crossed the Rio Bonito, and started up Salazar Canyon. He stopped at the home of José Córdova just long enough to get help removing the shackles that had been pestering him and the stolen horse, and then he rode on, circling back east across the Capitan foothills and canyons to Agua Azul (Blue Water). A few miles more brought him to the small settlement of Las Tablas, where his friend Yginio Salazar lived. Salazar, a brother-in-arms from Billy's Lincoln County War days, fed him and gave him some blankets to sleep out a safe distance from his house. Salazar urged Billy to head across the border into Mexico, but Billy was not sure what he would do. Maybe he would go to Texas, he said.

Before leaving the Las Tablas area, Billy Burt's pain-in-the-butt horse got away from the Kid, and this time no one was standing around to catch the animal. The horse loped off for home. The Kid managed to get another horse and saddle (perhaps it was a gift of a confederate, perhaps not), and left young Yginio with the memories of a friendship he held on to for the rest of his life (carved on Salazar's tombstone are the words "Pal of Billy the Kid").

Billy now seemed to be headed south to Texas and then Mexico, but he only got as far as the upper Peñasco River, approximately forty miles south of Lincoln. He showed up unannounced at the cabin of his friend John Meadows just as Meadows and ranching partner Tom Norris were inside preparing supper, their backs to the open door.

"I've got you covered," the Kid said as he stepped into the cabin.

"Yes, and what in hell are you going to do with us—" Meadows replied as he turned. "By God, that's the Kid," he blurted out, both surprised and elated.

Meadows told Billy to sit down and join them for a plate of beans, and the three men talked till late into the night. The Kid told the story of how he had pulled off his escape from the Lincoln County courthouse in broad daylight, and how he had killed James Bell and Bob Olinger. He also told them how much he deeply regretted shooting Bell.

"It was a case of have to, not of wanting to," Billy said.

"You'd better go into Mexico while the going's good," Meadows told the Kid.

"You can make it there now, and you can do well there."

"I haven't any money," Billy said. "What could I do if I went to Mexico or some other place with no money? I'll have to go back and get a little before I can leave."

"You go back to Fort Sumner and Garrett will get you as sure as you go back," Meadows warned. "He ain't laying down on his job."

"Garrett will get me if he can," Billy said, "but I've got too many friends there."

What Billy did not tell Meadows was that he had another reason besides money to return to Fort Sumner. Whatever he had been thinking when he arrived on the upper Peñasco, Billy left that place with only one destination in mind, and neither Meadows nor anyone else could talk him out of it. The Kid was going home, to his friends, to where he was loved.

Back in Lincoln, while residents were still excitedly talking over the escape and trading stories and rumors of the Kid's whereabouts, Billy Burt's horse wandered into town. It was dragging a rope.

8

The Darkened Room

I am not going to leave the country, and
I am not going to reform, neither am I
going to be taken alive again.
—BILLY THE KID

Let those doubt who will.
—PAT F. GARRETT

SANTA FE, APRIL 30, 1881. Governor Lew Wallace sat at his desk in his office in the Palace of the Governors. Before him was the death warrant for one William Bonney, alias Kid, alias William Antrim. This handwritten document directed Sheriff Garrett to carry out Billy's death sentence on Friday, May 13, as ordered by the district court in Mesilla, but before any of this could happen, the governor had to sign the warrant.

The fifty-four-year-old Wallace, a native of Indiana, was an extremely intelligent man who could speak knowledgeably on any topic. Known for his dry wit, he was also slightly pompous, opinionated, and rather defensive. His father, a West Point graduate, had served as both lieutenant governor and governor of Indiana. Wallace, who as a child dreamed that he would become victorious and famous on the battle-field, interrupted his law school studies to join an Indiana regiment in the U.S.–Mexican War of 1846–1848. Thirteen years later, when the Civil War broke out, he again gave up his law practice to become a soldier. As his state's adjutant general, he raised and organized six regiments of Indiana men and then accepted the command of one of those regiments as its colonel. By March 1862, Wallace had achieved the rank of major general of volunteers—he was only thirty-four years old. General Wallace was not tall, but he was a dashing figure with his

Lewis "Lew" Wallace, territorial governor
of New Mexico and author of *Ben-Hur: A
Tale of the Christ.*

long beard and bushy mustache, jet black hair, and piercing dark eyes. His men affectionately nicknamed him "Louisa."

But unfortunately, Wallace's glory days were short-lived. At the bloody Battle of Shiloh, on April 6–7, 1862, he became the scapegoat for the Union's near defeat and its shocking loss of men when more than thirteen thousand were killed, wounded, or captured. When General Ulysses S. Grant ordered him to rush reinforcements to the front, Wallace had sent his division over the wrong route, and by the time the mistake was caught, hours had been lost. Wallace's men did not unite with the rest of Grant's force until after the first day's fighting was over. His division fought during the next day's battle, but even though that day ended in a victory for Grant, Wallace's Civil War career was subsequently sidetracked and forever tainted with charges of tardiness at Shiloh. The accusations caused Wallace to spend the rest of his life defending his actions.

One episode demonstrates just how sensitive Wallace became to the subject of Shiloh. In June 1881, while sitting in a State Department reception room, Wallace noticed on a table a copy of the first volume of Adam Badeau's three-volume *Military History of Ulysses S. Grant*. Wallace picked the book up, immediately flipped to the pages covering Shiloh, and then became incensed at Badeau's criticism of his performance. Wallace grabbed a pen and wrote a stinging rebuke in a margin of the offending page: "There are more willful falsehoods in the foregoing paragraph than in any other of the same length in English literature. Lew Wallace."

President Rutherford B. Hayes had appointed Wallace territorial governor of New Mexico (at an annual salary of $2,600) in September 1878, with the primary task of ending the Lincoln County troubles. So far, Wallace had failed, despite good intentions and considerable effort. His amnesty proclamation had allowed some of the worst offenders in the war to go scot-free while effectually leaving others the choice of either fleeing the Territory or living outside the law. He had failed to get anyone convicted for the murder of Huston Chapman, and although he got Gold Lace Dudley removed from command at Fort Stanton, that officer was later exonerated of any wrongdoing for his actions during the Big Killing in Lincoln.

And then there was William H. Bonney and the exasperating talk of a pardon. For one thing, Wallace never understood the boy—of course, not many did—nor did he understand the sympathy and friendship the outlaw enjoyed with native New Mexicans. Wallace's haughty estimation of Bonney was revealed early on in a letter written at Lincoln on March 31, 1879: "A precious specimen nick-named 'The Kid,' whom the Sheriff is holding here in the Plaza, as it is called, is an object of tender regard. I heard singing and music the other night; going to the door, I found the minstrels of the village actually serenading the fellow in his prison." Not surprisingly, Wallace's opinion of the Kid failed to improve over time.

Now, that precious specimen was a problem and an embarrassment. Every mention of the outlaw in the newspapers was a reminder of the governor's failings in Lincoln County. Surely with some satisfaction, then, Wallace signed the death warrant for the Kid, after which the great seal of the Territory of New Mexico was affixed. Wallace knew his term as governor was quickly coming to an end, but with Billy waiting in jail, he would likely still be in Santa Fe when the Kid dropped through a trapdoor and was hanged. So be it.

Later that same day, a wire arrived at the Palace of the Governors. Wallace may have been enjoying a pleasant smoke at the time—something he was fond to do—or he may have been replying to correspondence from some early fans of his new novel, *Ben-Hur*. The book had been released by Harper & Brothers on November 12, 1880, and had sold out of its first printing of five thousand copies by December 22. It continued to sell steadily. At any rate, a telegraph message usually indicated a matter of some importance, and Wallace read the telegraph immediately. Sent from Deputy Sheriff Ethan W. Eaton at Socorro,

138 miles to the south, the message contained but one sentence: "Billy the Kid escaped from Lincoln yesterday evening, killing Deputy Sheriffs J. W. Bell and Bob Olinger."

Like a deadly contagion, the news that Billy had escaped again raced from person to person throughout the Territory, even if few people knew the particulars of what had happened. Not until two days later did the *Daily New Mexican* have enough details of the escape to publish an extra edition. And on May 3, the *New Mexican* devoted even more space to the escape and somehow managed to find new respect for Billy in his ruthless act:

> [It was] as bold a deed as those versed in the annals of crime can recall. It surpasses anything which the Kid has ever been guilty of so far that his past offenses lose much of their heinousness in comparison with it, and it effectually settles the question as to whether the Kid is a cowardly cut throat or a thoroughly reckless and fearless man. Never before has he faced death boldly or run any great risk in the perpetration of his bloody deeds.

News of Billy's sensational escape spread across the front pages of the nation's newspapers as fast as it could be transmitted over the telegraph, and he became even more notorious, and more feared than ever before. The words *Billy the Kid* danced off the tongues of shopkeepers and housewives, butchers and bakers, schoolchildren and ministers, and he immediately rose to a status alongside the most famous outlaw of that era: Jesse James. Jesse, unlike the Kid, was a hardened professional bank and train robber of many years' experience, but like the Kid, he was daring, a media favorite, and quite adept at evading the law (even more so than Billy). Whatever was to come for the Kid, the Lincoln courthouse escape had earned him a place in the American consciousness.

And what was to come began to haunt many in the Territory.

"This is terrible," wrote a Lincoln correspondent to the *New Mexican,* "and the Kid is free with his threats of murder thick in the air. He said, I understand, that he wanted to live long enough to kill Governor Wallace, or as he put it, 'that damned old son of a bitch Wallace.' He [Wallace] cannot be too vigilantly on his guard."

Wallace did have to worry that Billy might just show up in the plaza one dark night like some rabid animal, seeking vengeance. Wallace immediately posted another $500 reward for the Kid's capture, and then put together a plan for his own personal safety. Every morning, he stepped outside the rear of the Palace with a revolver in his hand. He walked quietly to a thick adobe wall where he had had a chalk outline drawn of a human form. He squared himself, took aim and fired several practice shots at the faceless figure. He then returned to his office, laying the pistol on a table at his side within easy reach. "Forewarned, forearmed," the former Union general told a friend. If Billy ever did ride into Santa Fe, it would be a different Lew Wallace confronting him. This Wallace had turned himself into an expert pistoleer.

THE NEWS OF THE Kid's escape and the murder of his two guards quickly reached Pat Garrett in White Oaks. Garrett departed the mining camp for Lincoln the evening of April 29 with a former Colfax County deputy by the name of Goodlett. The sheriff faced not only the gory mess Billy left behind, but also pangs of guilt. True, Bell and Olinger died because of their own carelessness, but Garrett was not completely without blame, as he freely admitted later: "I knew the desperate character of the man whom the authorities would look for at my hands on the 13th day of May—that he was daring and unscrupulous, and that he would sacrifice the lives of a hundred men who stood between him and liberty. . . . And now I realize how inadequate my precautions were."

In his own defense, Garrett maintained that his explicit instruc-

BILLY THE KID.

$500 REWARD.

I will pay $500 reward to any person or persons who will capture William Bonny, alias The Kid, and deliver him to any sheriff of New Mexico. Satisfactory proofs of identity will be required.

LEW. WALLACE,
Governor of New Mexico.

Governor Wallace's reward notice for Billy the Kid, published in the *Santa Fe New Mexican* beginning May 3, 1881.

tions to the guards were not followed. But as sheriff, it was his responsibility to correct the unacceptable behavior he observed in Bell and Olinger before leaving for White Oaks, or, one might argue, either relieve the deputies from duty or postpone his trip. He did neither. All Garrett could do at this point, however, was to see to the final affairs of his former deputies and once again take up Billy's trail. This time, though, there would be no taking the Kid alive.

"I knew now that I would have to kill the Kid," Garrett later told writer Emerson Hough. "We both knew that it must be one or the other of us if we ever met."

Garrett arrived back in Lincoln the next day and immediately organized a party of volunteer scouts and followed the Kid's route out of town, hoping to pick up his trail. But the Kid left little to follow, and folks along the way were not talking, at least not to Garrett. Garrett then sent out his deputy, Barney Mason, to see what he could find. Garrett figured that a single man would likely have an advantage over a sheriff's posse, considering how Kid-friendly the countryside was. Mason, undoubtedly a bit nervous about doing this alone, actually did have better luck tracing Billy's movements and was able to trail the Kid all the way to Fort Sumner and arrived there on May 7. The next morning, a Sunday, a mulatto stock raiser named Montgomery Bell told Mason that his horse had been stolen. Bell thought the animal had been taken by a "Mexican," by which he meant a native New Mexican. He asked Mason to catch the thief.

Mason started out from Fort Sumner with cattleman Jim Cureton. After riding fifteen miles, the two arrived at a sheep camp at the head of Buffalo Arroyo, where they suddenly came upon the stolen horse, as well as its rider—Billy the Kid. The Kid was with four Hispanic men who rapidly positioned themselves as if to shoot it out with the intruders. Mason was the only one carrying weapons, but as soon as he recognized Billy, he whipped his horse around and dug his spurs in deep, leaving a stunned Cureton wondering what had happened.

As the *Las Vegas Gazette* reported, and everyone knew, Billy "never had any great love for Barney . . . especially since he assisted in the capture of Billy and party at Stinking Springs." Mason, of course, knew this better than anyone else. Cureton supposedly spoke to Billy, who asked him to tell Montgomery Bell that he had taken the horse because he had no other way of getting around, and that he would either arrange to return the horse or pay him for it.

Back at Fort Sumner, Mason and Cureton tried to raise a posse to go out after the Kid, but they could not find anyone who wanted anything to do with it. Everyone said it was a foolhardy mission. A fellow could get shot—or worse (probably worse). And besides, many people there liked the Kid. Mason eventually sized up the situation for what it was and realized it was unsafe for him to remain in the area. He promptly loaded up his family in a wagon and headed out of town to Roswell.

Billy had no intention of leaving the Fort Sumner vicinity. He was staying, or being given refuge, in the outlying sheep and cow camps, the small Hispanic settlements, and, of course, within Fort Sumner itself. His friends, mostly native New Mexicans, were always watching out for strangers or suspicious activity, and they brought him the latest newspapers, in which Billy must have read some of the crazy stories being written about him, the wildest being that he had murdered three Chisum cowboys in cold blood because of his grudge against the Pecos cattle king. It was a complete fabrication, but the story was taken for the truth by a public who only knew the Kid as a vicious killer.

In early June, in a story first published in the *Denver Tribune* but picked up by several other newspapers, including the *Chicago Tribune*, it was reported that Billy was staying close to Fort Sumner because of a sweetheart. This information had come from Colonel George P. Buell, post commander at Fort Stanton. Sheriff Garrett knew all about Billy's favorite girl at Fort Sumner, and that girl, of course, was Paulita Maxwell, Pete's teenaged sister. Billy had had his fair share of female companionship, but Paulita appears to have been the only girl who wrote to him when he was in jail in far-off Mesilla (the Kid had proudly shown Paulita's letter to Sheriff James W. Southwick). As an elderly woman, Paulita admitted she might have married Billy—if he had asked. Perhaps the Kid intended to, but if so, he waited too long.

Despite reports that Billy was on the Pecos, Garrett did not seem to be doing much in the weeks following Billy's bloody escape. He remained at home a good part of the time, enjoying his small family and tending to his modest ranch. This brought Garrett criticism from those who wanted Billy swiftly brought to justice, or, better yet, dead. Although Billy still had his sympathizers, they were in the minority, and the brutal courthouse murders, as well as Billy's threats to kill his enemies, from Garrett on up to Governor Wallace, sent chills through most of the Territory's citizens. They did not want this heinous murderer in their midst any longer. But the Lincoln County sheriff kept his own counsel. He was not one to be pushed into anything, and if he was going to go after the Kid—and no one doubted that he would

Paulita Maxwell, Billy's girl.

at some point, hazardous though it would be—he was going to do it his way.

While Garrett was willing to believe that Billy had returned to his old haunts in the Fort Sumner vicinity, he also had serious doubts. He thought it absolutely incredible that the Kid, the most wanted man in the Southwest, would linger in the Territory when there was nothing to stop him from slipping across the border into Mexico, girl or no girl. Garrett knew the Kid was not stupid, and so he was often skeptical about each report of Billy's whereabouts. Garrett did not dismiss the rumors, but he also knew he could wait. "If my seeming unconcern deceived the people and gave the Kid confidence in his security," he wrote later, "my end was accomplished."

Billy did feel comfortable and secure in and around Fort Sumner.

His friends there included Garrett's own sister-in-law, Celsa Gutiér-rez, a twenty-five-year-old married woman with whom Billy may have had an affair (some people said she bore Billito children), and her husband, Saval. And most of those who were not the Kid's friends were too scared to cross the fugitive. Billy must have enjoyed the no-toriety and deference he received at Sumner. In Mexico, he would be just another gringo on the run. The Kid also possessed enough hubris to explain why he chose to remain within Garrett's reach. In his fast twenty-one years, Billy had rarely encountered a man he had not bested or outsmarted, and he had survived numerous tight spots and had escaped many captors. Billy, like other young men his age, probably thought he would live forever.

SOMETIME IN LATE JUNE or early July, Garrett got a letter from a merchant at Fort Sumner (probably his old partner Beaver Smith), telling him the Kid was hanging around Pete Maxwell's place. A very few brave individuals at Fort Sumner, it seems, were willing to secretly correspond with the Lincoln County sheriff. Garrett, now at his office in Lincoln, also got a reply to a letter he had written to Manuel Brazil, asking if he knew anything about Billy's current whereabouts. Garrett knew he could trust Brazil, who had been a useful ally in the Stinking Spring capture. In his letter, Brazil said he knew he was on the Kid's hate list, so he was being very careful in his movements. He had not personally encountered the outlaw. Even so, he had good reason to believe that the Kid was in the area. Brazil closed his letter by offering Garrett any help he could give in capturing the Kid.

Around this time, John W. Poe arrived in Lincoln from White Oaks with an intriguing story for Garrett that also placed Billy at Fort Sumner. Poe, a twenty-nine-year-old from Kentucky, was work-ing for the Canadian River Cattle Association to recover stolen Texas cattle and also to help put the clamps on the rustling of Texas herds

(Frank Stewart's old job). Like Garrett, Poe had spent time as a buffalo hunter on the Texas plains during the big killing years of the 1870s. He even later claimed that he single-handedly harvested twenty thousand bison. By helping to finish off the buffalo herds, though, he had also killed his livelihood, so Poe became a lawman, first accepting a one-year appointment as Fort Griffin's town marshal. In 1879, he moved to Mobeetie, Wheeler County, Texas, where he served as a deputy sheriff and deputy U.S. marshal. After losing the election for county sheriff by one vote, he became a livestock detective for the Panhandle cattlemen.

Poe was six feet tall with a solid build. He had a thick, drooping mustache much like Garrett's, and the two men shared a similar determination and nerve. After assuming his duties as a stock detective, Poe had traveled to White Oaks in March 1881, where he first met the new Lincoln County sheriff, and he and Garrett formed an alliance. Garrett commissioned Poe as a deputy sheriff. This gave Poe the legal authority in New Mexico to make arrests, and he began doing so, becoming quite good at locating stolen Texas cattle and even finding the hides of stolen cattle that had been processed. Poe later wrote that the Lincoln County sheriff impressed him as a "very brave and efficient officer."

White Oaks remained Poe's headquarters, and in early July 1881, he was approached by George Guinn, a forty-year-old miner, who said he had information about Billy the Kid. Back in Texas, Poe had known Guinn as a decent man, but the miner had fallen on the bottle and hard times in White Oaks. Having no other place to stay, Guinn slept in a vacant room in the livery stable of Sam Dedrick and William West, both of whom were known to be associates of the Kid and his gang. Guinn emphasized that what he was about to tell Poe must be kept in the strictest confidence, because he feared his life would be in danger if word got out about what he knew. And what he knew was this: a night or two ago, he had overheard a conversation between

Garrett, James Brent (standing), and
John W. Poe.

Dedrick and West in which they said the Kid was at Fort Sumner.
Guinn also picked up from this same conversation that Billy had been
in the White Oaks vicinity twice since his escape, and both times, he
had met with these two men. Poe had trouble believing Guinn's story,
but the man was so insistent and sincere that he decided to report it
to Garrett.

Garrett decided that the time was right to make a little jaunt to
Fort Sumner. He wrote a quick note to Manuel Brazil to meet him
at the mouth of Taiban Arroyo, five miles south of Sumner, one hour
after dark on July 13. Garrett knew better than to travel with a big

posse on such a touchy job—the more men who knew what the sheriff was doing, the greater the risk that someone would tip off the Kid. Instead, he would ride with only two deputies, Poe and Thomas C. "Kip" McKinney.

Garrett liked the twenty-five-year-old McKinney, who had ridden with the Roswell posse when Garrett made his first raid on Fort Sumner back in November. Raised a cowpuncher in Uvalde County, Texas, McKinney was a gangly man with a dark, bronzed face, pale green eyes, and the requisite lawman mustache sprouting out beneath his distinctive Roman nose. Garrett told Poe what the plan was, but he did not inform McKinney at first, telling him only that he was about to make a business trip to Arizona and he wanted McKinney to accompany him. They would first travel to Garrett's home in Roswell, where Garrett had some small matters to attend to, and from there they would leave for Arizona. Garrett believed it a good idea to plant a false story in Lincoln, knowing that at least one or two townspeople would not be able to stop themselves from asking McKinney what he was up to. Once they were well on their way, Garrett told McKinney the truth: they were going after the Kid.

After a brief stop at his ranch to see Polinaria, Garrett led his men north, up the Pecos, on the night of July 11. The manhunters stayed off the main road and traveled mostly after sundown. They purposely made no stops at ranch houses along the way. They reached the meeting place at the appointed time, but Brazil was not there to greet them. He probably had not gotten Garrett's letter. After waiting for about two hours, they rode off the road some distance, picketed their horses, and made camp for the night. Shortly after the dawn, they mounted up and rode to some low hills where they could use their binoculars to scan the countryside. They did not see anything out of the ordinary and figured it was time to come up with a plan.

Poe had never been to Fort Sumner before, and no one there knew who he was, so they decided that he would visit Sumner alone and try to determine if the Kid was anywhere close. Poe would then ride to the nearby settlement of Sunnyside and look up the postmaster, Milnor Rudolph, a friend whom Garrett trusted. The three of them would meet back up that night at moonrise a few miles north of Sumner at a place known as La Punta de la Glorieta (the point of the intersection).

Poe rode into Fort Sumner before noon that day and was immediately aware that he was being noticed and watched. Just as soon as he tied his horse to a hitching post outside a saloon and store, a small crowd of men gathered around and pleasantly asked where he was from and what his business was. The deputy said he had tried his hand at mining in White Oaks and was now on his way back to his home in the Texas Panhandle. The story seemed logical enough to the locals, who invited Poe to have a drink in the saloon. It was never really just one drink, but Poe was very careful to have only a small amount of liquor and still not offend his new friends. Not surprisingly this led to a meal in the store, the first square meal he had eaten in days.

For the next hour or two, Poe lounged about the plaza, striking up a conversation now and then with the people he ran into. But he could tell that the folks of Fort Sumner were noticeably on edge, and no matter how gingerly he tried to get them to talk about the Kid, his inquiries were met with suspicion. Disappointed, he left for Sunnyside without having learned a thing.

Poe reached Sunnyside late in the day and handed Rudolph a letter of introduction from Garrett, saying that he needed a place to stay for the night. The postmaster warmly invited Poe to his home, where the deputy received his second meal of the day. Poe had been careful not to mention the purpose of his visit, but after supper and some small talk he began talking about Billy's escape from Lincoln. He then told Rudolph he had heard the Kid was hanging around Fort Sumner. Rudolph's demeanor changed abruptly. He nervously said that he had heard about these rumors but he did not believe them; the Kid was too smart to risk his life by remaining in the Territory.

"We talked on about other things," Poe wrote later, "but every time I mentioned the Kid the same agitation showed in the old man's actions and talk."

Finally, Poe decided to tell Rudolph that he was working with Garrett to track down the Kid, and Garrett had specifically sent him to Sunnyside because he believed that Rudolph could provide information on Billy's whereabouts. At this, the old man became even more agitated, and it was Poe's turn to become suspicious. In Rudolph's defense, he did not know this man who was asking such pointed questions about the Kid, and like many others in the area, he was terrified of Billy and what he might do. Rudolph was very aware of the Kid's bloody record—which included the murder of a sheriff and three deputies—and that no one had been able to hold him in jail for very long. So Rudolph denied that the Kid was anywhere close to Fort Sumner, and that convinced Poe that he was onto something. Poe ended the conversation by saying he had changed his mind about spending the night. His horse was now well rested and fed, and it would be more comfortable to ride during the cool hours of the night. A look of relief came over Rudolph's face.

AFTER POE SEPARATED FROM Garrett and McKinney that morning, the sheriff and his deputy had ridden over to the Pecos and spent the day out of sight in the brush and willows near the river. Once darkness flooded the valley, they mounted up and Garrett led McKinney in a circle around Sumner. As they approached the meeting place, they recognized Poe riding up from the opposite direction. Poe told Garrett that although he had failed to gather any positive information in Sumner, the townsfolk's reticence to discuss the outlaw and, more especially, Rudolph's strange behavior, led him to believe that their man must be close.

Garrett now wanted to see Pete Maxwell. After all, he had made the long trip from Lincoln based on information, credible or otherwise, that the Kid was hanging out around Fort Sumner and a woman, a "sweetheart," had been keeping him there. Maxwell would know if his sister had seen the Kid, and, as the town's patriarch of sorts, he would likely have heard if the Kid had recently been in Sumner. But Garrett knew he needed to approach the Maxwell residence with extreme caution. The moon was shining brightly now, and Garrett's six-foot-four frame would be easy to spot out in the open. If the Kid was in Sumner, there were several places he could be staying—and looking out of. Garrett was not about to offer himself up to the young killer like that fool Olinger.

Garrett led his two deputies back south to a small peach orchard at the edge of the village; just beyond the orchard was Fort Sumner's open plaza, formerly the fort's parade ground. Near the orchard, they came upon a small campfire tended by a single man. Poe recognized the man from back in Texas and said his name was Jacobs. Jacobs invited his guests to some coffee, and the three got down and unsaddled their mounts. After some quiet conversation, the lawmen staked their horses and prepared to enter the orchard. Garrett pulled his Model 1873 Winchester carbine from its saddle scabbard. He had taken the carbine, as well as the hefty Colt six-shooter on his hip, from Billy Wilson at Stinking Spring. At the time, Garrett had noticed that the weapons were practically brand-new, so he confiscated both guns for himself—and had not regretted it.

With Garrett in the lead, the manhunters stepped into the peach orchard and crept toward the plaza. From there, Garrett knew they would have a view of the old officers' quarters (one of which was the Maxwell place) on the west side of the plaza, as well as the quartermaster depot across the plaza to the south. The depot was where his in-laws, Celsa and Saval Gutiérrez, lived. As he, McKinney, and Poe neared the plaza, Garrett began to hear voices; they were speaking

Spanish. He silently motioned to his men to hide themselves. They listened for some time but it was impossible to determine what was being said or even to recognize who might be speaking.

Suddenly, Garrett saw a man stand up from the ground. The man was in the orchard, but not near enough for Garrett to tell who it was, especially because the man's broad-brimmed hat was shading his face. He was in his shirtsleeves—that, Garrett could see—and he was wearing a dark vest and pants. The man said something more to an unseen companion, then turned and hopped over a fence and into the plaza. Garrett watched as the silhouetted figure walked away toward the Maxwell residence. Garrett would learn later that this man was the very desperado they were after—Billy the Kid.

Garrett decided it was unwise to continue to Pete Maxwell's place from their position, so he and his deputies quietly backed out of the orchard and took a long circuitous route behind the row of officers' quarters and eventually approached the Maxwell place from the opposite side of the plaza. Garrett stopped at the open front gate and whispered to his deputies: "This is Maxwell's room in this corner. You fellows wait here while I go in and talk to him." The deputies watched as Garrett walked through the gate and stepped onto the porch. The door to Maxwell's room was open, as were the windows. During the warm New Mexico summers, residents opened the doors and windows of their adobes in the evening to let in the cool night breeze and during the day they shut them to keep out the hot air.

Poe took a seat on the edge of the porch, just inside the open gate, while McKinney squatted on the ground outside the fence. Garrett had been inside Maxwell's room only a few minutes when Poe saw someone rapidly come toward them along the fence. As the man got closer, Poe noticed that he was not wearing a hat and he was walking in his stocking feet. And the man seemed to be fiddling with his trousers, as if he was fastening them. Poe assumed it was either Maxwell or one of his friends. But he was wrong.

CRS

WHO BILLY LEFT BEHIND in the peach orchard that night is a mystery. It could very well have been a woman—and it probably was. There is no doubt that a beautiful moonlit evening in July and the nearby peach orchard offered idyllic conditions for a romantic tryst. But whoever he was with kept that memory to herself for the rest of her life.

From the orchard, Billy walked to the home of Celsa and Saval Gutiérrez. They were letting Billy sleep in their quarters, even though their brother-in-law was the man who had been elected to hunt him down. But Celsa and Saval had made their choice long ago, like Barney Mason had made his. Billy stepped into the Gutiérrez place carrying a small piece of raw meat. Saval, Celsa, and Celsa's seven-year-old son, Candido, watched as Billy walked past them and set the meat down in the kitchen.

"Celsa, I brought some meat for you to make my supper," Billy said.

Although the hour was late, nearly midnight, Celsa walked into the kitchen to begin the Kid's meal. Billy then made himself comfortable, taking off his hat, vest, and gun belt, and pulling off his boots. But Celsa soon interrupted him.

"Billy, this meat that you brought is no more than a bone. It doesn't have any meat," she said.

"Give me a knife to go get some good meat," Billy replied, "and tell Don Pedro [Pete Maxwell] that I took the meat so that he doesn't think that another stole the meat."

The Kid picked up the butcher knife Celsa motioned to, stuck his pistol in his pant pocket, and walked out the door for Maxwell's house, where a freshly slaughtered beef was hanging.

Billy did not see the men outside of Maxwell's home, at least not initially. The gatepost partially hid Poe, but Billy must not have been really paying attention. When he walked through the gate, though, he came face-to-face with Poe on the edge of the porch. Startled, the Kid pulled his six-shooter and pointed it at him.

"¿*Quién es?*" (Who is it?), Bonney asked urgently as he jumped onto the porch. "¿*Quién es?*"

Poe had never seen the Kid before, and neither had McKinney, so they were not sure who this was. But Poe tried to calm the agitated stranger.

"Don't be afraid," he said as he straightened up and stepped onto the porch with Billy. "There is no one here to hurt you."

"¿*Quién es?*" Billy repeated as he backed down the porch, his six-shooter in one hand and the butcher knife gripped in the other.

Poe took a step toward Billy, still trying to reassure him, an extremely foolish act considering that a pistol was pointed at his chest. Instead of firing, Billy slipped into the doorway of Maxwell's bedroom, the thick wall concealing him from Poe's view, but just as he was gone, he leaned his head back out: "¿*Quién es?*"

Pat Garrett heard the commotion on the porch. Just moments earlier, he had walked straight up to Maxwell's bed, which sat in a corner of the unlit room, and had taken a seat on the edge of the mattress, near the headboard. He had prodded Maxwell awake and then asked him if the Kid was anywhere nearby. Maxwell had seemed agitated and evasive—he was frightened of Billy. Finally, Maxwell had whispered to Garrett that the Kid was not at his place, but he was nearby. At that instant, they both heard the voices outside, and shortly after that, a man appeared in the doorway.

Billy stepped into the darkened room and approached the bed. At first, Garrett thought this might be Maxwell's son-in-law, Manuel Abreú, coming to ask Maxwell who the strange men were. Not realizing how deadly this situation was, Garrett did not try to grab his pistol at first.

"Pete, who are those fellows on the outside?" Billy said, still coming closer. He reached out and placed his hand on the end of the bed.

"That's him," Maxwell breathed to Garrett, who had just figured this out. Garrett instantly reached around for his Colt.

Billy, his eyes adjusting to the darkness, saw the sheriff's movement and sprang back, simultaneously bringing up his six-shooter and beginning to point it. *"¿Quién es?" "¿Quién es?"*

The Kid sensed danger, but he hesitated to fire his weapon. He did not recognize the person sitting on Maxwell's bed; he (or she) might be a friend. That hesitation of not more than a heartbeat or two, that split-second confusion born of the Kid's conscience, was all Garrett needed.

A Colt Single Action Army revolver makes four distinct clicks when its hammer is pulled back to full cock. When the hammer is pulled back rapidly, however, the clicks are nearly indistinguishable, resulting in a quick, ratchetlike sound. Billy heard this sound, and then he was blinded by a bright flash of light, followed by a deafening roar. He felt a powerful, paralyzing blow to his chest, and he fell limp to the floor.

Garrett had jerked his pistol from its holster and fired it in one swift motion. Although he, too, was blinded by the handgun's muzzle flash, he quickly lunged to his side and fired a second shot in the same direction, filling the room with acrid blackpowder smoke. Garrett then ran for the door. Maxwell bolted upright and jumped over the foot of his bed, getting tangled in the sheets and blankets and falling to the floor. After Garrett dashed out onto the porch, he put his back against the adobe wall next to the door. A wide-eyed Poe rushed up to him, his gun drawn. When Maxwell finally came out of the bedroom, Poe instinctively pointed his pistol at him.

"Don't shoot Maxwell," Garrett warned, at the same time pushing his deputy's six-shooter down with his hand.

"That was the Kid that came in there onto me, and I think I have got him," Garrett told his deputies.

"Pat, the Kid would not come to this place," Poe said. "You have shot the wrong man."

Poe's remark shook Garrett but only for a moment. He quickly reviewed in his mind what had just happened. "I am sure that was him," Garrett finally said, "for I know his voice too well to be mistaken."

Following the gunshots, Poe had heard a groan and some gasps or gurgling sounds, but the room was now silent. Still, no one wanted to go in without making damn sure Billy the Kid was dead, or at least incapacitated. Maxwell retrieved a tallow candle and put it in one of the open windows. The candle's flickering flame revealed the body of a young man, spread-eagle on the floor. Garrett and Maxwell confirmed that the body was indeed that of William H. Bonney. A butcher knife could be seen on the floor near his left hand and a pistol near his right. Garrett could also see his Winchester carbine leaning up against the door facing, where he had placed it just minutes before.

The lawmen and Maxwell filed into the room and carefully examined the Kid's body. Garrett's first shot from his .44 had pierced Billy's chest just above his heart; his second had gone wild. There was some confusion, though, as to whether or not Billy had gotten a shot off at Garrett. Poe and McKinney swore they heard three shots come from the room. Garrett believed the Kid had fired one shot between his two, and Maxwell was certain that the Kid had fired. After carefully examining the room for bullet marks, however, they found only the two created by Garrett's pistol. They then inspected Billy's pistol. It was a Colt double-action identical to his Lightning (which had been confiscated at Stinking Spring), except this pistol was in .41 caliber. Five of the cylinder's six chambers contained cartridges while one contained an empty shell casing. The hammer rested upon this empty shell, a common safety practice (if the hammer rested on a live cartridge, a harsh jar might set the gun off accidentally). The men were forced to conclude that the Kid had not fired his weapon, but they could not explain why they had heard three shots.

BY NOW, MANY OF Fort Sumner's residents had heard about the shooting and were gathering outside the room to see if it was true that Billito was dead. Most of these were friends or sympathizers of the Kid. Deluvina, the Maxwell family servant, had been especially fond of the outlaw. Short, dark-skinned, and decidedly unattractive, Deluvina was also strong, a hard worker, and loyal. A well-known healer, she was often seen far out on the prairie gathering various flowers, leaves, and roots for her elixirs. In her spare time, she enjoyed a good drink and good smoking tobacco. She was about twelve years older than the Kid, and she was one of those who wanted to mother Bonney. "Billy the Kid was Deluvina's idol," remembered Paulita, "she worshipped him; to her mind, there never was such a wonderful boy in all the world."

Deluvina went into Maxwell's bedroom with Jesus Silva, a Maxwell cowhand and a friend of Billy's. She burst into tears when she saw Billy's face, and between her sobs, she was loudly cursing Pat Garrett. As she left the room, she cried out, "My little boy is dead!"

Paulita Maxwell also had a long look at the body. Her room was in the same building, and the gunshots had startled her awake. John Poe studied the girl carefully. Garrett had told him about her love for the Kid, and the deputy was surprised by how little emotion she showed as she stared down at the corpse. Poe had not seen the girl before that night, of course, and only Paulita knew the thoughts that raced through her mind when she saw that poor Billito would never again whisper in her ear, bring her a treat, or crack that funny grin.

Several Hispanic women begged Garrett to let them remove the body, and he agreed. Maxwell suggested they take it to the old carpenter shop near the quartermaster's corral. The shop contained a sturdy workbench where they could place the body. Jesus Silva, who helped transport the corpse to the workshop, found it odd that the chest wound did not bleed until approximately two hours after Billy had been shot. Only a small spot of red on the front of the Kid's light-colored shirt gave away the fatal bullet's entry point. The women carefully prepared the body for a wake, placing lighted candles all around it, and for the rest of the night, a number of Fort Sumner's residents, both men and women, kept quiet watch over their friend Billito.

Garrett and his men also kept watch that night, but not over Billy the Kid. The sheriff was concerned that some of Billy's distraught friends might attempt to exact revenge. Local sheepherder Francisco Lobato said later that if they had had a leader, they would have done just that. But Sumner's natural-born leader, the one who specialized in revenge, was dead. The rest of the night passed without incident.

Garrett had ordered Alcalde Alejandro Seguro to hold an inquest on the killing, and the following morning, the alcalde named six men to what was essentially a coroner's jury. Among the members of the jury were Garrett's brother-in-law, Saval Gutiérrez, and Garrett's friend from Sunnyside, Milnor Rudolph, who served as foreman. No inquest had been held at Fort Sumner for Billy's pals Charlie Bowdre and Tom Folliard, but then again, there had been no reward for either of those men. With $500 cash at stake, Garrett was very particular that there be a legal paper trail to document his success. He had gone through hell collecting the last reward from the Territory, so he was determined to give Santa Fe's bureaucrats as little to doubt as possible.

The jury viewed the body in the carpenter's shop to confirm the cause and manner of death, after which they visited Maxwell's bedroom and took testimony from Don Pedro, the only eyewitness to the shooting other than Sheriff Garrett. The men promptly came up with a verdict: "We of the jury unanimously find that William Bonney came to his death from a bullet wound in the left breast near the region of the heart fired by a pistol in the hand of Pat F. Garrett and our judgment is that the action of said Garrett was justifiable homicide and we are united in opinion that the gratitude of all the community is due to said Garrett for his action and whom is worthy of being compensated."

The reference here to compensation suggests that Garrett must have been involved in the verdict's wording, and the jury may not have been united in this expression of gratitude. Gutiérrez and two other jury members, for example, never read the verdict in its finished form—they were illiterate. In any case, Garrett now had the documentation he needed to present his claim to the Territory.

The Kid's funeral took place that afternoon. Garrett had arranged with Maxwell to make sure the body was "neatly and properly dressed." Jesus Silva constructed a crude coffin, after which he and Fort Sumner resident Vicente Otero dug a grave in the old post cemetery. The coffin was transported to the burying ground in Otero's wood wagon and was followed by a procession of nearly every resident of Fort Sumner. The words spoken over the grave came from Job, chapter 14: "Man that is born of a woman is of few days and full of trouble. He cometh forth like a flower, and is cut down: he fleeth also as a shadow, and continueth not." The next day, a marker made out of a stave from the fort's picket fence was placed at the head of the grave. Stenciled on the board's eroded surface were the words "Billy the Kid." No last name. No date. No quaint Victorian sentiment.

Garrett got himself ready to leave for Las Vegas and Santa Fe, and Pete Maxwell would ride with him for part of the trip. The sheriff dismissed his two deputies, who set off down the Pecos, McKinney for his home near Roswell and Poe for White Oaks. John W. Poe was never able to come to understand why Billy had hesitated and had not killed him that night when he came upon Poe and McKinney outside of Maxwell's residence. If anything, Billy had an uncanny knack for staying alive. Poe puzzled over the strange events of that night on his long ride back to White Oaks—and for years to come. Toward the end of his life, he came to a single conclusion: Billy Bonney's demise had been foreordained.

9

Both Hero and Villain

I sometimes wish that I had missed fire [and] that the
Kid had got in his work on me.

—PAT F. GARRETT

KILLING THE KID.
Pat Garrett's Nervy Feat.
He Catches and Shoots Billy Bonney.
A Wound Through the Heart Which
Wrought Good for New Mexico.
Quickness and Bravery Required and
Found in a Sheriff's Arm and Eye.

THOSE WERE THE HEADLINES in the *Santa Fe New Mexican.* News of the Kid's death had reached Las Vegas on Monday morning, July 18, brought there direct from Fort Sumner by the mail contractor. The *Las Vegas Gazette* scooped its rival, the *Daily Optic*, getting a brief report to the Western Union office by 8:00 A.M., which gave several newspapers across the country the chance to feature the news in their afternoon editions. In Santa Fe, the intelligence had first been communicated in a telegram sent from Las Vegas to Billy's old antagonist, John S. Chisum, who was then in the capital and no doubt euphoric at the news. Sent by military contractor Marcus Brunswick, a friend of Chisum's, the telegram was only one sentence: "Pat Garrett killed Billy Kid near Sumner Friday night."

Garrett and Pete Maxwell arrived in Las Vegas later that same Monday, which allowed the *Daily Optic* to get the first interview with the lawman. The *Optic* fawned over Garrett while demonizing the Kid, a pattern repeated in newspapers throughout the Territory, and, to a lesser extent, the nation. Garrett was the "terror of all evil-doers" who deserved to be well rewarded for his "cool, brave conduct." Billy Bonney, on the other hand, was "a bold thief, a cold-blooded murderer, having perhaps killed more men than any man of his age in the world. . . . All mankind rejoices and the newspapers will now have something else to talk about." The Kid's death was covered in the *New York Times, Chicago Tribune, Boston Globe, Rocky Mountain News, Salt Lake Herald, Minneapolis Tribune, Tombstone Daily Nugget* (which used as its headline, "A Corner in Hell Filled"), *Indianapolis News,* and scores of others, even the venerable *Times* of London, England.

The *Albuquerque Daily Journal* wanted Garrett appointed the U.S. marshal for the Territory. The *Kansas City Journal* opined that Garrett was just the man to solve Missouri's outlaw problem: "He who will follow the James boys and their companions in crime to their den, and shoot them down without mercy, will be crowned with honors by the good people of this commonwealth, and be richly rewarded in money besides." When a Colorado newspaper suggested that Garrett be sent to Washington to serve as a guard for Charles J. Guiteau, President James A. Garfield's assassin, the *Daily New Mexican* commented that a better idea would be to let Guiteau loose and then offer Garrett a reward for him. Garrett had "achieved a fame which will be undying," the *Rio Grande Republican* observed, which was all too true. Pat Garrett was now, and forevermore, the man who shot Billy the Kid.

Garrett arrived in Santa Fe by rail on July 19, and one of the first things he did was to defend Pete Maxwell. The buzz around the capital was that Maxwell had somehow been in cahoots with the Kid, that he had been knowingly harboring the desperado. This was fueled by rumors about Billy's relationship with Pete's sister. In a long interview with the *Daily New Mexican*, Garrett denied that Maxwell had been hiding the outlaw and said that fear alone had prevented Pete from letting anyone know where the Kid was. Maxwell had assured Garrett that if there had been a safe way of letting the sheriff know, he would have done so. Although Garrett's explanation satisfied the reporter, it makes little sense because others at Fort Sumner found that informing on Billy was as easy as licking a postage stamp and sticking it on an envelope. Did Pete Maxwell fail to inform on the Kid because he did not want to hurt his sister? Garrett was most likely protecting Paulita's reputation. Like Billy, Fort Sumner had been the sheriff's home; he still had friends and relatives there.

Garrett's main business in Santa Fe was to see about the reward money. Unfortunately, he had to deal with William G. Ritch, secretary of the Territory and acting governor (the new governor, Lionel Sheldon, had rushed to Washington, D.C., upon hearing that his friend President Garfield had been shot). Ritch had made it difficult for Garrett to collect the first reward, after Garrett's capture of Billy at Stinking Spring. The lawman had already forwarded his report to the Palace of the Governors, where it had been received Monday evening. The next Wednesday afternoon, Garrett called on the acting governor, and he brought reinforcements: Thomas B. Catron and Marcus Brunswick. Catron was one of the most powerful men in the Territory and an extremely skilled attorney. Undoubtedly having received legal advice from Catron, Garrett presented Ritch with a bill for $500 for the "capture" of William Bonney. He also submitted as evidence for his claim an affidavit from the editor and manager of the *Daily New Mexican* confirming that the reward offer had been published, the Fort

Sumner coroner's jury verdict, and his own statement summing up how he killed the Kid.

Ritch put the men off. But, having been roundly criticized for delaying the first reward, Ritch made sure it did not appear that he was refusing to honor the Territory's offer. He assured Garrett and his supporters that he was willing to pay the reward and was glad to do so. But he needed some time to go over the Territory's records and confirm the reward offer. Garrett could not have heard this as good news. The sheriff possessed the published reward notice and proof of Bonney's death. How much more confirmation did Ritch need? A lot more, it turns out. The attorney general advised Ritch that the reward notice appeared to be a *personal offer* of the former governor, as there was no record in either the governor's office or the secretary's office that Wallace had offered the reward as an executive act. Consequently, if the reward was to be paid with territorial funds, it would have to be approved by the legislature. On July 21, Ritch suspended any action on Garrett's claim until it could be brought before the next Legislative Assembly.

Fortunately, Garrett would have cash to hold him over in the meantime. The day after the sheriff's arrival in the capital, Jimmy Dolan pounded the streets of Santa Fe, asking for cash donations for Garrett to reward him for slaying "the worst man the Territory has known." Dolan had collected $560 by the end of the day; he would eventually give Garrett $1,150. The same thing was going on in other New Mexico communities, from Las Vegas to Las Cruces. Las Vegas had a similar collection, contributing nearly $1,000 in a few hours' time. John Chisum was reportedly prepared to hand the sheriff $1,000 of his own money, and it was expected that another $1,000 would come from the citizens of Lincoln County (the ones who were not Kid sympathizers). Even without the reward, the many donations represented a small fortune for someone of little means such as Garrett.

On Thursday, July 28, Pat Garrett purchased a horse and rode out of Santa Fe, alone, for Las Vegas. It was much quicker to go by train, of course, but lately things had been moving pretty fast for the lawman, and if he was on a train ride, he might have to talk and be sociable with the other passengers. Better to sit astride a good horse, enjoy the smell of sage, feel the warm sun from a turquoise sky, and just let the mind wander.

EVEN WITH ALL THE adulation Garrett received for ridding the Territory of young Billy, there were the whispers—and they started when the Kid was hardly in his grave. Within a matter of days, some people were saying that Garrett had not fought fair—Billy did not have a gun that night—and the way Bonney was killed was murder. These things were openly spoken, and even printed in newspapers far beyond the Territory. A good example of this line of thinking appeared in the *Globe* of Atchison, Kansas, which called Garrett's act "more or less cowardly. The Kid was stopping at the house of a supposed friend, who betrayed him, and allowed Garrett to hide in the house. In the darkness of the night Garrett crawled upon him, and shot him dead."

These stinging slanders were one thing, but Garrett was also upset by some outrageous reports that the Kid's body had been exhumed and mutilated. In its July 25 issue, the *Las Vegas Daily Optic* said it had received the Kid's "fatal finger," the one that had "snapped many a man's life into eternity." The trigger finger was preserved in a jar of alcohol, and so many visitors wanted a peek at it that the paper considered purchasing a small tent so it could operate a kind of sideshow. A month and a half later, the *Optic* ran an elaborate piece claiming that five days after the Kid's funeral, his body had been exhumed by a local "skelologist." The body was then taken to a Las Vegas doctor, who boiled and scraped the head to get the skull. This was when the *Optic* was supposedly given Billy's trigger finger. The rest of the corpse had been buried in a corral so the flesh could decompose, leaving the bones that would be retrieved and pieced together with wires into a skeleton.

A follow-up article in the September 19 issue reported that a Miss Kate Tenney of Oakland, California, had read about the Kid's preserved finger and had written the paper to request the appendage, as well as a photograph of the outlaw. Tenney, the *Optic* said, was the Kid's sweetheart. The newspaper sent Tenney a letter of condolence that also told her that her beau's finger had been sold and shipped east for the cash price of $150. The *Atchison Globe* jokingly suggested that the Tenney letter was a scheme of the *Las Vegas Gazette* to get the notorious finger, which had apparently led to a nice increase in subscriptions and advertising for the *Optic*. Several newspapers accepted the *Optic*'s stories at face value. After all, stranger things had happened to the bodies of dead outlaws. After "Big Nose George" Parrott was lynched in Wyoming in March 1881, a local physician took the body and had a medicine bag and a pair of shoes made from Parrott's skin.

Then there were the cheap nickel novels (known today as dime novels) that purported to tell the story of the outlaw William Bonney. Five showed up on newsstands in 1881, three in early September, just seven weeks after Billy's death. Two of these novels bore the title *The True Life of Billy the Kid*, even though they were anything but. One of the authors, a Don Jenardo (otherwise known as John Woodruff Lewis), wrote that Billy's first devilish deed occurred in Arizona when he shot a friend in the back of the head. The friend, a young miner, was to be married the next day to a beautiful senorita Billy had feelings for. Jenardo's version of Billy's death is just as imaginative. He describes Garrett receiving a tip that the Kid is sleeping at Maxwell's house and that the outlaw will arrive at midnight. Garrett gets to the house just before midnight and, finding it deserted, hides behind Maxwell's bed with his rifle. When Billy walks in, he immediately senses that someone is there and draws his *pistols* (what kind of a gunslinger would he be with just one pistol?), but Garrett steadies his rifle faster. "Thus died," wrote Jenardo, "the youngest and greatest desperado ever known in the world's history."

Garrett's answer to the insinuations and lies was to produce his own book. And if he made a little money on the venture, that would be okay, too. He partnered with the boozing but fun-loving journalist, postmaster, and justice of the peace Ash Upson, who did much of the writing for the book. Upson and Garrett became friends after Garrett relocated to Roswell; Upson actually moved into the Garrett household in August 1881. And Upson had known Billy as a youth in Silver City and later as a Lincoln County Regulator, which seemed to make him the perfect choice for a ghostwriter. Upson may have proposed the idea to Garrett in the first place.

Upson wanted to try a book publisher back east, but Garrett insisted on shopping it in Santa Fe. He knew the editor and publisher of the *Daily New Mexican,* Charles W. Greene, who immediately drew up a contract between Garrett and his New Mexican Printing and Publishing Company for a 128-page book. They agreed the printed copies would sell for 50 cents each. When the book appeared the following March—at 137 pages—it carried a title that put the cheap novels to shame: *The Authentic Life of Billy, the Kid, The Noted Desperado of the Southwest, Whose Deeds of Daring and Blood Made His Name a Terror in New Mexico, Arizona and Northern Mexico.* Garrett was identified as the Lincoln County sheriff who "Finally Hunted Down and Captured" the Kid "By Killing Him." The title page made the final claim that the book was "A Faithful and Interesting Narrative."

Although Garrett stated in the book's introduction that his volume was a response to the innumerable inaccuracies contained in the yellow-covered cheap novels about the Kid, the first half of his book is little different from the nickel novels he criticized. The meat of the book begins slightly past the middle, when Garrett enters the story. Significantly, this is when the narrative changes to the first person.

Straightforward and matter-of-fact, Garrett's account of the hunt for the gang and their capture at Stinking Spring, and the fatal encounter with the Kid in Pete Maxwell's room, makes for a gripping tale, a true classic of western Americana. Not surprisingly, Garrett does not mention that the Kid had been staying with his in-laws at Fort Sumner. Nor does he bring up Paulita Maxwell, the Kid's sweetheart. It would not do to associate the respectable young woman with an outlaw, even though some newspapers had already published stories about her affair with Billy.

Garrett saved the last few pages to answer his critics and to address the obnoxious rumors about Billy's remains. He did not shoot the Kid from behind a bed or from underneath a bed. There was no way to get behind the bed, as it was crowded against the wall. And he had not been under the bed because he was not expecting the Kid to burst into the room; he was taken completely by surprise. If Garrett had had fair warning, then hell yes, he would have been under the bed or behind anything else that might have provided a little protection.

Was he scared? Garrett considered that a damn fool question. "I started out on that expedition with the expectation of getting scared. I went out contemplating the probability of being shot at, and the possibility of being hurt, perhaps killed; but not if any precaution on my part would prevent such a catastrophe."

As far as fighting the Kid fairly, critics essentially suggested that Garrett should have given Billy a chance to kill him. The Kid had made it known that he would never be taken alive again, and Garrett had no intention of giving the Kid any chance whatsoever. The Kid had walked into a situation much better than Garrett had intended. "What sort of 'square fight,' or 'even show,' would I have got," Garrett posed, "had one of the Kid's friends in Fort Sumner chanced to see me and informed him of my presence there, and at Pete Maxwell's room on that fatal night?"

Concerning the whereabouts of Billy's corpse, Garrett wrote that the body had been interred in the Fort Sumner cemetery, and that is where it remained still. "Skull, fingers, toes, bones and every hair of the head that was buried with the body on the 15th day of July, doctors, newspapers editors and paragraphers [reporters] to the contrary notwithstanding. Some presuming swindlers have claimed to have the Kid's skull on exhibition, or one of his fingers, or some other portion of his body, and one medical gentleman has persuaded credulous idiots that he has all the bones strung upon wires. . . . Again I say that the Kid's body lies undisturbed in the grave—and I speak of what I know."

Thirty-eight years after the publication of Garrett's *The Authentic Life*, Charlie Siringo, who had been a member of the Texas posse, claimed that Garrett had Billy's body dug up to make sure that the trigger finger was still attached—it was. But like Upson, Siringo could not resist improving upon a story.

Unfortunately for Garrett and Upson, their book was not a best-seller—far from it. The Territory was hardly a large market, and as Upson had feared, the publisher did not have the experience or wherewithal to market the book nationally. But Pat Garrett had had his say, and his say would profoundly influence countless authors, historians, and screenwriters. The newspapers may have given birth to the legend of the Kid, but Pat Garrett's slim volume was the legend's memory book.

Just five months after the publication, Garrett had an experience that could have come straight out of a nickel novel, except for its staid ending. It occurred on August 1, 1882, in the billiard room of Albuquerque's Armijo Hotel, the city's newest and finest. The hotel's dining room was so nice the male guests were required to wear coats. Garrett had just arrived from Santa Fe, and as he stood in the billiard room, perhaps watching a game or about to join one, in walked Joseph Antrim, the brother of Billy the Kid. Antrim, a professional gambler, had been in Albuquerque for the last several days, and more than a few people in the room recognized him. Rumors had been circulating for months that Antrim wanted to avenge his brother's death; or, as one newspaper reported in dramatic fashion, he "hankers for the blood of Pat Garrett, the man who killed The Kid."

Those who recognized Antrim tensed as he headed straight for Garrett, but their anxiety soon turned to surprise and curiosity when they saw Garrett and Antrim begin a long discussion, their voices staying frustratingly low. It was not until the next morning that a newspaper reporter was able to pry from Garrett the gist of the conversation. Garrett said Antrim strongly disavowed the rumors floating around, and said he had no ill will toward the lawman. Antrim "merely intended talking over the killing of the Kid with the man who killed him." Perhaps Joseph Antrim was trying to get straight in his own mind how the likable boy he bid good-bye to in September 1877 had become such a wanted and hated criminal and why that boy, above all others, had deserved to die in such a cold, ruthless manner. Garrett would not have had an answer to that (it is a hard thing to get straight even now), but he did tell Antrim that he did not understand why he would hate him in the first place, because he had only done his duty, which "demanded the homicide." The two then parted, not as "the best of friends," the happy ending reported by the newspaper, but not as enemies, either. They never met again.

WITHIN A WEEK OF killing the Kid, Garrett threatened to resign as sheriff of Lincoln County. The job did not pay well, he explained at the time, and he did not think the county's citizens had given him the support he needed. He said he would have quit months before had the Kid not escaped from the Lincoln courthouse. He had stayed on the job to see the Kid business through to the end and that had kept him wearing his badge. The sheriff did not say it, but those hair-raising few seconds in Maxwell's bedroom likely had something to do with his surprise announcement. Garrett's threat to retire, however, came before the grateful people of the Territory had had a chance to show their appreciation. The substantial cash donations presented to Garrett appear to have given him something of an attitude adjustment, and he decided to stick it out until the end of his term.

On February 20, 1882, the Territory finally delivered on Wallace's $500 reward offer. But money was not the only thing Garrett received as thanks for doing in Billy the Kid. He was also presented with some very impressive mementos. One of these was a handsome sterling silver pocket watch manufactured by the Elgin National Watch Company of Illinois. Inscribed inside the case were the words "From Grateful Citizens/of/Lincoln County/September 1881/To/Pat Garrett." Much more remarkable—stunning, actually—was the solid gold sheriff's badge from Albert J. Fountain, the Kid's old attorney and a political ally of Garrett. The oddest memento, though, was a walking cane commissioned by several "Grant County citizens" in 1883 as a gift for Garrett. The cane was to be made from the wood of Billy's old cabin in Silver City and fitted with a gold head bearing an "appropriate inscription"—just what the six-foot-four lawman needed.

Toward the end of his term, Garrett made it known that he would not be seeking reelection as sheriff. He supported his deputy, John W. Poe, to be his successor. Garrett had bigger things in mind. Encouraged by Albert Fountain and his loyal benefactor, Captain Joseph C. Lea, Garrett ran for a seat in the Territorial Council, and he seemed to have a good chance at victory in the fall election. But not everyone felt the former lawman was a good choice. One particularly harsh critic, who signed himself in the *Rio Grande Republican* as "X," accused Garrett of being ungrateful to his former political supporters whom he was now running against. He also claimed that Garrett was illiterate and was being played by his associates. In another letter, this one signed "Texan" but possibly written by the mysterious "X," the writer argued that Garrett, though a good sheriff, was not qualified to serve in the Council. "The trouble with Mr. Garrett is . . . that the praise of the newspapers, together with the toadying flattery of those surrounding him, has made him egotistical in a superlative degree."

Garrett fired right back with a well-reasoned and, at times, witty letter of his own. But Garrett was not finished. The letters critical of Garrett had both originated in Lincoln, and when Garrett thought he had figured out who the author was, he sought the man out. That man was a twenty-seven-year-old attorney from West Virginia named William M. Roberts. Garrett had also heard that Roberts had said some unpleasant things about his wife, Polinaria. Garrett was particularly sensitive when it came to his wife because he was well aware of the racist attitudes of many Anglos in the Territory who looked down on interracial marriages.

Garrett found Roberts visiting with several other men in La Rue's store and interrupted their conversation. He asked Roberts if he had written the letter, and Roberts denied it. Garrett then asked Roberts to step outside because he wanted to say something in private. Once outside, Garrett again accused Roberts of writing the letter. Roberts, a little haughty now, replied that anyone who said he wrote the letter was a goddamn liar. With that, Garrett yanked out his Colt and slammed it down on Roberts's head. The poor man crumpled to the ground, blood flowing from his scalp. Garrett then paced up and down, saying he had better be respected, and if it took a shooting iron to get that respect, so be it. Roberts, who fully recovered from Garrett's assault, did not press charges.

Garrett made a strong showing in the election that November, but not strong enough to gain the seat. Although he won Lincoln and Grant counties, he failed to carry Doña Ana County, the home of the anti-Garrett *Rio Grande Republican*. No matter, he had plenty to keep him busy. Garrett directed his energies to carving out a future as a successful cattleman—not on the scale of the Chisum brothers, but successful enough to make him a player in the region. The cattle business was booming in eastern New Mexico, in large part due to Garrett's success in putting an end to the thieving of the Kid and his pals. In 1883, more than 81,000 cattle ranged over the grazing lands of Lincoln County, the highest number in the Territory (sheep in the county numbered 113,000). Some of those cattle wore Garrett's distinctive brand: PAT. That same year, Garrett partnered with John Poe, now the sheriff of Lincoln County, to buy a herd of cattle near Lincoln; Garrett operated a ranch not far from Fort Stanton.

In the spring of 1884, troubles on the Texas Panhandle's cattle ranges put Garrett once again on the trail of rustlers. Like John Chisum on the Pecos a few years before, the large Texas cattlemen were feuding with the small-time operators, who were stealing from their big neighbors. But the cattlemen were also having problems with their own cowhands. A year earlier, nearly two hundred Panhandle cowboys went on strike for better pay. When the strike failed, the owners refused to rehire a number of the punchers, which left some disgruntled cowboys out of work, and so destitute they were more than willing to turn to rustling to earn a living. The owners of the bigger ranches called on Garrett to put a stop to the rustling and to enforce the law in cow country. They offered Garrett $5,000 a year to organize an independent company of rangers, and to make it legal, Garrett would receive a captain's commission from the Texas governor. The *El Paso Lone Star* described this arrangement as the "finest means of protection that has ever been tried." The owners of the small ranches, however, were not nearly as exuberant. They were afraid that Garrett's rangers would be little more than the tools of the big cattlemen.

Just before Garrett headed over to the Panhandle, he paid $5,000 to purchase a ranch in Lincoln County. Then, sometime that April, he departed for Texas, accompanied by Barney Mason and another man. Garrett's ranger company, which numbered about nine men, operated for less than a year. During that period, Garrett made some key arrests and strictly enforced a recent proclamation of the Texas governor prohibiting civilians from wearing six-shooters (the governor was apparently unfamiliar with the Second Amendment, although for a time, New Mexico Territory had an identical law). Garrett and his rangers circulated among all the roundup camps, sometimes inspecting two hundred punchers in a day. In the opinion of Garrett's friend, John Meadows, this gun control effort might have been Garrett's biggest success. "They got Pat Garrett just in time to save another Lincoln County War, and Pat he understood it, and he disarmed every doggone one of them." But Garrett became convinced that his cattlemen bosses had hired him to simply kill the worst rustlers, not bring them to justice, and he would have none of it.

In January 1885, Garrett moved his small family to Las Vegas so they could be close to his new position as the chief of the Southwest Livestock Detective Agency. In March, Garrett took the oath as cattle inspector for the Territory's third district. That same month, he arrested two rustlers in Tascosa and a third, a man named Tom Ruby, in Las Vegas. In commenting on the arrests, the *Lincoln Golden Era* reminded its readers, "As we said before, Pat will get 'em."

Despite Garrett's continued success in corralling rustlers, he soon stumbled into a more lucrative—and safer—payday in the form of an eccentric and apparently wealthy Scotsman by the name of Brandon C. Kirby. The adopted son of James Cree, a prosperous ship owner, Kirby was said to have served in South Africa as a captain in the Royal Scots Fusiliers. He had come to America looking for a place to invest Cree's fortune and eventually settled on Lincoln County. Kirby immediately chose Garrett to help him as his agent in acquiring lands and cattle. Within a few weeks' time during the summer of 1885, they spent $300,000 of Cree's money. Kirby acquired several ranches, including Garrett's, and made his headquarters on Eagle Creek, a few miles from Fort Stanton. Of the eleven thousand head of cattle he purchased, most were "she cattle," as Kirby was importing 140 Black Angus bulls to breed with them. The ranch was named the Angus

VV (locally known as the Double V), and Garrett became the ranch's first manager at $5,000 a year for five years. On the ranch's printed stationery, Garrett proudly used the title he had acquired from the Texas governor: Captain Pat F. Garrett, Manager.

In a way, Kirby was an exaggerated version of John Henry Tunstall of Lincoln County War days. He wore fine suits of Scotch tweed and overcoats of Irish frieze, and it is hard to imagine a stranger pair than Garrett and Kirby. Their relationship did not last a year. Garrett reminded the Scotsman that in the American West, a deal is a deal, and he walked away with his first year's salary. The next year old man Cree sent his natural son to the ranch, and Cree followed with his wife two years later. Kirby was out as manager of the Angus VV and disappeared from New Mexico in 1890.

Garrett left the cattle business at a good time. In 1886, a harsh drought hit the region, which was rapidly becoming overstocked. A sudden fall in the price of cattle only made matters worse. Garrett went to his home just east of Roswell and poured himself into farming, with some horse breeding and racing on the side, of course— Garrett would always be a gambler at heart. The dry climate made it impossible to grow anything without irrigation, and he set about purchasing existing irrigation ditches and building new ones. Garrett believed that with strategically placed dams, flumes, and canals, the entire Pecos Valley could be transformed into a Garden of Eden for farmers. Garrett partnered with his old publisher in Santa Fe, Charles Greene, and cattleman Charles B. Eddy, and by 1889, their Pecos Irrigation and Investment Company had become a juggernaut. They had several new investors, more than 40,000 acres of irrigated land (with a goal of 220,000), and a new town that Garrett and Eddy had laid out named, appropriately enough, Eddy (present-day Carlsbad, New Mexico).

Garrett's farm was one of the most valuable in the valley. Four hundred acres of his twelve-hundred-acre place were being cultivated, he had started a nursery with seven hundred apple trees, and he also operated a dairy. But he was also spending a lot of money. He partnered in livery stables in Roswell and Eddy and in a blacksmith shop in Roswell, and he was a large investor in a Roswell hotel. There was also the stage line that Garrett and friend James Brent, who had succeeded John W. Poe as Lincoln County sheriff, operated between Eddy and Roswell. With everything he had going on, Garrett and his fellow investors were forced to travel in order to secure more capital for the irrigation company, and that ultimately led to Garrett's downfall. When the big capitalists stepped in, Garrett could not match their contributions and purchases of company stock. The man who had originated the visionary idea to green the Pecos Valley was forced out.

Garrett ran for sheriff of Chaves County in 1890, one of two new counties carved out of the insanely large Lincoln County. Because of his hard work and many investments in the Pecos Valley, Garrett was a front-runner in the election. But Garrett's fame and popularity spawned something of a backlash. Another problem—a big problem, actually—was Garrett's onetime friend John W. Poe. Garrett and Poe had had a falling-out over some money Garrett had borrowed, and the relationship had gone south from there. Poe publicly announced his support for another candidate, and Garrett lost the election. If the loss of control of his dream to irrigate the Pecos Valley had been a bitter pill, his failure to become the first sheriff of Chaves County was absolutely intolerable. Garrett wanted nothing more to do with New Mexico and its people.

The year before, Garrett had made a trade in Uvalde, Texas (eighty miles west of San Antonio), that involved an irrigation ditch project. Ever the optimist when it came to speculating (in other words, gambling), he had sent Polinaria a letter at the time that said he would make $20,000 off the deal. Garrett now told his wife and kids to start packing; they were moving to Uvalde.

At this time, Garrett and Polinaria had four children, Ida, Elizabeth, Dudley Poe, and Annie. Dudley Poe had been named for John W. Poe, when the former deputy was still a close friend. Elizabeth, called Lizzie by family and friends, had lost her eyesight in early childhood. According to one story, her eyes had troubled her from birth, and when a supposed "eye specialist" in Roswell told Garrett he could cure Lizzie's problem, Garrett was eager to try, regardless of the cost. So Garrett paid the money and Lizzie received the treatment, but it only accelerated her blindness, and the specialist accelerated his exit from town. Lizzie, who loved her father dearly, as did her brothers and sisters, remembered his insistence that she grow up like any normal kid, and also his extreme patience. "Think your way out, daughter," he would tell her, "and keep your head clear, above your heart" (as an adult, Elizabeth Garrett would compose the New Mexico state song, "O, Fair New Mexico").

Pat and Polinaria eventually had four more children—Patrick, Pauline, Oscar, and Jarvis—making a total of eight. There was a gap of several years between the first four and the second four, and Garrett jokingly referred to his offspring as his first and second crops.

On Monday, April 13, 1891, the Garrett clan, and also James Brent and family, pulled out of Roswell for their new homes in Texas. Ash Upson, known to the Garrett kids as "Uncle Ash," stayed behind in Roswell for another year settling his and Garrett's interests before moving to Texas. Nine-year-old Ida Garrett wrote to her uncle Ash three months after the family's arrival and told him that she and her mama "like Roswell better than we do here. It is so hot and dry." Ida's letter also revealed that her papa's time was now mostly occupied by horse racing. The fairgrounds at Uvalde included horse stables and a racetrack. Garrett favored trotters, the sleek animals being hitched to low two-wheeled carts, or sulkies, for racing. Ida told Uncle Ash that her papa had gone to Eagle Pass, Texas, on July 4, where he raced a trotter named George Selden and outran seven other horses. Her papa had set up another race in San Antonio, but his opponent abruptly backed out after Garrett arrived. Papa made the man pay his expenses to San Antonio.

Six months after Garrett relocated to Uvalde, the *Uvalde Herald* wrote about the increasing number of blooded horses in west Texas. Garrett had much to do with that. He raced his horses at fairgrounds in New Mexico and Texas and as far away as New Orleans. In a San Antonio newspaper, he was the "horseman from Uvalde," with no mention of Billy the Kid. Yet Garrett's Uvalde years were filled with growing frustration and growing losses, both personal and financial. He dropped $1,500 on a single steam engine for his Uvalde irrigation project, and that did not include transportation costs from St. Louis. On March 21, 1894, an obviously depressed and tired Garrett wrote Polinaria from an unknown race venue:

Dear Wife

I have been [a]wake for two hours. Woke at one o'clock and cant sleep so have got and lit my Pipe. What a terrible thing it is for a man to be so poor that he is compel[led] to stay away from his wife and children this way. I hope you are not bothered as I am. It seems now as if I will not be able to leave here until the races are over. I still hope to make some money so I can pay what we owe when I come. . . . Will be home by the 10th of April sure and hope I will never have to go anywhere again without you are with me. . . .

P. F. Garrett

≈ 10 ≈

Another Manhunt

That's the history of New Mexico: kill somebody or
steal something and you can sure get a good office.
—J. A. WOODWARD

SINCE HIS BRIEF STINT as Billy the Kid's attorney in 1881,
Albert Jennings Fountain had solidified his power and influence in southern New Mexico Territory. The fiery Republican had
served in the territorial legislature as Speaker of the House. He had
chased raiding Apache warriors, rustlers, and thieves, as the leader of
a mounted militia unit he had organized himself, and he served ably
as assistant U.S. district attorney in the county seat of Las Cruces. In
1894, when a group of prominent cattlemen formed the Southeastern New Mexico Stock Growers' Association, they hired Fountain
as a special investigator and prosecutor. In less than a year's time,
Fountain's dogged efforts resulted in fifteen men finding new lodgings
in the territorial prison—and that was only the beginning. In January 1896, in the same Lincoln County courthouse from which Billy
Bonney had escaped nearly fifteen years before, Fountain obtained

Albert Jennings Fountain.

thirty-two indictments against twenty-three men for cattle theft and the defacing of brands.

The accused in these latest indictments knew they could be looking at as much as ten years in prison. But on February 1, as Fountain and his eight-year-old son, Henry, were returning from Lincoln to their home in Mesilla, something terrible happened. At Chalk Hill, a low rise just west of the windblown gypsum dunes known as White Sands, a mail carrier noticed that the tracks of Fountain's buckboard turned off the road. There were additional sets of tracks from horses and sharp-edged cowboy boots, and a pool of dried blood the size of a man's wide-brimmed hat soaked the sand next to the road. Behind some nearby bushes, three empty brass cartridges glistened in the sunlight.

A hastily organized posse discovered the abandoned buckboard about ten miles away. Fountain's valise had been rifled, with various papers strewn about upon the ground—and the indictments were missing. Also missing were the prosecutor and his boy, although evidence near the buckboard suggested that their blood-dripping bodies had been wrapped in a blanket and tied to the back of a horse, which was then led away.

This crime was particularly revolting because the killers had also taken the life of the innocent child, thus breaking an unspoken code of decency, even among outlaws. Outrage swept the far reaches of New Mexico, from the governor on down, as one posse after another looked for both the victims' bodies and for the men behind the murders.

With no progress in the case, New Mexico's governor, William T. Thornton, urged that Pat Garrett be made a special deputy to investigate the murders. The current Doña Ana County sheriff would hear none of it, however, nor would he resign to allow Garrett to take his place. But Thornton had a backup plan for the famed manhunter. Garrett revealed the high points of his meeting with Thornton and other power brokers in a February 25 letter to Polinaria, who was pregnant with their fifth child:

> Dear wife:
>
> . . . I made a trade yesterday to go to work for the committee that has been selected by the most prominent men of New Mexico to hunt and bring to justice the murderers of Col. Fountain and his little eight year old boy. They pay my expenses and $150.00 per month, and $8,000.00 in case I succeed in arresting and convicting the murderers.
>
> I arrived in Las Cruces night before last. I never saw a family so much disturbed as his family. People think that Mrs. Fountain and one of his daughters will go crazy.
>
> I dislike very much as you know Dear Wife to be away from

you, especially at this time, but here is an opportunity for me to make money and a chance for me to get the Sheriff's Office of Doña Ana County, which is worth $6,000 a year.

Governor Thornton thinks he could put me in the office at once, but he cannot yet. However, he has not given up yet, and thinks that within a month or two he can do so. . . .

Now wife, don't feel despondent but be the good and brave little wife that you always have been and everything will come out alright. Get Mrs. Nelson to come and stay with you when you get sick and a Doctor if you need him. You know, if it were not that we are so poor, I would not be away from you a minute, so, if I am successful we will get located in this country, and I will never be away from you and the children again. Tell the children to be good and study hard at school.

Yours,

P. F. Garrett

Four days later, Garrett was in the saddle looking for the bodies. The bitter cold, wind, and blowing sand made the solemn task miserable as well. At Garrett's side was Sheriff Charles C. Perry of Chaves County who had captured Indian Territory outlaw Bill Cook and his partner Jim Turner, a feat that was widely celebrated in the press, and entitled the sheriff to several thousand dollars in reward money. Now the forty-one-year-old Perry had a reputation for manhunting that nearly rivaled Garrett's. Perry was related to one of Garrett's old Roswell neighbors, where the two had first met. The Chaves County sheriff was as brash and loud as he was brave, and Garrett liked that.

Garrett and Perry rode back into Las Cruces after a week of fruitless searching. Garrett wrote Polinaria that he was not about to give up, and that he would start out again in a few days. "It is only a matter of time when I will succeed," he assured her. "You know when I make up my mind to do something I never quit as long as there is any hope."

Yes, Polinaria knew. Those words—*when I make up my mind to do some-thing I never quit*—revealed the essence of the lawman. He would see the job through to the end, even if it killed him—or got him killed.

The likely perpetrators had been identified by the posses within a few days of the disappearance. One set of tracks leading from the Fountain buckboard belonged to the horse of Dog Canyon rancher Oliver Lee, and Lee's bootprints matched those found at the crime scene. Another set of bootprints at the crime scene were linked to William McNew, who was married to Lee's niece. A third suspect, Jim Gililland, had been heard to say that if the Fountains' bodies had to be found before someone could be convicted, that conviction would be a long time coming. And when prompted about the Fountain child, whose mother was a native New Mexican, Gililland had chillingly replied that the boy was "nothing but a half-breed and to kill him was like killing a dog."

All three suspects were allies of Fountain's rabid political adversary, Albert Bacon Fall, a former legislator, district court judge, and the driving force behind the Democratic Party in southern New Mexico. Fall had been responsible for these men having received appointments as deputy U.S. marshals and, later, deputy sheriffs for Doña Ana County. Lee and McNew were among the twenty-three men named in the indictments obtained by Fountain at the last term of court in Lincoln.

Garrett's great challenge was securing evidence strong enough to convict the suspects, not the least of which was the Fountain bodies. To assist Garrett, Governor Thornton turned to the world-famous detective agency established by Allen Pinkerton in 1850. Its creepy logo featured a single human eye (with eyebrow) and the compelling motto "We Never Sleep." Pinkerton operative John C. Fraser traveled from his Denver office to Las Cruces, where he would base himself while conducting an open investigation. Fraser met with Garrett at the Lindell Hotel in El Paso on March 8. Garrett, who had been on the job less than two weeks, told Fraser what he had concluded about the case. He believed that Lee, McNew, and Gililland had held up Fountain at Chalk Hill, but as many as five men may have been involved in the plot. Garrett did not believe that Albert Fall was there, but Fall may very well have known what was happening. He felt certain the bodies would be found within five miles of the ambush site.

Although Garrett was a man of action—that reputation got him hired by Governor Thornton—he famously reserved that action for the time and place of his choosing, regardless of any outside pressure or criticism. Ever the poker player, he was extremely adept at using psychology and deception to his advantage. He had given Billy the Kid the impression that he was disinterested, and the Kid let down his guard, and that is when Pat got him. Now Garrett was concerned that the Pinkerton's activities might do more harm than good.

"I saw very plainly that he did not want me to go out and cause a stir by an open investigation," Fraser wrote in his daily report. "He told me that what he wanted me to do was to try and pull everybody off from the idea that Oliver Lee, Gililland, and McNew are the [suspected] men and to stop them from talking so much."

Garrett also cautioned Fraser that it would be impossible for a stranger to approach the Lee camp without getting shot full of holes. The outfit was cold-blooded and jumpy, he told the Pinkerton. "[I]t would be nothing for them to kill anyone whom they suspected."

As Fraser pursued the case, he became increasingly frustrated with Garrett and Perry. Garrett never volunteered anything. Any information Fraser got came from direct questions. Often, Fraser would begin to brief Garrett about having interviewed someone, and Garrett would reveal that he or Perry had already talked to the person. "[H]e is a man who says very little," Fraser wrote the governor.

Garrett remained cordial with both Fall and Lee, occasionally seeing them on the streets of Las Cruces or El Paso. On Fraser's prompting, Garrett arranged a meeting with the two men in Fall's Las Cruces law office. The attorney was quite chatty with Garrett and Fraser, freely admitting that he did not care for Fountain any more than he did a snake. He then tore into Fountain's character, something Fountain would have willingly reciprocated if still alive—their animosity toward each other had been that great. At one point, Fall passed along a scandalous rumor from a "reliable citizen who got it from someone else" that Fountain had been caught in a "compromising position" with his daughter before leaving with his young son for Lincoln, which perhaps gave credence to some reports that Fountain had left the country of his own volition (those reports were published in Fall's *Independent Democrat*). When Fraser tried to question Oliver Lee, Fall interrupted and made sure Lee did not give Fraser anything of any use to the investigation.

Governor Thornton called the Pinkertons off the case in May 1896. In July, Charles Perry, Garrett's partner in the investigation, absconded with more than $7,000 in Chaves County tax monies and reportedly ended up in Johannesburg, South Africa. Garrett finally received his appointment as Doña Ana County sheriff in August (with the help of, surprisingly enough, Albert Fall). But Garrett's term of office would expire at the end of the year, so in November, he ran for sheriff as an independent. At a Republican rally held in Las Cruces shortly before the election, Garrett won over the crowd with his "quiet wit and sarcasm," but the individual who stole the show was Miss Maggie Fountain, the daughter of Albert Fountain and sister of young Henry. Loud cheers greeted Maggie as she stepped up to the podium, but the spectators quickly grew silent when the young woman began to speak. She spoke passionately in support of Pat Garrett. Only at his hands, she told the crowd, would her father's murderers soon be brought to justice. When she finished, many in the crowd had tears in their eyes. Garrett won the election.

Garrett, now a deputy U.S. marshal as well as the county sheriff,

looked into occasional leads on the Fountain case, but little of signifi-
cance surfaced to add to the limited findings from the first few weeks
or so of the investigation. As month after month rolled by with no
progress on the Fountain case, the Territory's patience with Garrett's
slow, deliberate methods grew extremely thin. Part of Garrett's hesitation to act revolved around Albert Fall's influence over the courts.
Garrett had observed firsthand how skillfully the attorney could ma-
nipulate the system, and he did not look forward to facing Fall in
the courtroom with the evidence he then possessed. Yet Fall was not
going anywhere, or so it seemed, and when the grand jury met for
the March 1898 term of the district court, several indictments in the
Fountain murders were expected to be handed down.

A short time before the grand jury convened, Garrett stopped in
at Tobe Tipton's saloon in Tularosa. Seated at a table, deep into a
game of poker, were Oliver Lee, Albert Fall, Jeff Sanders, and George
Curry. The men asked Garrett to join them, and Garrett sat down
directly opposite Lee, who faced the door and windows. As the hours
passed, Garrett and Lee remained courteous, but little more. At various times, one or two of the players got up from the table for a bite
to eat or to take a short nap, but the game never stopped. On their
return to the table, the players often took a different seat. Not Garrett
and Lee; they always faced each other. According to Curry, the game
lasted for three days and three nights. Garrett was a serious poker
player, but it is hard to imagine he neglected his duties as sheriff for
that long. Whether it was an afternoon or seventy-two hours, when
the game finally broke up, Garrett told Curry, a good friend of Lee's,
that he had something to say to Lee and he wanted Curry to listen
in. The three went to Curry's office, where Garrett asked Lee if the
grand jury issued an indictment for him, how the sheriff should serve
the warrant.

"Pat, you'll have no trouble serving a warrant on me," Lee said. "I
have no reason or desire to resist the law."

To the surprise of many, perhaps to Garrett most of all, the grand jury met and adjourned without issuing a single indictment on the Fountain case. On April 3, an angry sheriff marched down to Judge Frank W. Parker's courtroom and petitioned the judge for bench warrants for the arrest of Lee, McNew, Gililland, and William Carr for the murder of Albert and Henry Fountain. Carr was accused of trailing the Fountains for Lee and the others. In support of his petition, Garrett filed affidavits—sworn to by himself and two members of the posse that had discovered Fountain's buckboard—that outlined the sheriff's evidence. With the warrants in hand, Garrett promptly collared McNew and Carr. The news of the warrants rapidly spread through Las Cruces, accompanied by a number of wild rumors. George Curry heard that Fall had been arrested as well, and he rushed down to the sheriff's office to see the attorney. When Curry saw Garrett, he asked if Fall was in the county jail. "No, but he ought to be," was Garrett's terse reply.

Lee and Gililland were another matter. Garrett sent a posse out to arrest them, but they could not be found. Lee was soon spotted on the streets of El Paso, where he was overheard to say that if the court would promise him a reasonable bond, he would go to Las Cruces and turn himself in, but he would not be arrested if it meant he would languish in the county jail indefinitely.

Tall and good-looking with coal-black hair and mustache and burning dark-brown eyes, Lee was also intelligent—he was said to have one of the best libraries in New Mexico. Widely recognized as a crack shot with both pistol and rifle, the thirty-two-year-old was just as dangerous as Garrett, and like Garrett, he had done his fair share of killing. He had been on the winning side in a vicious range war, eventually carving out a small cattle empire in the southern portion of the Tularosa Basin, his headquarters being his well-known ranch at the mouth of Dog Canyon. According to some, Albert Jennings Fountain being one, he built that empire at the expense of others.

Susan E. Barber, the most successful female rancher in New Mexico history, was convinced that Lee had conspired with her foreman to rob her Three Rivers ranch of a substantial number of cattle—Lee had a brand that conveniently covered Barber's. (Susan Barber was formerly Susan McSween, the widow of Lincoln County War victim Alexander McSween. She had achieved alone the fortune Scotsman McSween had dreamed of.)

On July 11, 1898, Deputy Sheriff José Espalín stopped at W. W. Cox's San Augustin Spring ranch on the east face of the Organ Mountains. He said he was looking for horses, but he had left Las Cruces that morning with Garrett and three other deputies on a mission to track down and arrest Oliver Lee and Jim Gililland. Garrett had sent Espalín to the ranch to see if he could pick up anything on the fugitives—Lee was known to be sweet on Cox's sister-in-law. Espalín got more than he bargained for when Oliver Lee, James Gililland, and A. P. "Print" Rhode, Lee's future brother-in-law, rode up. Wisely, Espalín did not try to arrest the fugitives, and Lee and Gililland did not say anything about surrendering. They exchanged pleasantries, and after a few minutes, Lee and Gililland headed off toward the low-lying Jarilla Mountains. Beyond the mountains, Lee owned a satellite ranch known as Wildy Well. Espalín left San Augustin shortly after the fugitives and hurried to Garrett's ranch, about ten miles to the north. Garrett guessed that Lee and Gililland would stop for the night at Wildy Well and ordered his deputies to mount up. Riding with Garrett, in addition to Espalín, were Clint Llewellyn, Ben Williams, and H. K. Kearney, Garrett's chief deputy.

Garrett's posse set out after sundown and did not stop once across the thirty-eight dry, hard miles to Wildy Well, arriving at about 4:30 A.M. the next day. Clustered together on an open, treeless plain were a flat-roofed adobe dwelling, a nearby frame building with an attached wooden shed, a windmill, a pumphouse, a metal water tank about eight feet in diameter, and a corral. Lee's and Gililland's horses were in the corral, as were their saddles. Garrett, who had lost none of his bravado in the years since riding down Billy the Kid, opted to go in through the front door and surprise the fugitives.

Their Winchester rifles leveled and cocked, the posse burst into a large room where they found several sleeping forms in the darkness. Garrett used the muzzle of his Winchester to poke one body and ordered the man to throw up his hands. At the same time, someone did the same with a man lying next to him. Both of them bolted upright, terrified, their hands in the air. And that is when the confusion began. The first man shouted that the person next to him was a woman, his wife, and for God's sake not to excite her, because she had some kind of a nervous constitution. The man repeated this two more times before the befuddled posse members stopped pointing their rifles at the trembling woman. Also in the room were the couple's four children. The man, James Madison, worked for Lee. The posse also discovered another man in the house, Dennis McVeigh. Garrett asked Madison where Lee and Gililland were and Madison said he had no idea, but they were not around there.

Garrett ordered Madison to take him through the cellar, which he did—and there was no Lee and Gililland. The sheriff told his men to keep cool; the fugitives had to be close. Garrett left Llewellyn in the house while he and the others explored the outbuildings. By now, the sky was beginning to fill with morning light. One of the posse saw McVeigh making hand signals to someone up on the roof of the house, and then Garrett spotted a ladder leaning up against the side of the house. Lee and Gililland, it turned out, had not taken any chances after meeting Espalín at the Cox place and had taken their bedrolls to the roof. Garrett ordered Madison to climb the ladder and tell the fugitives to surrender, but Madison had no interest in sacrificing his life for the law. Garrett could not do much with the outlaws from the ground, so he and his men clambered up on top of the shed, which was less than fifty feet away from where Lee and Gililland were. Ben Williams found a spot behind the water tank.

Kearney stood up on the shed roof, and yelled at the men to surrender—and then a split second later he inexplicably fired his Winchester at them. His shot was answered instantly with rapid gunfire, and Kearney winced in pain as a bullet struck and broke his shoulder. As he crumpled, another bullet pierced his thigh. Inside the house, Mary Madison grabbed her frightened children and raced to the cellar. Garrett fired two or three shots and then ducked down below the roofline of the frame building the shed was attached to. Lee and Gililland had the advantage because they were firing from small openings in the house's thick adobe parapet, and the possemen were crouched behind the metal roof and thin boards, which were hardly bulletproof. Garrett received several wounds to his face as the fugitives' slugs cracked and splintered the wood. At one point, Lee thought he killed the sheriff, but Garrett had ducked his head at the last second. Williams did not have it any better behind the water tank, as Lee and Gililland's well-placed bullets ripped through the tank's sheet metal, sending a flood of water on top of him.

Kearney was badly wounded, and Garrett helped him down from the roof and got him in the bed of a wagon that was inside the shed. As he comforted Kearney, two more shots plowed into the shed; one of the bullets pierced the roof and lodged in a wagon wheel next to the sheriff.

"You are a hell of a lot of bastards to order a man to throw up his hands and shoot at the same time," Lee shouted angrily when the gunfire stopped.

Garrett admitted that Kearney had fired "a little too quick."

"Are any of you hurt?" Garrett asked.

"No," Lee yelled back.

"You have got yourself in a hell of a close place," Lee said.

"I know it," Garrett replied.

Garrett tried to get them to surrender, but Lee said he had heard that Garrett intended to kill him. Garrett assured Lee that any such story was a lie; they would be perfectly safe in his hands. Lee then said that if Garrett and his posse would pull out and give the fugitives a little time to put some distance between them, he and Gililland would not shoot at any of the posse when they left their positions to retrieve their horses.

"You won't shoot us in the back, will you?" a distrustful Garrett asked.

"You know damn well we won't!" Gililland shouted back.

Kearney needed help, and even though Garrett still had Lee and Gililland outnumbered, the wanted men's fortified position made any kind of assault a suicide mission. Humiliating as it was, the best thing to do was to break off the fight for now and hope to catch up to the gunmen at another time. As the posse retreated to their horses, tied to a nearby fence, Lee said he would come to Las Cruces and turn himself in if Garrett would fix a bond for him. Garrett said he had nothing to do with Lee's bond and then rode off with his men. Sometime later, after determining that Lee and Gililland were gone, the posse came back and took Kearney by wagon to the railroad two miles away. He died from his wounds two days later. Garrett was not at his deputy's side. He had already started back after Lee and Gililland.

WILDY WELL HAD BEEN Garrett's best chance to apprehend Lee and Gililland. It was reported in El Paso that Lee withdrew a large amount of money from a bank there the day after the gunfight, July 13, and then disappeared into the remoteness of New Mexico Territory. Lee was not so remote that he could not plead his and Gililland's case in several letters to Fall's *Independent Democrat*, which championed the pair, railing against what the Democratic organ painted as a vendetta plotted by the large cattlemen and Lee's political opponents. In late September, a Doña Ana County grand jury did hand down murder indictments for Lee, Gililland, and McNew. By then, Lee had publicly said he would never be taken by Pat Garrett. Lee promised he would come in peaceably if Garrett were removed from office or defeated in the upcoming election. Garrett, running again as an independent, handily won the November contest, and Lee and Gililland continued the life of fugitives. It was a less than ideal time for them to submit to arrest anyway, because their ally, Albert B. Fall, was then serving as the captain of a regiment of New Mexico volunteers enlisted for service in the Spanish-American War. Fall had desperately wanted to see action in the Cuban campaign, but the fighting had ended so quickly that he and his men never made it out of the States. The forty-eight-year-old Garrett had also sought a military commission, but the governor, Miguel Antonio Otero, refused to grant Garrett a commission until after he had arrested Lee and Gililland.

The fugitives spent all of their time constantly looking out for New Mexico's famed manhunter, the slayer of Billy the Kid. On one occasion, Lee and some cowboys were immersed in a poker game at the Cox ranch and somehow failed to notice that a couple of cowpunchers had arrived until the two young men stepped onto the porch. Surprised, Lee and the others sprang to their feet, scattering cards, knocking chairs back, and tipping the small table over as they reached for their guns—they were that jumpy. When Lee's staunch friend, George Curry, was appointed sheriff of the newly created Otero County, Lee saw an opportunity to end their ordeal, retain their pride, and defy Pat Garrett—all at the same time. Lee sent Sheriff Curry a letter with his terms for surrender: he would not give himself up to Garrett, nor would he spend one hour in Garrett's Doña Ana County jail. As Lee expected, Curry traveled to Santa Fe and pleaded Lee and Gililland's case to Governor Otero, the man who had appointed Curry sheriff. After securing the governor's acceptance of the terms, Curry next sought out Judge Frank W. Parker in Las Cruces, who also agreed to the deal.

On the morning of March 13, 1899, Lee and Gililland boarded the southbound Santa Fe at Rincon, thirty-three miles north of Las Cruces, and took seats in the smoking car. They had heavy beards and long hair, the result of their months on the dodge. Lee also wore an uncharacteristic derby hat, one that had seen better days. Gililland concealed his eyes with a pair of wire-framed blue sunglasses. Accompanying the fugitives was their friend, a cowpoke by the name of Eugene Manlove Rhodes. Rhodes later gained fame as a writer of western fiction, his inspiration drawn from New Mexico's mesas, mountains, and deserts, and its people, larger-than-life characters like Billy the Kid, Pat Garrett, and Oliver Lee. Before boarding the train, Lee and Gililland handed their weapons over to Rhodes, so that they were essentially traveling in his custody until they surrendered to Judge Parker at Las Cruces. Lee had telegraphed Parker from Rincon that they were on their way.

The one thing Lee, Gililland, and Rhodes did not figure into their plan was Pat Garrett being on the same train. Garrett and Captain John R. Hughes of the Texas Rangers were escorting a prisoner from the territorial prison at Santa Fe to El Paso; their prisoner was chained to a seat in the same car that the fugitives and Rhodes were occupying. Garrett, of course, did not know about the secret negotiations of Sheriff Curry, and he still held warrants for the arrest of Lee and Gililland. After the train pulled out of Rincon, Garrett walked down the aisle of the smoker and stopped beside Lee, who was holding a newspaper in front of his face. Garrett stared out the window at the passing telegraph poles and beyond at the irrigated fields lining the Rio Grande. Lee's heart raced, as did those of his two companions, expecting any moment to feel Garrett's pistol sticking him in the belly. Finally, the sheriff continued down the aisle and into the next car.

When the train pulled into the station at Las Cruces, Judge Parker was waiting on the platform. The fugitives stepped off the smoking car and walked straight up to the judge, who immediately accepted their surrender. Garrett, who had stepped off the train at the same time as the fugitives, had no idea as to what had just transpired on the station platform. But when it was revealed to him that he had been riding in the same car as Lee and Gililland, he was, according to one newspaper, "considerably chagrined." Many later wondered if Garrett had in fact recognized the fugitives—perhaps he had been tipped off to Sheriff Curry's plan and chose to be on hand simply to make things interesting. Captain Hughes never believed that possible, because he knew that Garrett was so intent on apprehending Lee and Gililland he would have gladly risked death to arrest them. Garrett later told Curry that while he did not recognize the bearded men, he certainly did notice them and considered them suspicious. He had made up his mind to hold them for questioning if they had continued on the train to El Paso.

THE TRIAL OF LEE and Gililland began on May 26, 1899, at Hillsboro, New Mexico, a rapidly declining mining town in Sierra County (the defense had won a change of venue from Las Cruces). The prosecution had opted to try the accused for the murder of little Henry Fountain first. The trial of their associate, William McNew, for the murder of Albert Fountain had occurred a few weeks earlier but the Territory had decided to drop the case, fearing that an acquittal would weaken the case against Lee and Gililland. So McNew, who had been twiddling his thumbs in Garrett's jail while his buddies were on the run, was released on bail—he was still charged as an accomplice in Henry's murder. William Carr, arrested with McNew in April 1898, had been granted his freedom after a preliminary hearing failed to produce convincing evidence against him. The entire focus of the

Territory, then, was Lee and Gililland. Albert B. Fall, who had recently returned from his Spanish-American War service, headed up the defense team. The lead attorney and big gun for the Territory was the ringmaster of the Santa Fe Ring, Thomas Benton Catron.

Unlike Billy the Kid's Mesilla trial in 1881, which only grew in stature as Billy's legend grew, the Lee-Gililland trial received immediate national attention. A special telegraph line was installed between Hillsboro and the railroad, twenty miles away, so the numerous reporters present could file their stories on what happened each day. And what developed was a masterful defense by Fall, who relentlessly badgered prosecution witnesses, easily confusing them. Fall was especially merciless when it came to Jack Maxwell, the prosecution's chief witness. Maxwell claimed to have been at the Lee ranch on the day of the Fountain disappearance and to have observed the defendants arrive on jaded horses, after which they slept outside with their guns for the next two nights. But Maxwell had also signed a contract with Garrett and Perry that promised him $2,000 if he delivered information leading to the conviction of the killers. Obviously, Fall argued, the powers that be were out to get the defendants from the beginning, when they should have been searching for the "real murderers."

The one witness Fall failed to rattle was Pat Garrett. The sheriff was not the star witness, but he was a star attraction. On the day of his testimony, there was a noticeable increase of the "gentler sex" present in the courtroom. One reporter, overawed by Garrett's physical presence, described the sheriff as standing over *seven feet* in his stockings. He was, the reporter continued, the "terror of evildoers in New Mexico for a generation." Of course, any mention of Garrett in the newspapers included the obligatory reference to his fame as the killer of Billy the Kid. Garrett had a lot riding on this trial, and it was more than just the substantial reward money. He had assembled much of the evidence against the defendants, the men also responsible for the death of his deputy at Wildy Well. He firmly believed them guilty of the Fountain murders. A conviction would validate the decision to bring him back to New Mexico Territory to ferret out the killers. It would mean the Doña Ana County voters had been right to keep him in office, and it would validate his dogged detective work. It would make him something more than the slayer of the Kid.

On June 13, after seven minutes of deliberation, the jury returned a verdict of not guilty. Although evidence presented during the trial had been fairly incriminating, much of it was circumstantial. Fall had done a superb job of casting doubt on witness testimony—there were no eyewitnesses to the crime—and the victims' bodies had not been found. More than all of this, though, the trial had become something larger than the defendants, larger than the victims. It had become another battleground for Republicans and Democrats, the big cattlemen and the small ranchers, the Santa Fe Ring and those outside the Ring. When the verdict was announced, the spectators in the courtroom jumped up, clapping and cheering. Lee and Gililland were mobbed with well-wishers, receiving slaps on the back and countless handshakes. Although the Territory's prosecutors put on a good face, holding out the prospect of a future trial for the murder of Albert Fountain, they had essentially bet the house on the outcome in Hillsboro. No one would ever again face the bench for the murders of Albert and Henry Fountain, nor would Lee and Gililland ever go to trial for killing Deputy Sheriff Kearney.

Whether or not justice was served in Hillsboro will never be known with certainty. Garrett did not think so, nor did the Fountain family. Two years before, Pinkerton detective John C. Fraser had written Governor Thornton that he "felt satisfied that this entire matter will come home to Oliver Lee." Indeed, Lee remains a suspect even now. But the cattleman also had plenty of supporters, and over a ten-year period beginning in 1918, he was elected three times as a state representative and three times as a state senator. While serving in the legislature, Lee was said to have always carried a .45-caliber pistol in a holster hidden by his long dress coat. He died in 1941, and today his old Dog Canyon ranch house has been restored and is open to the public as part of the Oliver Lee Memorial State Park.

The bodies of Albert and Henry Fountain have never been found. The entire affair has earned a place as the Southwest's most enduring murder mystery.

Unwanted Star

Some folks hated him, some loved him,
but whatever he did, whatever happened
to him was always big news.

—DR. WILLIAM C. FIELD

ON FRIDAY, OCTOBER 6, 1899, Pat Garrett was sitting in his Las Cruces office when a well-dressed stranger walked in and introduced himself as Sheriff George Blalock of Greer County, Indian Territory. He was hunting a fugitive named Norman Newman, who a year before had robbed and killed Blalock's partner. Although Newman had been quickly apprehended, he had escaped from jail on July 1. Since that time Blalock had followed the outlaw across the Texas Panhandle and all over southern New Mexico, having already made three trips to the Territory. Blalock understood that Newman, who was using the alias Billy Reed, was currently employed as a cook at W. W. Cox's San Augustin Spring ranch. Blalock showed Garrett a warrant for Newman's arrest that he had earlier sworn out at the Doña Ana County courthouse, and he asked for help in apprehending the fugitive.

Garrett called for his deputy, José Espalín, and the three set out for the Cox place. Blalock warned Garrett that Newman was a desperate character and they had to be prepared for a fight—Garrett knew the type. He decided they would surround the house and approach it from opposite sides. Newman did not know Garrett, so he thought it best if he went in and confronted the outlaw. No one at the Cox place noticed the officers closing in on the structure except for two of Cox's little girls in the yard, and as they easily recognized Garrett, they paid him no mind. The twenty-five-year-old Newman was standing in the kitchen, just having finished washing the dishes and wiping his hands on a towel.

"Are you Mr. Reed?" Garrett asked.

"Yes."

"My name is Garrett. I am sheriff of this county and have a warrant for you."

"All right, Mr. Garrett," Newman calmly replied.

Garrett reached out with his handcuffs, and the next thing he knew, Newman had punched him in the head. Garrett grabbed hold of Newman, who lunged through the kitchen's open French door, dragging the two-hundred-pound Garrett out with him. Espalín ran up to the door and shoved his pistol in Newman's face and shouted at him to stop. Garrett ordered Espalín not to shoot the man, who continued to struggle. Espalín turned his six-shooter around and struck Newman a sharp blow or two on the head with the pistol's butt, causing him to collapse, taking Garrett down with him. The two officers held on tight, and Garrett fished again for his handcuffs. It was then that an aged bulldog named Old Booze saw the fight, charged across the yard and, growling and snapping his teeth, leapt on Espalín. The deputy let go of Newman and did his best to fight off the crazy dog, cursing, yelling, and kicking at the animal.

With only Garrett holding him, Newman sprang to his feet, fighting and throwing punches at the sheriff. He finally broke free of Garrett's grasp when his shirt tore apart, leaving Garrett clutching the tattered pieces of fabric. Garrett and Espalín chased after Newman and ordered him to halt. The outlaw went in the house and ran down a hall toward his room when Espalín, assuming that Newman was going for his gun, blasted him with two shots to the back. Newman fell forward, a dead man.

The coroner's inquest in Las Cruces exonerated all three lawmen of any wrongdoing. Sheriff Blalock transported Newman's body back to Greer County, Oklahoma, for burial. But when the sheriff went to apply for the reward on the outlaw, it was pointed out that the governor had offered the reward for Newman's "arrest and conviction." Garrett knew all about that, too.

This incident did not endear Garrett to the Cox crowd, who had taken a liking to the young Newman. Cox's wife, pregnant at the time, had been in the pantry when Garrett came after Newman in the kitchen. Her brother, Print Rhode, was so mad about the deadly scuffle and shooting—which could have injured his sister and the Cox girls—that he threatened to kill Garrett on sight. Rhode, whose full name was Archie Prentice Rhode, had been born to a dry goods merchant in Lavaca County, Texas, in July 1868. At about the age of twenty, he had traveled to southern New Mexico with the family of W. W. "Bill" Cox. He was stocky, with strong arms and hands, standing nearly five and a half feet tall and weighing around 140 pounds. He had pale blue eyes and a light, sandy complexion that easily burned in New Mexico's intense sunlight. When he was not wearing his wide-brimmed hat, it was plainly evident that Rhode's reddish brown hair was fast disappearing from his forehead.

One old-timer remembered Rhode as someone who wanted to be a tough guy and had a hard time getting along with folks. That did not seem to be a problem with the Cox clan, who thought he was dependable and fiercely loyal. That loyalty also found its way to Oliver Lee, who married Winnie Rhode in October 1898, making Lee a

brother-in-law of both Bill Cox and Print Rhode. Rhode, in fact, took
the stand for Lee at the Hillsboro trial. Pat Garrett was a neighbor
so Bill Cox tried to stay on friendly terms with the lawman and his
family, but Rhode did not care for Garrett, and the sheriff, who had
dealt with a number of outlaw wannabes, felt the same way about
Rhode. The two had even more reason to dislike each other after the
robbery of the George D. Bowman & Son Bank in Las Cruces on
February 12, 1900.

That anyone would dare rob a bank in Garrett's town in broad
daylight seems beyond foolhardy, but then again, criminals are not
always known for their intelligence. Still, William Wilson and Oscar
Wilbur nearly pulled it off. After riding into Las Cruces and sticking their guns in the face of the bank's cashier, they quickly collected
more than $1,000 in greenbacks and then calmly walked out the door
and got back on their horses. They slowly rode away until someone
in town fired two pistol shots to sound the alarm. The robbers then
spurred their mounts into a gallop and struck out to the east toward
the Organ Mountains. Twenty minutes later, Garrett started two
posses—with Deputy Ben Williams leading one while Garrett rode
in front of the other. The posses had no luck tracking down the suspects the first day, but by the end of the next day, six men had been
arrested who either fit the robbers' descriptions or were thought to be
connected in some way to the holdup. None of the bank's money was
found, and all six were soon released. Garrett and his men continued
to scour the Organs for the robbers, but by the end of the week, they
seemed to have gotten away.

Wilson and Wilbur did get away, but not clean. Garrett was given
a tip that told him who the robbers might be, as well as information
that they had been living in Hanover, in Grant County. Garrett sent
Ben Williams there to investigate, and the deputy found out that Wilbur's wife had told her friends a short time before the robbery that she
was moving to San Antonio. Williams traveled to San Antonio, nearly

six hundred miles from Las Cruces, where he soon located Wilson and Wilbur, and, with the help of a local deputy sheriff, captured them. Once back in Las Cruces, Wilbur turned state's evidence on the promise of a lesser sentence. He said that Print Rhode and Will Cravens had provided the horses for the robbery and that they had been paid $100 each as their share. On March 22, Rhode and Cravens were arrested and charged as accessories to robbery. They were released after each posted a $1,000 bond.

The four men's cases were brought before the court on April 20. Both Wilbur and Wilson pled guilty and awaited their sentence while Rhode and Cravens pled not guilty. Judge Parker presided over the four-day trial of Rhode and Cravens, and, once again, Garrett had to sit still while he heard the defense attorney, Albert B. Fall, ridicule a case he had put together. Fall was not the prosecution's biggest worry, however. Their primary problem was Wilson, who contradicted all of Wilbur's claims concerning Rhode and Cravens's involvement. Garrett took the stand and did his best to vouch for the truthfulness of Wilbur's confession, but at that point, even if Honest Abe Lincoln had come back from the dead, he would have had trouble overcoming the doubt cast in the minds of the jury. Rhode and Cravens were found not guilty. Garrett was not happy, but at least he had put two of the robbers away.

PAT GARRETT PROBABLY COULD have held the sheriff's position in Doña Ana County for the rest of his life, but he chose not to run again in 1900. He told a newspaper reporter that times had changed in the Territory, and the sheriff's office no longer needed his "peculiar talents in the line of good marksmanship and quick action at the head of posses." Polinaria and the children may have had something to do with his decision, and there was also his ranch and his mining investments that could always use more of his attention. His decision is puzzling, though, because the sheriff's office provided a steady income, and the way Garrett liked to gamble—both at the poker table and in business—the Garrett family definitely needed that income. Nevertheless, Garrett's term as sheriff expired on December 31, 1900, after which he retired to private life—for just twelve months.

In December 1901, Pat Garrett's name was once again in the nation's press, and in a very big way. Teddy Roosevelt, the hero of San Juan Hill ("that damned cowboy" to his critics), became the nation's president after the assassination of President William McKinley, and as the position of collector of customs at El Paso was set to expire at the end of the year, Roosevelt decided to put his own man in the position. He soon set his sights on ex-lawman Garrett.

It is unknown how Garrett's name first came into consideration, but El Paso was practically his second home (not really a good thing), where his penchant for stiff-bosomed shirts, high collars, and Prince Albert coats had earned him the nickname "dandy sheriff." Garrett likely learned that the present collector would not be reappointed and began building support to get the nomination. By December 5, he was on a train to Washington, D.C., to lobby the president in person. Traveling with him was nemesis-turned-strange-bedfellow Albert B. Fall. In a highly sensational move, Fall had switched from the Democratic to the Republican Party after the 1900 elections. Once in Washington, Garrett and Fall stepped up the pressure on the president, by making sure he received written endorsements and telegrams, as well as visits from prominent New Mexico politicians—all good Republicans, of course. On December 9, Garrett met with an old associate from New Mexico's bloody outlaw days: Lew Wallace.

"He said he would do anything I asked him to do," Garrett wrote Polinaria about the meeting, "says I did him a great favor once (in the 'Kid' affair), so he is anxious to express his gratitude."

Wallace went with Garrett to the White House, after which several newspapers reported that Roosevelt had decided on Garrett for the collector of customs and that the president would send the appointment to the Senate. Texas Republicans were not pleased, feeling that the post should go to a Texan. Telegrams began to pour in opposing Garrett's nomination. Many in the anti-Garrett crowd claimed that the ex-lawman was unfit for the office; others attacked his character. One letter writer argued that the appointment of a man who had made a record for himself as a killer would reflect poorly on Roosevelt's administration.

Garrett visited the White House once again on December 15 to make his final appeal for the El Paso post.

"Garrett, they say you're a drunkard," Roosevelt said, bluntly.

"It isn't true, Mr. President. But I've been drinking all my life."

"You are charged with being a gambler," Roosevelt added.

"I know the difference between a straight and a flush, Mr. President, and in my section of the country, a man who doesn't know this doesn't know enough to keep the flies off in fly season."

"I am told you are an atheist and an infidel."

"I have pronounced views on some subjects, Mr. President, but I know enough to keep them to myself when they don't agree with the men around me."

Roosevelt liked the straight-shooting Garrett and forwarded his appointment to the Senate, where it was soon confirmed. On December 20, Roosevelt invited Garrett back to the White House for the signing ceremony. The president signed Garrett's commission with a gorgeous gold-clad and engraved Wirt fountain pen. Handing the pen to the ex-lawman, Roosevelt looked his new collector in the eye and said, "Mr. Garrett, I am betting on you."

"Mr. President, you will win that bet," Garrett replied, a proud smile breaking across his face.

THIS APPOINTMENT OF PAT GARRETT created a surge of new interest in the story of Billy the Kid. A reporter for the *Silver City Enterprise* hunted up sixty-four-year-old Harvey Whitehill, former sheriff of Grant County, and prodded him for his recollections of the Kid, which White-hill gladly gave. An El Paso reporter tried to do the same with Garrett, but he had no interest in revisiting that part of his life for the press. When the reporter asked him where he might find a copy of Garrett's *The Authentic Life of Billy, the Kid*, Garrett refused to tell him. "The new collector, if he has his way," wrote the reporter, "will bury the event."

Garrett had buried Billy back in 1881, but there was no way he could bury the legend that was already taking on a life of its own. The Kid was a double-edged sword for Garrett. The ex-sheriff's reputation and fame had been established by hunting down and killing Billy. That act put many people in Garrett's debt, not the least of whom was Lew Wallace, who easily could have ignored Garrett's request for assistance in swaying the president. It was, in fact, Garrett's reputation as the killer of Billy the Kid that got the attention of Roosevelt, who was famously infatuated with the American West. But at the same time, the Kid cast a dark shadow over Garrett. He had never been able to escape the accusations that he was nothing but a coward and a murderer. This, coupled with Americans' fondness for transforming their outlaws into heroes, left Garrett exasperated and, at times, bitter.

Garrett's presidential appointment finally gave him a status and respectability he had not known as a county sheriff. The El Paso cus-tomhouse monitored a flood of goods coming from Mexico, every-thing from livestock to tourists' trinkets. The annual duties collected amounted to some $40,000. Unfortunately, Garrett did not have the autonomy in his new position he had known as sheriff. There were plenty of critics, disgruntled about his appointment, and politically sensitive Washington bureaucrats watching his every move. Com-plaints against Garrett's interpretation of Treasury Department rules soon appeared in the newspapers. One story, which ran under the headline "Made the General Pay," reported on how Garrett refused

Pat Garrett as collector of customs, El Paso, circa 1903.

to refund the duties collected of General Harrison Gray Otis for items he was bringing into the United States as gifts for his grandchildren. Otis, editor of the *Los Angeles Times,* filed a protest with the Treasury Department. A much bigger flap, however, came over Garrett's appraisal of three-thousand-plus cattle imported by the Corralitos Ranch of Casas Grandes, Mexico. The cattle company vigorously protested the duties charged by Garrett, who ended up traveling to New York City to argue the case before the Board of Appraisers—not very successfully.

Other complaints revolved around Garrett's alleged lack of "tact and common politeness" in performing his duties. It is easy to imagine the fifty-three-year-old Garrett, who was once *the* law in New Mexico, exhibiting a decided lack of patience, even a short temper, with anyone who attempted to get around their customs duties, sought some personal favor, or simply argued with him about a decision. The Treasury secretary reprimanded Garrett via letter, essentially ordering him to be more polite. Garrett was outraged. But he received an even harsher rebuke from the secretary after he got into a fistfight with a former customhouse employee, George M. Gaither. Garrett had been forced to accept Gaither as a temporary inspector because of the criticism over Garrett's cattle appraisals, a sore point with the collector. Gaither's appointment was for a thirty-day trial period, and Garrett had no intention of keeping the man at the customhouse a single minute after the trial period expired. But after Gaither was dismissed, he went about El Paso claiming that Garrett had reneged on a promise of a full-time job. When Garrett ran into Gaither on the street, he called the man a goddamned liar—Garrett hated liars— and that was when the fistfight broke out. This made the papers as well, but Garrett still held on to his collectorship.

What many believed finally cost Garrett his job occurred in San Antonio in April 1905. President Roosevelt was visiting the home of the Alamo for a reunion of his famed regiment of Rough Riders. He had invited Garrett to join him there and to sit at his table at an outdoor lunch planned for the Rough Riders. But Garrett brought along as a guest his good friend Tom Powers, the owner of a saloon and gambling establishment called The Coney Island, which was Garrett's favorite watering hole in El Paso. Garrett even arranged to have a photograph taken of himself and Powers with the president. But Garrett did not tell the president anything regarding Powers's well-known reputation as a professional gambler, and when Roosevelt found out later, he was extremely upset. Eight months later, as Garrett's four-year term as collector was coming to an end, he learned that Roosevelt had decided not to reappoint him.

Roosevelt told Garrett and others that the Powers incident had not had anything to do with his decision, but there is no question that it put an end to Garrett's political career. First, the Texas Republicans had never forgiven Roosevelt's administration for not giving the collectorship to a Texan. Then there was the icy relationship between Garrett and the Treasury secretary. The secretary told the president that Garrett had been an inefficient collector, and that he had heard reports from El Paso that Garrett was often absent from his post, was in debt, and had not curbed his gambling and drinking. Last, Roosevelt had not fared well in the press for handing government appointments to men with what were perceived to be notorious pasts. His appointment of Bat Masterson as a deputy U.S. marshal for New York had prompted the *New York Evening World* to write, "The President likes killers."

As soon as Garrett realized his job was in jeopardy, he rushed to Washington to plead his case with Roosevelt. Against the advice of friends, Garrett insisted on taking Tom Powers with him. Powers had considerable influence in El Paso, and he somehow believed he could help his friend with the president. But Roosevelt would not see Powers, though Garrett stuck up for his friend, telling the president that he would gladly introduce Powers to anyone. Even so, it quickly became

Garrett with President Theodore Roosevelt at the San Antonio Rough Riders reunion, 1905. Tom Powers is the man in the Stetson, second from the right.

clear to Garrett that the president had already made up his mind. The *Washington Post* noted that Garrett looked dejected after visiting the White House and in other ways exhibited "the bitterness of defeat." In a last-ditch effort, Garrett's writer friend Emerson Hough wrote a letter, pleading with Roosevelt, even promising that Garrett's resignation would be on the president's desk no later than July 1, 1906. This six-month reprieve would allow Garrett to maintain his pride and say he left the job himself. By the time Hough wrote his letter, Roosevelt had appointed a Texas Republican to take Garrett's place.

When he returned to Texas, Garrett answered a few questions from a Fort Worth reporter about his future prospects. "I have a ranch in New Mexico," he said. "And I will go there for a time. Just what my future plans will be I do not know. However, I am going to do something and don't expect to remain idle. I have no complaint to make against anyone for my removal. I simply take my medicine."

GARRETT HAD LITTLE TIME to dwell on this. By January 1, 1906, he was in Santa Rosalía (present-day Camargo), Chihuahua, Mexico, investigating a brutal slaying involving an American rancher named O. E. Finstad. The Mexican authorities believed that Finstad had murdered his brother-in-law and another man; Finstad said they were attacked by "assassins." Garrett, who was licensed to practice law in Mexico, had been employed by either Finstad or, more likely, Mrs. Finstad to help with the defense. The Finstads no doubt believed that Garrett's notoriety as a lawman would bring attention to their case, and it did. Garrett conducted his own investigation and determined that Finstad and his associates were assaulted by Mexican bandits. He then appealed directly to President Roosevelt, asking for the American government's assistance in the case. But despite Garrett's efforts, which were substantial, the Mexican court convicted Finstad in early March and sentenced the rancher to twelve years in the penitentiary. It was Garrett's one and only Mexican legal case.

Garrett was always looking for the big "trade," the deal that would make him thousands of dollars all at once. The Finstad case had simply represented some quick cash, but while Garrett was in Mexico, he thought he found the next moneymaker: a silver mine in Chihuahua. Garrett wrote Emerson Hough in Chicago that the property could be acquired for $50,000 in cash and $50,000 in stocks. If Hough could interest some of his friends, Garrett believed they would all make a handsome profit. But Garrett had not had the best of luck with earlier mining speculations in New Mexico, and it is unlikely that he was able to convince Hough or his Chicago associates. And like most of Garrett's friends, Hough knew the ex-lawman was in debt—to just about everyone.

Some of Garrett's debts had been outstanding for years, and instead of using the income from his El Paso collectorship to pay down his creditors, he had used it to speculate, gamble, and, incredibly enough, help out any friends who were a little short. When Thomas B. Catron sent an outstanding Garrett note to El Paso for collection, three banks refused it. They had plenty of their own notes against him.

"He might pay for politics or for some other reason of that kind," Catron was advised, "but he pays no one down here. He figures in lots of deals, but do not think he puts up a cent in any of them."

Just a few days after Garrett wrote to Hough about the Chihuahua mining scheme, the Doña Ana County sheriff seized all of Garrett's property, including the family home on his Black Mountain ranch (near San Augustin Pass), so that it could be offered at public auction. This was the result of a long-running legal tussle with an Albuquerque bank over a debt Garrett had incurred sixteen years earlier when he cosigned a $1,000 promissory note for George Curry. In the end, Garrett retained some control of his land, not because he paid up, but because he had already mortgaged most of it, and his "homestead" was protected by New Mexico statute. The livestock he had not mortgaged or snuck off his property was sold to pay his back taxes.

Louis B. Bentley, who owned a store in Organ, kept a small, leather-bound book upon which he had scratched the words *Dead Beats*. The book contained the names Pat Garrett and two of his children, Poe and Annie; Garrett owed Bentley $35.30. In Las Cruces, Garrett had also stopped paying his bill at the May Brothers Grocery, although he continued to buy his foodstuffs there. When Albert Fall learned about the situation and asked the grocers why they did not demand payment, they said they did not want any trouble and were afraid to cut Garrett off. In a remarkable gesture, Fall decided it was not right for the grocers to suffer this debt, and he and another man shared the cost of Garrett's groceries. Fall truly felt sorry for Garrett, an extremely proud man who was fast becoming a penniless has-been.

"I don't know how you are fixed," Fall wrote to Garrett in December 1906, "but suppose you are broke as usual, so I enclose a check for fifty dollars which amount you can return to me if your stock, which I have turned over to the Bank, goes to par or above."

A couple of weeks later, Garrett wrote Fall: "I have got into a fix where it seems impossible for me to get along without using the $50 I was to send to you. . . . Be patient with me and I will try and never do wrong again."

But things suddenly looked up for Garrett when Roosevelt announced in April 1907 that he was appointing George Curry the next governor of New Mexico Territory. Rumors floated about Las Cruces that Curry would make Garrett the superintendent of the territorial penitentiary at Santa Fe. An excited Garrett wrote to Polinaria from El Paso, asking her to send him his dress suit and Prince Albert coat. Not only was Garrett going to attend Curry's inauguration in Santa Fe, but Curry had invited Garrett to go to Washington with him. "He will do anything he can for me," Garrett wrote about Curry. "I am going to try hard to do something and feel very much encouraged." But Garrett was doomed for another disappointment. Curry did not come through with the prison appointment, nor did he really do anything to assist Garrett in a substantial way—odd considering that Curry was partly, if not entirely, responsible for Garrett's trouble with the Albuquerque bank.

By the end of August, Garrett had begun another business scheme. The *Rio Grande Republican* announced that he had become a partner in an El Paso real estate firm. How Garrett insinuated himself into this partnership is unknown, but it gave him yet another reason to make frequent visits to the border town. During Garrett's entire term as collector of customs, he had kept his family in New Mexico, and they remained there still, either at a house in Las Cruces or at the Black Mountain ranch. For extended periods, Polinaria was left alone to take care of their children, of whom the youngest, Jarvis, was just two years old. Garrett's favorite El Paso hangout was Powers's Coney Island saloon, where he was known to frequently buy a round of drinks for the house. Just as well known, it seems, was that Garrett spent his nights with a prostitute while in El Paso, a woman remembered only as Mrs. Brown. Emerson Hough may have been referring to this relationship when he wrote to President Roosevelt in December 1905, and said he knew of "only one sort of indiscretion of which Garrett has been guilty. This has nothing to do with his integrity. Would rather not state this but can do so if necessary."

There is no question that Pat Garrett deeply loved his wife, Polinaria, and his children—his numerous letters to his family reveal a man who was devoted, doting, and, more often than not, worried— but Garrett also led another life away from his family, and that other life drained his already shattered finances and compounded his rapidly deteriorating mental state.

AS WINTER SET IN and, little by little, the days became shorter and cooler, Garrett became more bitter, angry, desperate, and depressed. Earlier in the year, he had written Hough that "Everything seems to go wrong with me." By February 1908, the thing most wrong in Garrett's mind involved a young cowpoke named Wayne Brazel. Born Jesse Wayne Brazel in December 1876, Brazel had gone to work at Cox's San Augustin Spring ranch at age fourteen, and it was said that Bill Cox treated the boy like a son. He grew up to be a big, good-natured, albeit slow, cowhand, who did not have an enemy in the world. He did not even carry a gun. Albert B. Fall employed Brazel to take care of his horses at his ranch, just east of the Garrett place. More often than not, though, Brazel was looking after Fall's children, who adored the young man. On days when the weather forced everyone inside, they sat at his knee while he spun some wild tale to their immense delight. He taught one of the little Fall girls to say,

"By-golly-gosh-darn-double-duce-damn," explaining that that simple line of cussing was all one needed to get through life. Remembering back years later, Fall's daughter, Alexina, thought Brazel was a little feebleminded.

Brazel generally wore a black, broad-brimmed Stetson with a high crown that he pulled down close to his ears. His ruddy face was invariably clean shaven, and he kept his sandy hair cropped short. A scar ran down from the right corner of his mouth and over his chin. It came from either a knife cut, boyhood horseplay with his brother, or from being thrown by a bronc—take your pick. He got crossways with Pat Garrett after leasing the Bear Canyon ranch from Garrett's twenty-five-year-old son, Poe, in March 1907. The Bear Canyon ranch was situated in the San Andres Mountains a few miles north of Garrett's Black Mountain ranch, and although the lease agreement between Poe and Brazel clearly states that the ranch belonged to Poe, most contemporary accounts agree that it was Pat Garrett's property, and Garrett certainly acted as if the ranch belonged to him. Garrett no longer had any stock to put on the place, and as he was intent on building his herds back up, he came up with a deal that said each year Brazel would give him ten heifer calves and one mare colt in exchange for the five-year lease. Garrett later claimed that Brazel said he was going to put three hundred to four hundred cattle on the place, but instead of cattle, Brazel moved in a herd of more than twelve hundred goats. Garrett was furious; five years with that many goats nibbling the sparse grass to bare nubs would spoil the place for all other livestock. Garrett was also upset to learn that his neighbor, Bill Cox, had fronted the money for the operation. Worse still, though—Print Rhode was Brazel's partner in the goat herd.

Garrett tried to get the lease voided in court. He went to see the justice of the peace in Organ and swore out arrest warrants for both Brazel and Rhode based on an antiquated New Mexico statute that made it illegal to herd livestock closer than a mile and a half to a house

Wayne Brazel (seated) with Jim Lee and Will
Cravens. Brazel had shaved his head as a joke.

or settlement. The hearing took place in an Organ butcher shop in
January 1908 and drew a large crowd; some of the onlookers, relatives
and friends of the accused, were armed and tempers ran high. Rhode
tried to pick a fight with Garrett, but as Print's brother, Sterling, remembered, "Pat was too smart for it." In a rather anticlimactic move,
the justice dismissed the case—just one more thing that went wrong
for Garrett. Soon there was talk that Garrett, Brazel, and Rhode were
making threats against one another. Someone even overheard Garrett
say that "they" would get him unless he got them first.

Garrett became more brutish and quarrelsome than ever. He got into three or four fistfights in Las Cruces, and at fifty-seven years of age, the ex-sheriff came out of each one in worse shape than the one before. One day he wrote the governor in desperation: "Dear Curry: I am in a hell of a fix. I have been trying to sell my ranch, but no luck. For God's sake, send me fifty dollars."

But then something happened to offer the perfect solution to Garrett's headache with the Bear Canyon outfit. Garrett was approached by James B. Miller in El Paso with an offer to buy the ranch. Miller told Garrett he had purchased a thousand head of Mexican cattle and they were to be delivered to El Paso on March 15. Although he had a ranch in Oklahoma, Miller preferred not to ship the cattle there until the fall and needed a place not far from El Paso to graze them. Garrett was not about to let this opportunity slip by because of a cussed herd of goats. He went to Brazel and talked the cowpoke into going to El Paso to see what might be worked out with Miller. After a short meeting, Brazel agreed to give up his lease as long as a buyer could be found for his goats. Miller found a buyer, his partner Carl Adamson, who also happened to be related to Miller by marriage. Adamson would take all twelve hundred goats at $3.50 apiece. Brazel returned to Bear Canyon and carefully counted his herd—instead of twelve hundred, he had eighteen hundred. Adamson was unwilling to buy that many, and Brazel was unwilling to give up the lease unless he did. Nevertheless, Adamson agreed to meet with Garrett and Brazel in Las Cruces to see if they could all come to some kind of agreement to save the deal.

Adamson traveled to Garrett's ranch on February 28 and spent the night, and Garrett sent a note to Brazel that the meeting was still on for the next day. The next morning, a Saturday, Garrett got up early and took what was said to be "unusual care" dressing himself. At about 8:30 A.M., Garrett said good-bye to Polinaria and the children and stepped into the two-horse top buggy with Adamson. He placed beside him a rather unusual folding shotgun manufactured by the

Burgess Gun Company of Buffalo, New York. Specifically designed for law officers, the 12 gauge, when folded, fit into a custom leather holster that allowed the wearer to quickly draw the gun and flip up its barrel into a locked position, ready to fire. This particular Burgess bore an inscription that identified the weapon as having belonged to Robert G. Ross of the El Paso Police Department. Ross had died of complications from appendicitis in 1899, and Garrett apparently bought the gun from the man's widow.

Garrett grabbed the leather reins and slapped them against the rumps of the team, and they scooted off down the dirt track leading away from his ranch. At the Walter livery stable, about a half mile west of the Organ store and post office, Garrett drove the buggy right into the corral and up to the water trough so the horses could drink. The day had begun to warm up, but Garrett was still wearing his signature Prince Albert coat. Garrett spotted the fifteen-year-old Walter boy, Willis, hitching some horses to a box wagon and asked if the young man had seen Brazel. Willis pointed down the road at the wisp of dust still hanging in the air and said he had just left. Garrett waited for his horses to finish their drink and then backed the team up and started them down the road to Las Cruces. Willis watched them for a moment as they drove out of sight and then returned to hitching his horses.

About two hours later, Deputy Sheriff Felipe Lucero sat at his desk in Las Cruces thinking he needed to get some lunch. Suddenly, the office door burst open and in stepped a visibly distressed Wayne Brazel.

"Lock me up," Brazel stammered. "I've just killed Pat Garrett!"

Deputy Lucero laughed at Brazel and accused him of pulling his leg. But Brazel insisted that he had shot Garrett, and Lucero, after pausing a moment to carefully study the man, decided he was serious. After locking Brazel in a cell, Lucero stepped outside to see Adamson, who was waiting in the buggy just as Brazel said he would be. Adamson confirmed Brazel's story and Lucero retrieved the revolver that

Brazel had surrendered to Adamson. The sheriff then put Brazel's horse in the stable and saddled up his own. Lucero had Adamson follow him in the buggy as he rounded up a coroner's jury, which was not hard to do, as there were now several excited people out in the street dumbfounded at the news of Garrett's death. Within a short time, Lucero led Adamson and the seven-man jury out of town, accompanied by Dr. William C. Field. The group rode in an easterly direction toward the storied Organ Mountains, their jagged, serrated peaks like one great claw reaching up to scratch the sky.

After traveling approximately five miles, they came upon Garrett's body next to the road in the bottom of the wide Alameda Arroyo. Someone carefully removed the lap robe Adamson had used to partially cover the corpse. Garrett was lying on his back, his arms outspread and one knee drawn up. About three feet from the body and parallel to it was Garrett's Burgess shotgun, still folded and in its holster. Dr. Field noticed that there was no sand kicked up around the holstered gun, suggesting that it had been carefully placed there. Field and the jury also noted that Garrett's trousers were unbuttoned, and although he wore a heavy driving glove on his right hand, his left hand was bare. Two bullet wounds were identified, one in the head and the other in the upper part of the stomach.

After Garrett's body was taken to H. C. Strong's undertaking parlors in Las Cruces, Field conducted a careful autopsy and found that the bullet to the head entered from behind—the doctor discovered several of Garrett's hairs pushed into the entry wound. The bullet exited just over the right eye. Field also determined that the bullet in Garrett's stomach ranged up through his body, suggesting that the bullet had been fired when Garrett was on the ground or falling down. Field found this bullet behind the shoulder and cut it out. One other item of interest was discovered, probably by undertaker Strong as he undressed the body: a check made out to Patrick F. Garrett in the amount of $50 and signed by Governor George Curry.

News of Garrett's death flashed across the nation's telegraph wires, with many newspapers running the story in their Sunday editions. These first published reports repeated what both Brazel and Adamson had told the deputy sheriff and the coroner's jury: Brazel fired his pistol in self-defense when he saw Garrett go for his shotgun. First thing on Monday, Poe Garrett filed an affidavit against Brazel, charging him with the murder of his father. A preliminary hearing took place the next day, with the Territory's attorney general, James M. Hervey, handling the questioning for the prosecution. There were high hopes that Carl Adamson's testimony would provide some answers to exactly what had happened that day in the arroyo, but he was somewhat of a disappointment. Adamson testified that he and Garrett overtook Brazel about three-quarters of a mile from Organ. When they first spotted the cowboy, Brazel had been talking to someone in the road, but by the time they caught up to him, he was alone. The three continued on together, with Brazel sometimes riding alongside the buggy and at other times falling behind by a hundred yards or so. At a certain point, as Brazel was riding alongside, the conversation turned to the goats. The talk began calmly enough, Adamson recalled, but soon became heated as Garrett berated Brazel for somehow underestimating his herd by six hundred goats. Brazel tersely repeated his position that unless he could sell all of the goats, the deal was off.

Adamson, who claimed he was driving the buggy, said that Garrett and Brazel argued for about fifteen minutes as he guided the team along at a walk.

"Well, I don't care whether you give up possession or not," he remembered Garrett saying. "I can get you off there anyway."

"I don't know whether you can or not," Brazel replied.

At this point, Adamson suddenly felt a need to urinate, so he pulled back on the reins and brought the team to a halt. After handing the reins to Garrett, he stepped out of the buggy on the right side, walked near the front of the team, turned away from Brazel and Garrett, and unbuttoned his trousers. Brazel had stopped his horse a few feet forward of the buggy, reining his horse around a bit so that he was facing Garrett sideways, on the buggy's left side.

Adamson next heard Garrett say in a high-pitched voice, "God damn you, I will put you off now!"

A second or two later, Adamson was startled by a "racket" followed by a gunshot. He spun around to see Garrett stagger and fall backward. He then saw Brazel, pistol in hand, fire a second shot. The second shot had come, Adamson said, just as quickly as a man can cock a pistol and shoot it.

The team jumped at the sound of the gunfire, but Adamson quickly grabbed the lines and wrapped them around the hub of one of the buggy wheels. Adamson then ran around the vehicle just in time to see Garrett stretch out his body and make a grunting noise. The famed lawman died without saying a word.

"This is hell," Brazel said. "What must I do?"

Adamson told Brazel he better surrender to him. After covering Garrett's body and tying Brazel's horse to the back of the buggy, the two hurried to Las Cruces and the sheriff's office. Adamson remembered that Brazel "seemed as cool as any man I ever saw as we drove into town."

In the courtroom, Brazel appeared nervous and uncomfortable. His attorneys chose not to put him on the stand at the hearing, preferring to wait for the grand jury to take up the case. Bail was set at $10,000, which was promptly guaranteed by seven men, among them Bill Cox. Just one hour after the hearing, Brazel was walking the streets of Las Cruces.

Garrett's body remained in state at Strong's parlors for six days, where it was "viewed by thousands of people." The funeral occurred on Thursday, March 6. It had been delayed for twenty-four hours to give two of Garrett's brothers time to travel to Las Cruces from Louisiana. Governor Curry and Tom Powers were among the six pallbearers. Powers, the El Paso friend Garrett stuck by at great cost to himself, also read the funeral sermon, which was a eulogy originally delivered by Robert J. Ingersoll, the famed orator and agnostic, over the grave of his brother. This choice for a tribute, as well as the speaker (Powers was also an agnostic), only seemed to confirm many people's suspicion that Garrett was an atheist.

Nevertheless, few of Garrett's friends and family would argue with the eulogy's concluding sentence: "There was, there is, no gentler, stronger, manlier man." Garrett's body was interred at the Odd Fellows cemetery outside of Las Cruces.

Before and after the funeral, Garrett's friends and family fumed about what they considered to be not only a murder, but a conspiracy. It was clear to them and others that Garrett's death had not occurred the way Brazel and Adamson described it. For one thing, it was obvious that Garrett, too, had been urinating when he was killed—he had been found with his trousers unbuttoned and his glove off his left hand. And Garrett's assassin, whether it was Brazel or someone else, had shot him from behind because the first bullet, they believed, had been to the back of Garrett's head. They were also suspicious of the several men connected with the affair, and with good reason. James B. "Jim" Miller had an unsavory reputation as a killer—but not just any killer. Dr. J. J. Bush of El Paso, a friend of Garrett's, wrote Governor Curry with a chilling assessment of Miller, whom he claimed to have known intimately for years.

"[H]e is today the most dangerous man in the whole Southwest. He is deep and burrows beneath the surface like a mole. He is either an open face-to-face gun fighter or a midnight assassin as the case may be. He is a chief of conspirators and a planner of dark deeds."

Bush told Curry he had recently learned that a half brother of Oliver Lee said that Miller was Garrett's killer. "I doubt it," Bush wrote, "but I do not for a moment doubt that he knew Garrett was going to be killed." Understandably, Bush asked Curry to destroy his letter as soon as it was read. Instead Governor Curry filed it.

Disturbing as it was, Bush's description of Miller was actually dead-on. Miller, who had a reputation as an impeccable dresser, was believed to have killed at least seven men, but the number was generally thought to be much higher. At the age of eighteen, he was arrested for the murder of his grandparents in Coryell County, Texas, although he had never gone to trial for the crime. And he was related by marriage to notorious Texas gunfighters John Wesley Hardin and Mannen Clements. Garrett, as a former lawman and a fair judge of men himself, should have known about Miller and his background because Miller was well known to many El Pasoans. If Garrett did know whom he was dealing with, perhaps it was a sign of his desperation that he was willing to do business with such a shady figure. But then again, Garrett had dealt with many bad men and questionable characters during his career. Everyone had a past.

Questions also arose about the man Brazel was talking to on the road before Adamson and Garrett caught up to him. Adamson testified that he did not recognize the man, and there is no evidence that Brazel ever said who this was. There were rumors that it was Print Rhode. An anonymous letter sent to Annie Garrett accused Rhode of having played a role in the murder. Mailed from Las Cruces, the mysterious letter was handwritten using all capital letters:

DEAR FRIEND. WHY DONT YOU OR SOM OF YOUR
FRIENDS HAVE PRINCE RODES ARRESTE AND PUT
UNDER BOND FOR HELPING TO KILL YOUR FATHER
THERE IS NO DOUBT BUT THAT HE WAS WITH
BRAZEL AND ADAMSON ON THAT DAY.
HE WAS SEEN COMING FROM THAT PLACE THE
SAME DAY HE KNOWS ALL AND SO DO I AND IF I CAN
GET HIM UNDER BOND I WILL GET AROUND IN TIME I

AM AFRAID TO LET MY SELF BE KNOWN FOR A WHILE
YO SURELY KNOW THAT WAS WHY HE WAS IN THAT
COUNTRY COME THERE TO HELP DO THE DEED
    WHEN THINGS IS RIGHT I WILL MAKE MY SELF
KNOWN TO YOU AM YOUR FRIEND. EXPOSE HIM IF
POSSIBLE DONT LET HIM SNEAK OUT MORE THAN
ONE KNOWS ABOUT HIM BUT FRAID TO SAY SO DONT
DOUBT WHAT I SAY AN DO SOMETHING TO LET THE
PUBLIC KNOW ALL A PUT UP JOB.

As far as is known, the "friend" never revealed his (or her) identity
to the Garrett family.

Bill Cox of the San Augustin Spring ranch was also considered a
suspect. The fifty-two-year-old Cox supposedly had a personal friendship with both Garrett and Brazel. Indeed, Cox had forked over the
cash for some of Garrett's substantial debt—at least $3,000—and he
had acquired the mortgage on Garrett's ranch and livestock. The
surviving correspondence between Cox and Garrett and, later, Polinaria, is friendly and sympathetic. Yet Garrett's well-known proclivity
to ignore any and all creditors put a heavy strain on their relationship,
and the goat deal soured it even more (at least from Garrett's perspec-
tive). Cox was clearly in the Lee-Rhode camp—they were family. Jeff
Ake, who had worked at different times for both Garrett and Cox,
said years later that Cox was "deadly afraid of Garrett; we all knowed
that." Ake believed that Cox paid Brazel to kill Garrett.

ATTORNEY GENERAL HERVEY HAD real problems with Carl Adamson's testimony. He wanted to see the spot where Garrett died,
so on the day of the funeral, he located Adamson and asked to be
taken to the site. Hervey also brought along Captain Fred Fornoff,
chief of the New Mexico Mounted Police. The three rode to the site

in a buckboard, stopping at the place where Adamson said he had stopped his buggy before Garrett was shot. The arroyo's steep bank rose up on the south side of the road, and to the north there was quite a bit of black brush. The men stepped out of the buckboard, and while Adamson and Fornoff discussed the killing, Hervey walked off approximately thirty to forty feet and found a new Winchester shell casing on the ground. The place where he found the shell casing was not where Brazel said he had shot from. Back in Las Cruces, the attorney general listened to Brazel's story and became more suspicious. Hervey had been acquainted with Brazel for some time, and although he had only known him casually, he did not think the young man was the killer type. After returning to Santa Fe, Hervey told Fornoff that there was a lot about Garrett's death that did not feel right to him. Fornoff agreed, but they did not have the money to pay for a full-blown investigation.

Garrett had been a friend of Hervey's father, and the attorney general freely admitted that he had a personal interest in the case. If there had been a murder, he felt strongly that the culprits should be identified and prosecuted. Consequently, he visited El Paso and met with two of Garrett's old friends, one being Tom Powers. Hervey described his suspicions and asked if they would help finance an undercover detective to pursue the case for a few months. Much to Hervey's surprise and disappointment, both men were strangely uninterested in contributing. Hervey returned to Santa Fe and told Fornoff to dig into his meager expense account and find some reason to travel to El Paso and see what he could find. In the meantime, the grand jury convened in Las Cruces and indicted Brazel for the murder of Pat Garrett. The prosecution subpoenaed the Western Union Telegraph Company for all telegrams received or sent by Brazel, Adamson, Miller, Cox, Rhode, and Mannen Clements during February and March. They were taking the conspiracy accusations seriously.

Fornoff returned from El Paso with what he believed was a "real discovery." He heard that a "wealthy rancher" had paid Jim Miller $1,500 to kill Garrett. The money had been handed to Miller in a lawyer's office in El Paso, and as part of the bargain, the rancher was to supply a man to take the blame, as well as a witness to corroborate a self-defense plea. But while Fornoff's "discovery" included some interesting details, it was—like the other conspiracy rumors—derived from gossip on the streets. Hervey needed hard proof that would stand up in court, and to get that he needed time and money.

A few months later, Hervey met with Emerson Hough in Chicago. He hit up Hough just like he did Powers, asking if the published author and some of his Chicago friends would contribute $1,000 to allow the Territory to better investigate Garrett's murder. And like Powers, Hough declined. Garrett owed Hough a substantial amount of money, he explained, and the author was a little short just now himself.

Then Hough looked Hervey in the eye and said something that stunned the attorney general: "Jimmie, I know that outfit around the Organ Mountains, and Garrett got killed trying to find out who killed Fountain, and you will get killed trying to find out who killed Garrett. I would advise you to let it alone."

The Garrett murder case finally went to trial the first week of May 1909. Brazel's defense attorney was the biggest legal gun in the Southwest, Albert B. Fall, who was assisted by Las Cruces lawyer Herbert B. Holt. Mark Thompson, the district attorney, prosecuted the case, and Frank Parker, the district judge who had presided at the sensational Fountain murder trial ten years before, sat at the bench. The trial lasted only one day. Thompson, a friend of Fall's (keeping on Fall's good side was a prerequisite for any aspiring attorney in southern New Mexico), made only a halfhearted attempt to convict Brazel. The sole eyewitness, Carl Adamson, was not called to testify, and his name was inexplicably scratched off a list of witnesses subpoenaed by the Territory. Dr. Field, who had reported the findings of his autopsy to Thompson, was dumbfounded when he took the stand and the district attorney failed to ask him to explain the entry and exit wounds on Garrett's body. The case went to the jury at 5:55 P.M., and fifteen minutes later, the jurors were back in the courtroom with their verdict: Not Guilty.

Garrett's killing of Billy the Kid had made national headlines and so did his own death twenty-seven years later. But the verdict in the Garrett murder trial was mentioned in just a handful of newspapers. It was as if Pat Garrett had already been relegated to a distant past and had ceased to be significant to the present. The Territory, it would seem, had come to feel the same way. Garrett was an anachronism with considerable baggage. Better to get the murder trial over with quickly and not stir things up any more than they needed to be. Even Garrett's good friends, Tom Powers and Emerson Hough, were resigned to let it go. In later years, Dr. Field often wondered if it would have made a difference had he been allowed to elaborate on the autopsy.

"Who can tell," he once told a reporter. "Pat had lost his money; he'd lost many of his powerful friends. These circumstances are sometimes just as important as a country doctor's testimony."

Out at the Cox place, they held a big barbecue for Wayne Brazel. It was attended by punchers, friends, and ranchers from all over the range.

So who killed Pat Garrett? The standard outlaw-lawman histories go with Wayne Brazel, yet many of Brazel's acquaintances and friends doubted he did it. When Brazel was pressed about it, he gave conflicting answers. To some he confided that he had not been the killer, but to others he maintained that he had pulled the trigger. "I'm sorry I had to kill a man," Brazel supposedly told Albert Fall's wife. "But I'm sure glad he wasn't a good man." Decades later, those close to the affair began to open up, albeit to only a select few. In 1954, Oliver M. Lee Jr. admitted to historian C. L. Sonnichsen that his uncle, Print Rhode, was Garrett's killer. Lee claimed there had indeed been a meeting in El Paso at which Cox hired Jim Miller to do the job (Lee's father had been present). Yet before Miller could fulfill his contract, Rhode blasted Garrett in the back of the head with his Winchester that day in Alameda Arroyo. Because Rhode had a family, Brazel agreed to take the blame.

Unfortunately, Lee added, Cox still had to pay Miller to keep the assassin quiet. Toward the end of his life, Bill Cox's son, Jim, also implicated his uncle Print in an interview with local researcher Herman B. Weisner. "I want to tell you this," Cox said to Weisner, "I believed in letting a sleeping dog lie, but I want to tell you one thing. Never from the time that Wayne Brazel left Organ . . . to the killing of Garrett was his old friend and silent partner, Print Rhode, out of his sight." These revelations by Lee and Cox are in line with the anonymous letter received by Annie Garrett shortly after her father's death.

The reason Garrett had to die had to do with bad blood and plain fear. There is no question that Rhode despised Garrett, and, according to Oliver Lee Jr., Mrs. Cox was terrified that Garrett would eventually kill both her brother Print and Brazel. Albert Fall admitted as much in a letter to Eugene Manlove Rhodes, written just two years after the murder: "Everybody was afraid that he [Garrett] was going to kill someone and a sigh of relief went up when he was finally killed." As it turns out, Garrett was right when he said they would get him unless he got them first. He was also right when he predicted, on more than one occasion, that he would die with his boots on. Garrett seems to have shared the view of his friend Texas Ranger James B. Gillett, who once said that, "Men like myself, who spend their lives making enemies of the pests of society, must expect to be killed sometime."

As for Jim Miller and the thousand head of Mexican cattle, no one ever heard anything more about the cattle. They did hear about Miller, though. He was lynched with three other men in Ada, Oklahoma, on April 19, 1909, for the paid assassination of rancher and former lawman Gus Bobbitt. Carl Adamson, who had not made an appearance at Wayne Brazel's trial, did make an appearance at his own. In

December 1908, he was convicted of conspiring to smuggle Chinese nationals into the United States. Adamson appealed the ruling to the New Mexico Supreme Court where, on August 21, 1911, he received a sentence of eighteen months in the territorial penitentiary at Santa Fe. Adamson died November 1, 1919, in Roswell, New Mexico. Bill Cox, who became famous as a breeder of fine Hereford cattle, acquired Garrett's Black Mountain ranch from Polinaria in December 1908. By 1910, Cox's ranch was larger than the state of Rhode Island. He died of an unknown illness in 1923, and in 1945, the U.S. government condemned over 90 percent of the Cox holdings for a missile test site, known today as the White Sands Missile Range.

Albert Fall continued his political ascension after Garrett's death, serving in the U.S. Senate following New Mexico's admission to statehood in 1912 and becoming the secretary of the interior under Warren G. Harding in 1921. Ten years later, Fall was in prison. His remarkable downfall had come after he accepted "loans"—one for $100,000 in cash—from oil men to whom he had also authorized large federal oil leases. It became known as the Teapot Dome scandal. Fall died a broken man in an El Paso hospital in 1944.

At one time, Wayne Brazel wanted to join the New Mexico Mounted Police, and he asked Albert Fall for an endorsement. On February 7, 1908, just three weeks before Pat Garrett was killed, Fall wrote Governor Curry a short letter recommending the cowpoke. Brazel probably never had a chance of being accepted, but the Garrett murder quashed all hope of his joining the force. In September 1910, Brazel married a pretty, young schoolteacher named Olive Boyd. Exactly nine months later, she gave birth to a son, and two months after that, she died of pneumonia. Four years later, Wayne Brazel disappeared without a trace. Not even his brother had a clue as to where Brazel ended up. In 1935, Brazel's grown son, Jesse, hired a private investigator, El Paso attorney H. L. McCune, to track down his father. After much sleuthing, McCune reported back with an incredible tale:

Wayne Brazel had drifted to South America, where he was shot dead by Butch Cassidy and the Sundance Kid.

Print Rhode and his family moved to Yavapai County, Arizona, shortly after the Garrett killing. He purchased a farm there and leased part of it to a brother-in-law, thirty-six-year-old Henry L. Murphy. The two families were neighbors. In an extraordinary parallel to what had happened in New Mexico, an unknown dispute arose between Rhode and Murphy, with a vengeful Rhode deciding he wanted his brother-in-law off his land. But Murphy was just as determined to hold Rhode to the terms of the lease, even in the face of Rhode's angry threats. On July 8, 1910, Rhode confronted Murphy on a lane near their homes, pulled a .38-caliber revolver from his trouser pocket, and fired three shots at his unarmed brother-in-law. Only one bullet hit Murphy, but it was enough. He died quickly as his killer looked on, emotionless.

Arrested for murder, Rhode was transported to Prescott, where he received telegrams from Bill Cox and Oliver Lee offering financial aid and legal assistance. But no amount of money and legal firepower could save Print Rhode from justice this time. In May 1911, a jury convicted him of murder, and he entered the territorial prison at Florence as prisoner number 3585 with a twenty-year sentence. Even though Bill Cox was unable to help his brother-in-law in the courtroom, his influence in political circles was another matter. On December 23, 1913, Arizona's Progressive governor, George W. P. Hunt, released Rhode "on honor" to New Mexico's governor and Cox. Rhode received a parole a year later and a full pardon on April 28, 1916.

In San Elizario, Texas, a quiet town on the Rio Grande just a few miles southeast of El Paso, Print Rhode died peacefully in his home on October 14, 1942. There was no deathbed confession—at least not one that we know of.

Pat Garrett's killer took his secret to his grave.

Name of Convict *A. P. Rhode* ; Alias ; Registered No. **3585**

Property found on Convict

Expiration of Sentence with Credits *Sept 23rd 1933*

No. 5244 The Bryford Co. Printers, Phoenix, Arizona

TERRITORIAL PRISON AT FLORENCE, ARIZONA
DESCRIPTION OF CONVICT

Crime *Murder* : Sentence *20 Years from May 25th 1911* : No. of Commitment *970*

Fourth Judicial District; *Spring 1911* : Term of Court; Received *May 31 - 1911*

From *Yavapai* County; Race *American* : Nativity *Navajo Co Ariz* : Religion *Protestant*

Age *29* yrs. *0* mos.; Height *5* ft. *5 5/8* inches; Weight *143* lbs.; Complexion *Light Sandy* : Expression —

Size of Head *7 3/8* inches; Forehead *Med* : Color of Hair *Dark Brown* : Color of Eyes *Lt Blue* : Size of Foot *6*

Physical Peculiarities *Top front head bald* : Carriage *Erect* : Condition of Teeth *Bad*

Scars and Deformities *Head - White scar middle base back head - small brown mole above R Eye*
Small mole R cheek. forehead and face freckled - 2 horizontal scar under chin
Body - 1 vac upper L arm - brown spot top L shoulder - 3 brown spots R shoulder back
1 mole upper R hip - 2 hairy moles R shoulder blade - mole upper L calf - 2 small White
India Ink Marks 6 pole base of spine - mole upper R arm inside - upper back and upper arm freckled
- Right Baptism

Legitimate Occupation *Cowboy* : Knowledge of Other Trades

Temperate *Yes* ; Tobacco *Yes* : Opium *No* : Beard Worn When Received *No*

Married *Yes* ; Wife Living *Yes* : Has Children *Yes* : How Many *2* : Has Parents *Father*

Name and Address of Nearest Relation *Wife - Julia A. Rhode Las Cruces New Mex*

Can Read *Yes* ; Write *Yes* ; Where Educated *Texas* : What System *Public*

Had Former Imprisonment *No* ; in What Prison

When and How Discharged

PRISON RECORD

July 5 - 1912. Sent in honor to work on State Highway.

Returned to Florence Jan 10th 1913 - camp proven unstable.
Released on honor by Gov. Hunt to Gov. McDonald
of New Mexico + Mr. Cox - 12/23 - 13
Paroled 12/14/1914
Pardoned by Gov. Hunt April 28 - 1916

Print Rhode's Arizona prison record.

Epilogue

Fame is a food that dead men eat.
—AUSTIN DOBSON

IN OCTOBER 1905, PAT Garrett visited old Fort Sumner with Emerson Hough. Garrett had agreed to help Hough with a book to be titled *The Story of the Outlaw*, and they had an understanding that Garrett would receive a share of the royalties. Sumner was no longer the place Garrett had known in 1881. Its adobe buildings had been torn down some years back, and the large parade ground was a mess of weeds and sagebrush. After some searching, Garrett located the ruins of Pete Maxwell's residence, and he started taking Hough through the events of July 14—twenty-four years earlier.

"It was a glorious moonlight night," Garrett began. "I can remember it perfectly well."

As Garrett told the story of how he killed Billy the Kid, Hough listened in awe, keenly aware of his great fortune in being in the famed lawman's presence at the very place where justice had finally caught up with the Kid, where a snap shot in the dark had given birth to a legend.

The friends next drove their buckboard to the barbed-wire-enclosed cemetery, which also seemed to be falling down. The Kid's crude wooden marker had disappeared long ago, and Garrett spent some time kicking around the greasewood and cactus, trying to figure out where the grave was. He finally found it, and he stared down at the ground for a few moments in silence. Garrett then walked to the buckboard, dug out a canteen, and opened it.

"Well, here's to the boys, anyway," Garrett said, quietly. "If there is any other life, I hope they'll make better use of it than they did of the one I put them out of."

There was another life, of course, a robust mythic afterlife. By the 1930s, Billy the Kid had become a gold mine. Over the previous fifty years, his story had been revisited in the occasional newspaper article and magazine feature, but he officially achieved pop culture status with the 1926 publication of Walter Noble Burns's *The Saga of Billy the Kid*. Burns's book was just that, an enthralling, if not entirely accurate, full-blooded tale partially told by the participants themselves—Burns had interviewed several key Lincoln County old-timers about the Kid, the Lincoln County War, and Pat Garrett. Somewhat surprisingly, Burns saw Garrett as a heroic figure, the "last great sheriff of the old frontier," a characterization that drew criticism from the book reviewer for the *New York Times*. Like the typical Kid lover and Garrett hater—one always equals the other, it seems—the reviewer criticized the sheriff for shooting Billy in the dark "without giving him a chance to fight for his life." Be that as it may, Burns's book was a tremendous bestseller. Its success prompted New York trade publisher Macmillan to issue a new edition of Garrett's rare *The Authentic Life of Billy, the Kid* (Uncle Ash would have been pleased). And in 1930, Burns's book was the basis of the film *Billy the Kid*, directed by King Vidor and starring Johnny Mack Brown as the title character.

As the Great Depression wore on, the American public embraced

Billy the Kid, the young outlaw-hero who defied authority, just as they embraced the thrilling exploits of modern-day bank robbers John Dillinger, Pretty Boy Floyd, and Bonnie and Clyde. Some of those 1930s "public enemies" found Billy's story irresistible as well, perhaps even inspirational. After Bonnie and Clyde were shot to death in a horrific ambush on May 23, 1934, a book was found, among other things, resting in the backseat of their blood-spattered car—*The Saga of Billy the Kid*. Everyone fell in love with the myth, the legend, and that myth got another boost in October 1938, with the premiere of composer Aaron Copland's *Billy the Kid*, which featured a dancing, dudish Billy with iconic black-and-white-striped trousers. The ballet, its score overflowing with traditional cowboy songs, received glowing reviews, including one from Copland's proud mother, who told the composer that his piano lessons as a child had finally paid off.

By 1938, Billy's grave at old Fort Sumner (which had received a large tombstone six years previous) was getting hundreds of visitors annually, an impressive figure considering that Fort Sumner was not the easiest place to get to via automobile in Depression-era America. This prompted the cemetery's owner to consider building a museum and charging admission, until a grandson of Lucien Maxwell (Lucien and Pete Maxwell are buried in the cemetery) sued and won a permanent injunction that kept the cemetery free of charge. Also in 1938, the Works Progress Administration granted $8,657 to restore the old Lincoln County courthouse. The New Mexico legislature subsequently asked the federal government to designate the courthouse as a national monument. There were a few who viewed the creation of such a monument as immortalizing a cold-blooded killer, but their criticisms were ignored. Billy had become too much of a juggernaut. Although the courthouse failed to receive the federal designation, it was dedicated a state monument in a special ceremony featuring Governor John E. Miles on July 30, 1939. Also speaking that day were Billy's old friend George Coe and former territorial governor Miguel Antonio Otero. A crowd of approximately a thousand stood in the rain and watched the proceedings.

People like George and Frank Coe, Yginio Salazar, Jesus Silva, and Almer Blazer suddenly became minor celebrities, and tourists and newspaper reporters wanted to talk to them. George Coe was quick to catch on and published his own book, *Frontier Fighter,* in 1934. In addition to the people and places associated with the Kid, tourists and aficionados also wanted to see Billy artifacts, pieces of the True Cross, so to speak. The Kid had few personal possessions at the time of his death, yet certain individuals later claimed to have the Kid's gun, spurs, knife, the broken shackles from his courthouse escape, even a wad of hair from one of Billy's haircuts. Maybe some of these items were the Kid's, maybe none of them. One artifact that could not be disputed, one that would command a high price on the open market, had hung behind the bar in Tom Powers's Coney Island saloon since 1906. It was the gun that killed Billy the Kid.

Over the years, Powers had amassed an amazing collection of firearms that once belonged to famous westerners, including outlaw Sam Bass, Apache chief Victorio, El Paso marshal Dallas Stoudenmire, Texas gunfighter John Wesley Hardin, and Mexican revolutionary Pancho Villa. In 1906, Powers had talked his friend Garrett into letting him display the Colt pistol used to kill Billy the Kid and also Garrett's favorite Winchester rifle, both originally captured from Billy Wilson at Stinking Spring. Part of what made the saloon keeper's collection so valuable was that he had written documentation for each weapon. Garrett gave Powers a signed affidavit giving the history of the weapons (along with their serial numbers).

"These guns are my prize souvenirs," Garrett wrote, "because of their association with the Lincoln days and because I carried them through many trying times. During my life, I have owned many guns of all types and calabres [sic], but these two have been my favorites and the ones that I relied upon to protect and defend the people whom I have served."

According to the affidavit, Garrett gave Powers permission to display the weapons until he requested their return.

In October 1930, Powers, who apparently suffered from depression, took a pistol, pointed it at his chest, and shot himself just above his heart; he died three months later. Polinaria Garrett sued the Powers estate for the return of her husband's six-shooter, and the case received national publicity. The pistol that killed Billy the Kid was said to be worth more than $500. The Powers estate claimed that a financially desperate Garrett had finally sold the gun to Powers in 1907, and that

Polinaria Garrett with the gun that killed Billy the Kid.

may very well have been true. Even if Garrett had not sold the gun to Powers, he certainly owed Powers money when he died. However, Polinaria testified that Pat had given her the weapon in 1904, and two years later he had asked her permission to let Powers display it in his saloon. Polinaria also claimed that Powers had promised that the gun would be returned to her after his death. Garrett's widow was a small thing, but she could be just as feisty, if not more so, than her husband. The Garrett children loved to tell the story of how Pat once teased Polinaria about her English, and from that day forward, she never spoke to her husband in English again! She was not about to give up that pistol.

The El Paso County Court awarded the pistol to Polinaria, but the Powers estate appealed the decision to the Texas State Supreme Court. More than a year later, the appeals court affirmed the earlier ruling, that Pat Garrett had no right to sell the pistol without his wife's consent. The pistol belonged to Polinaria. On October 7, 1934, as a newspaper photographer snapped pictures, Mrs. Pat Garrett stood on the front porch of her Las Cruces home and received the prized weapon from her attorney, a man with the intriguing name U. S. Goen. It was a rare triumph for the Garrett family, which had struggled mightily after Pat Garrett's death. In early October 1936, Polinaria traveled to Roswell (the home of her daughter Elizabeth) where she was crowned Queen of the Old-Timers and rode in the annual Old-Timers parade. Two weeks later, she died from a heart attack. It seems strange that of all the surviving accounts and interviews from those who knew the Kid and Garrett, there is not one from Polinaria.

Fortunately, Polinaria was not around to see what film producer and director Howard Hughes did to her husband's memory. In 1939, after success with such movies as *Hell's Angels* and *Scarface*, Hughes chose Billy the Kid for his next big film. Hughes signed a contract with Garrett's surviving children, Oscar, Jarvis, Pauline, and Elizabeth, presumably for the rights to their father's story. Filming began in Arizona late in 1940. The finished movie, titled *The Outlaw*, had a limited release in 1943 and then a wide re-release three years later. Panned by critics and condemned by religious groups, *The Outlaw* became a true blockbuster, primarily because of the film's curvaceous new starlet, Jane Russell.

While most Americans were staring at Russell's breasts, Pat Garrett's children were looking at the disturbing portrayal of their father by character actor Thomas Mitchell. Mitchell's Garrett was a dumpy, conniving, vengeful weasel of a man, and the Garretts were furious and humiliated. In March 1947, they sued the Hughes Tool Company of Houston, Texas, of which Howard Hughes was head, for $250,000 for breach of contract. The memory of their father, they claimed in the suit, was "cruelly and unjustifiably besmirched." The result of their lawsuit is unknown. The family's goal, a rather naive one, was to correct the false impression of their father created by the film. But truly, no one cared much about Pat Garrett anymore but them.

Just three years later, in 1950, the Garrett family was angered once again over a perceived threat to their father's legacy. An old man living in the small town of Hico, Texas, was claiming to be Billy the Kid. A popular myth, one that existed even in Garrett's time, was that Billy had not been shot down that summer night in Fort Sumner but had somehow survived. One version of the story had Garrett killing another man and claiming it was the Kid so he could get the reward. Another version had Garrett in cahoots with the Kid to fake the outlaw's death. The myth played perfectly to the romantics, who hated the story about young, charismatic Billy, the Robin Hood of the Southwest, dying so tragically. But a living Billy meant that Garrett's greatest claim to fame was all a lie. It was as if the Garrett family could not win. Their father was either the villain for killing Billy, or he was unworthy of his dedicated-lawman reputation because he had not really killed the Kid and perhaps committed fraud in the process.

The Texas man's name was Ollie L. "Brushy Bill" Roberts, and he had petitioned New Mexico's governor Thomas J. Mabry for a pardon. Brushy, according to his El Paso lawyer, was old and tired of running, although exactly who or what he was running from at that late date is unclear. The governor agreed to meet with Brushy Bill in Santa Fe on November 30 to either verify Brushy's claim or dismiss it. The meeting took place in the governor's executive mansion in front of newspaper reporters, historians, Cliff McKinney (son of Garrett's deputy, Kip), and Oscar and Jarvis Garrett.

When Oscar Garrett's turn came to grill Brushy, he declined, saying he chose not to "dignify the occasion." Turns out, Oscar did not have to. Brushy seemed confused and had trouble answering several pointed questions. He did not know who the Kid fought with in the Lincoln County War, he denied killing James Bell and Bob Olinger, and he had to be prompted before he could come up with Pat Garrett's name. Perhaps Brushy was nervous in front of all those stern faces. The likely explanation is that Brushy Bill was a pathetic phony. The only thing he shared in common with Billy the Kid was a wild imagination. Mabry announced he would not consider a pardon, then or ever.

"Billy the Kid's Dead All Right" was the title of an editorial in the next day's *Santa Fe New Mexican*. "We're glad it was so bad," commented the paper on Brushy's performance. "It didn't fool anybody. Had the old boy been better versed and had he given a few right answers there would be confusion from now on as to whether the outlaw was killed in 1881 or whether he lived 70 years longer to apply for a pardon."

Brushy Bill Roberts, whoever he was, died in Hico, Texas, just short of a month after his interview with the New Mexico governor, but his story refused to go away. Billy the Kid and Brushy Bill returned to the spotlight in April 2003, when Sheriff Tom Sullivan of Lincoln County opened an official investigation (Case No. 2003-274) to examine the deaths of deputies Bell and Olinger in Lincoln and Pat

Garrett's killing of Billy at Fort Sumner. Sullivan pointed out as his motivation a recent visit to Hico, Texas, where today a museum touts Brushy Bill as the real Billy the Kid, thus contradicting what Sullivan knew of Lincoln County history. Assisted by his friend Deputy Steve Sederwall and the sheriff of DeBaca County, Gary Graves, Sullivan planned to collect DNA from the bodies of Billy the Kid, his mother, Catherine Antrim, Brushy Bill, and other Kid pretenders (Brushy was not alone) and make comparisons. Ultimately, the investigation was just as much about whether or not Pat Garrett had lied as it was about whether the Kid had survived. Sullivan vowed to remove Garrett's image from the Sheriff's Department's shoulder patch if he determined that Billy had not perished at Garrett's hands.

Governor Bill Richardson, seeing an excellent opportunity to bring media attention and more tourists to New Mexico, quickly joined the cause, offering state aid and the possibility that he might give Billy the pardon Lew Wallace had promised nearly 125 years earlier. The first news of the investigation generated a media frenzy. The story appeared on the front page of the *New York Times* and ran in some two thousand newspapers worldwide, and documentary filmmakers soon descended on Lincoln County to explore the "mystery" of Billy the Kid. In 2004, the investigation made the news again when forensic expert Henry Lee, made famous from his role in the O. J. Simpson murder trial, agreed to help with collecting blood samples and doing the DNA analysis.

The investigation also generated incredible controversy, with some critics arguing that the effort was a waste of time and money and others afraid of the consequences for New Mexico tourism if Billy's body was not found at Fort Sumner (a good possibility considering a major flood of the Pecos in 1904 and genuine confusion as to Billy's exact resting place within the cemetery). Sullivan and Sederwall were eventually thwarted in their attempts to exhume Billy, Catherine Antrim, and Brushy Bill, and Sheriff Graves was recalled from office.

The investigation did uncover some very intriguing, long-forgotten evidence connected with Billy the Kid, including the original carpenter's workbench where Billy's dead body had been placed, complete with human bloodstains. Considerable blood evidence was also revealed at the top of the Lincoln County courthouse stairs through a test using luminol, the same chemical employed in modern police forensic investigations. Unfortunately, the results of the DNA analysis of these blood samples, the DNA extracted from the remains of a Billy pretender, and any other findings of the investigation are currently in limbo. Sullivan and Sederwall, no longer associated with the Lincoln County Sheriff's Department, say their work was conducted on their own time and at private expense. "We left our badges, and we'll take our knowledge," Sederwall explained to the *Albuquerque Journal* in 2007. The two are currently being sued, along with the present Lincoln County sheriff, to force the release of their investigation's records. It seems that what started out as a "quest for the truth," to "set the record straight," has turned into a fight over just who gets to know that "truth."

The irony of all this is that Billy Bonney's fate is already known. It was known when Brushy Bill appeared in Santa Fe in 1950, just as it was known at Fort Sumner in 1881. Paulita knew. Pete Maxwell knew. Celsa, Deluvina, John Poe, Kip McKinney—they all knew. "He is dead, my friend Billy," said Florencio Chavez, who rode with the Kid as a Regulator. "Old Silva knows. And I am sure. These stories of another being killed, of the Kid slipping away, they have come with late years. My friend Bill he is dead."

NO LESS THAN SIXTY films have been made about Billy the Kid. He has been portrayed by Paul Newman, Kris Kristofferson, Val Kilmer, Emilio Estevez (who has the singular distinction of playing both the Kid and Brushy Bill Roberts), Roy Rogers, and a host of lesser B actors. Hundreds of books have been written about the outlaw, from comics and pulp westerns to works by novelists the likes of Michael Ondaatje, N. Scott Momaday, and Larry McMurtry. Bob Dylan, Billy Joel, and Jon Bon Jovi have written songs about him. Every year, countless tourists from around the world visit his grave at Fort Sumner and navigate Lincoln County's Billy the Kid National Scenic Byway. Nearly every spot Billy once touched is commemorated with a historic marker.

No one ever pretended to be Pat Garrett, to have survived the shooting in Alameda Arroyo. There are no Pat Garrett museums, no ballads about the Lincoln County lawman. By 1948, his grave in the Odd Fellows cemetery was neglected and covered with weeds; the family transferred his remains across the street to the Masonic cemetery in 1957. There are no signs on the highway pointing to Garrett's grave site, and it receives few visitors. Yet while Billy continues to get the glory and the empathy, Pat Garrett will never be forgotten. He remains, for better or worse, what he was at his death in 1908: the man who shot Billy the Kid.

The Kid and Pat Garrett are forever linked, and rightly so; today, in legend, but historically, in the memories of their friends and enemies. "I knew both these men intimately," Sallie Chisum told Walter Noble Burns in 1924, "and each made history in his own way. There was good mixed with the bad in Billy the Kid and bad mixed with the good in Pat Garrett. Both were distinctly human, both remarkable personalities. No matter what they did in the world or what the world thought of them, they were my friends. Both were real men. Both were worth knowing."

They need no finer epitaph.

Acknowledgments

I grew up in the heart of Missouri's Jesse James country, where I, like other boys my age, could not help but fall in love with the legend of the James and Younger boys (I'm still a little partial to Jesse today). As an adult, I embraced not only the history of my native state, but also the history of the American Southwest. So it seems fitting that I would eventually turn to another iconic outlaw—as well as the famous southwestern lawman who gunned him down. It has been an amazing journey, and I have had much help along the way. I would especially like to thank:

Marc Simmons, New Mexico's historian laureate and an exceptionally fine friend and mentor over the decades.

Robert M. Utley, who introduced me to my literary agent and graciously provided me with dozens of computer files consisting of his research notes for his excellent books on Billy the Kid and the Lincoln County War.

Robert G. McCubbin, who welcomed me into his home and gave me unlimited access to his superlative collection of historic photographs, documents, and rare books relating to the American West.

Ronald Kil, friend, solid westerner, and a damn fine artist. Thanks for letting me practice with your Frontier Six-Shooter.

Others who provided assistance include John P. and Cheryl Wilson, Las Cruces, New Mexico; Leon C. Metz, El Paso, Texas; Frederick Nolan,

Chalfont St. Giles, England; David Dary, Norman, Oklahoma; Durwood Ball, University of New Mexico; J. Randolph Cox, editor, *Dime Novel Round-Up;* Miles Gilbert, Show Low, Arizona; Elvis E. Fleming, Roswell, New Mexico; Joseph K. Treat, Santa Fe, New Mexico; Janean and C. W. Grissom, Taiban, New Mexico; Dave Woodwell, Las Cruces, New Mexico; Don McCubbin, Centennial, Colorado; Sally Faulkner, Coolidge, Arizona; Paul Andrew Hutton, University of New Mexico; Lynda Sanchez, Lincoln, New Mexico; Mike O'Keefe, Placitas, New Mexico; Elbert A. Garcia, Santa Rosa, New Mexico; Rex Rideout, Conifer, Colorado; Marcus Gottschalk, Las Vegas, New Mexico; Scott O'Malley, Colorado Springs, Colorado; Wade Shipley, Lovington, New Mexico; and the staff and professors of the Southwest Studies Department, Colorado College.

Those who assisted me at the numerous historic sites and research institutions I visited and corresponded with include John M. Murphy, L. Tom Perry Special Collections Library, BYU; Gwendolyn Rogers and Murray Arrowsmith, Lincoln State Monument; Nancy Sawyer, Arizona State Library, Archives and Public Records; Karen Mills, Historical Records Clerk, Lincoln County Clerk's Office; Ann Massmann, Donald Burge, and Mike Kelly, Center for Southwest Research, UNM; Jim Bradshaw, Haley Memorial Library and History Center; Tim Blevins and staff, Special Collections, Pikes Peak Library District; the staff of the interlibrary loan department, Pikes Peak Library District; Miriam Syler, Cobb Memorial Archives; Laura K. Hollingsed, Yvette Delgado, and Claudia Rivera, C. L. Sonnichsen Special Collections Department, UTEP; the staff of the Rio Grande Historical Collections, NMSU; Chris Reid, Pinal County Historical Society Museum; Cameron Saffell, Farm and Ranch Heritage Museum; the staff of the New Mexico State Records Center and Archives; Tomas Jaehn, The Fray Angélico Chávez History Library; and Susan Berry, Silver City Museum.

The long, tedious hours that were spent writing this book were made much more tolerable by four excellent radio stations that broadcast bluegrass, old-time, and classic country music live on the Web. They are WPAQ,

Mount Airy, North Carolina; WDVX, Knoxville, Tennessee; KOPN, Columbia, Missouri; and WSM, Nashville, Tennessee.

I must also make mention of my friend and hunting partner, Andy Morris, who also happens to be one hell of a blacksmith. He constantly asked me about this book as I was researching and writing it and eagerly listened to my numerous discoveries about Garrett and the Kid.

I thank my cousin David Wayne Gardner, Breckenridge, Missouri, for many pleasant hours spent in pursuit of Missouri wild turkeys each spring, my other passion.

My in-laws, Jack and Mary Ann Davis, Green Mountain Falls, Colorado, provided important child care services that allowed me to more easily leave home on several research trips.

I was most fortunate to have parents who had a keen interest in American history. With my two sisters, we visited countless forts, battlefields, historic houses, and museums each summer on our family vacations. So I thank my mom and dad, Claude and Venita Gardner, Breckenridge, Missouri, for turning me into a historian.

I am also indebted to my many teachers over the years. My high school English teacher, Mrs. Carol A. Cox, Chillicothe, Missouri, never failed to encourage me in my writing. In fact, I may not have become a writer if it had not been for her. At Northwest Missouri State University, I greatly benefited from the teachings of Dr. Harmon Mothershead, Mr. Tom Carneal, Dr. Richard Frucht, and Dr. George Gayler. At the University of Wyoming, I must thank my adviser and professor, Dr. Eric Sandeen, director of the American Studies Program.

My editor, Henry Ferris, devoted incredible energy and expertise to improving this manuscript. When he was not prodding me about getting to the action, he was telling me how excited he was about this book. He knew exactly what to say and when to say it. I feel extremely fortunate to have had the opportunity to work with him. Others at William Morrow to whom I am grateful include Jean Marie Kelly, senior marketing director; Dee Dee DeBartlo, publicity director; Lynn Grady, deputy publisher; Shawn

Nicholls, director of online marketing; Peter Hubbard; and Danny Gold-stein, editorial assistant. I would also like to thank my crackerjack copy editor, Laurie McGee.

My literary agent, Jim Donovan, a fine nonfiction writer in his own right, provided exemplary advice and insights at every stage of this book. If that was not enough, he spent hours copying articles and documents I needed. He's not only a great agent, he's a great friend.

My children, Christiana and Vance, have brought me much joy, and I hope this book will make them proud of their dad, at least someday. I'm certainly proud of them. I'll especially cherish the memory of the many gun-fights I had with Vance. Sometimes he was Billy the Kid and sometimes he was Pat Garrett, but no matter who played who, we stuck to the script—Billy always died in the end.

This book was started during very optimistic times and completed during very stressful times. My wife, Katie, lost her job of twenty years as the sole professional curator for the Colorado Springs Pioneers Museum. During those two decades, she contributed greatly to making it an award-winning institution, one of the most respected museums in the region. But when the City of Colorado Springs hit a budget crunch, they let her go without batting an eye. They didn't deserve her. I probably don't, either, but she happens to like me for some reason. This book would have been much more difficult to research and write had it not been for her support and enthusiasm. Thank you, Katie. Can't wait for us to get back out on the road in search of the next historical discovery.

Mark Lee Gardner
Cascade, Colorado
June 8, 2009

Notes

It is well known that Ash Upson did most of the writing for Pat Garrett's *The Authentic Life of Billy, the Kid, The Noted Desperado of the Southwest, Whose Deeds of Daring and Blood Made His Name a Terror in New Mexico, Arizona and Northern Mexico.* The two must have worked closely together on the manuscript, however, for Upson lived in the Garrett household during the time the book was being written. Unfortunately, the original manuscript has not survived, so it is impossible to say definitively what is purely Upson and what is Garrett, although most scholars tend to agree that the first fifteen chapters, which at times employ a dreadfully melodramatic style typical of the time, are primarily Upson, while the remaining chapters, which are written as a matter-of-fact, first-person narrative, more strongly reflect Garrett's contribution. To avoid clutter and confusion in my narrative and notes, I consistently refer to Garrett as the author of *The Authentic Life of Billy, the Kid.*

1. FACING JUSTICE

Garrett's arrival in Las Vegas with his prisoners and subsequent events were well reported by two Las Vegas newspapers, the *Daily Optic* and the *Gazette.* The Las Vegas newspaper accounts I have relied upon here and elsewhere in this book are found in *Billy the Kid: Las Vegas Newspaper Accounts of His Career, 1880–1881* (Waco, Tex.: W. M. Morrison Books, 1958).

Billy's greeting to Dr. Sutfin in front of the Grand View Hotel was recounted by Albert E. Hyde in his "The Old Regime in the Southwest," *Century Magazine* 63 (Mar. 1902). Hyde was indeed in Las Vegas at this time, but his version of events is highly romanticized and should be used with caution.

Garrett's account of the Las Vegas standoff is included in his *The Authentic Life of Billy, the Kid* (Santa Fe: New Mexican Printing and Publishing Co., 1882), 114–116.

Benjamin Miller's little-known version of the events at the Las Vegas depot is found in his rare *Ranch Life in Southern Kansas and the Indian Territory* (New York: Fless & Ridge Printing Company, 1896).

Train engineer Dan Daley was interviewed by a newspaper reporter in California in 1927, at which time he provided his memories of the Las Vegas standoff. Daley's fleeting brush with Billy the Kid, and this particular interview, have been missed by other historians and writers. See "When the Paths of Dan Daley and Billy the Kid Crossed," *The Decatur Review,* Decatur, Illinois, Jan. 23, 1927. Daley and his wife are enumerated in the 1880 U.S. Census, living in East Las Vegas. Daley's occupation is listed as "Engineer on R. Road."

Billy's words to Garrett after the lawman informed his prisoners he would arm them if the mob attacked are exactly as they were remembered by Garrett in his *The Authentic Life of Billy, the Kid,* 116.

Miguel Otero's role in the standoff is much embellished by his son, Miguel Antonio Otero, in the latter's book *My Life on the Frontier, 1864–1882* (1935; reprint ed., Albuquerque: University of New Mexico Press, 1987), 213.

J. Fred Morley's reminiscences were provided in two letters to James East dated Nov. 29, 1922, and June 29, 1924, transcriptions of which are in the Leon C. Metz Papers (MS 157), Box 16, C. L. Sonnichsen Special Collections Department, University of Texas at El Paso Library. James East gave his account of the Las Vegas standoff in an interview with J. Evetts Haley, Douglas, Arizona, Sept. 27, 1927, J. Evetts Haley Collection, Haley Memorial Library and History Center, Midland, Texas. The Morley and Garrett quotes are from East.

An article in the *Chicago Daily Tribune* of Dec. 29, 1880, but dated Las Vegas, Dec. 28, stated that a compromise was reached whereby Sheriff Romero and two men were allowed to travel with Garrett's party to Santa Fe to seek the governor's permission to return Rudabaugh to Las Vegas. Albert E. Hyde, in his 1902 article, wrote of a similar compromise, supposedly suggested by Garrett himself. No such compromise is mentioned by James East, J. F. Morley, Miguel Antonio Otero, or Garrett, and in fact, the *Las Vegas Gazette* of Dec. 27 chastised Sheriff Romero for *not* attempting just such an arrangement.

The pie episode is from Morley's letter to East of Nov. 29, 1922.

Billy's quoting the proverb "Those who live by the sword . . ." is from a letter of James H. East to Charlie Siringo, Douglas, Arizona, May 1, 1920, as quoted in Charles A. Siringo, *History of "Billy the Kid"* (Santa Fe: Charles A. Siringo, 1920), 105.

The now-iconic image of the Kid appeared in the Jan. 8, 1881, issue of *The Illustrated Police News,* which stated that it received the original from Las Vegas chief of police E. Roberts, who obtained it from Lincoln County. The engraving was printed again in the *Illustrated Police News* of Mar. 5, 1881. Chief of Police Roberts may have been Eugene Roberts, who is listed in the 1880 U.S. Census as a thirty-eight-year-old saloon keeper living in East Las Vegas. See Robert G. McCubbin, "The Many Faces of Billy the Kid," *True West* 54 (May 2007): 60–63.

Miguel Antonio Otero fondly recalled his visits to Billy in the Santa Fe jail in his books, *My Life on the Frontier,* 214, and *The Real Billy the Kid, With New Light on the Lincoln County War* (New York: Rufus Rockwell Wilson, Inc., 1936), 179.

The postal inspector was named Carson, and his letter of Jan. 11, 1881, is transcribed in James W. White, *The History of Lincoln County Post Offices* (Farmington, N.Mex.: James W. White, 2007), 83–84.

Billy's letters to Governor Wallace have been published many times. Scanned images of this correspondence, with the exception of Billy's letters of Mar. 13, 1879, and Mar. 2, 1881, are available on the Indiana Historical Society's website (www.Indiana-History.org) as part of a digital image collection titled "Lew Wallace in New Mexico."

For Billy's bay mare, see the *Las Vegas Gazette,* Jan. 4, 1881, and the *Las Vegas Daily Optic,* Mar. 12, 1881. The pistol W. Scott Moore presented to Frank Stewart, a Colt Frontier Six-Shooter in caliber .44-40, serial number 56304, was auctioned off by Rock Island Auction Company in December 2006, for a hammer price of $92,000.

Billy's escape attempt was reported in the *Santa Fe Daily New Mexican* of Mar. 1, 1881.

Governor Wallace's recollection of Billy's blackmail scheme is in the *Fort Wayne Morning Journal-Gazette,* July 13, 1902.

Incidents of Billy's trip to Mesilla were reported in the *Santa Fe Daily New Mexican* of Apr. 2, 3, and 7, 1881. The Kid's low opinion of the Mesilla jail was reported in *Newman's Semi-Weekly* of Apr. 20, 1881.

In 1876, 250 citizens of Grant County petitioned to have Judge Warren Bristol removed for various legal improprieties. Judge Bristol's record for murder convictions was praised in a long article in the *Rio Grande Republican* of Apr. 29, 1882. Two months later, however, the same newspaper condemned the judge for grossly undervaluing his real and personal property on his tax assessment. On the day of Bristol's funeral, Jan. 17, 1890, the business houses of Deming, New Mexico, Bristol's place of residence, were closed "as a mark of respect for the Judge's memory." See New Mexico Biographical Notes, Robert N. Mullin Collection, Haley Memorial Library and History Center, Midland, Texas; *Rio Grande Republican,* June 10, 1882; and *The Deming Headlight,* Jan. 18, 1890.

Editor Simeon Newman's rant against a delay in the Kid's legal proceedings is from the Apr. 2, 1881, issue of *Newman's Semi-Weekly.*

For Billy's plea of no jurisdiction in the Roberts case, see *Newman's Semi-Weekly,* Apr. 6, 1881.

My description of Simeon Newcomb is from Patrick H. Beckett, ed., *Las Cruces, New Mexico, 1881: As Seen by Her Newspapers* (Las Cruces: COAS Publishing and Research, 2003), 65–66. For Albert J. Fountain, see Gordon R. Owen, *The Two Alberts: Fountain and Fall* (Las Cruces: Yucca Tree Press, 1996); and A. M. Gibson, *The Life and Death of Colonel Albert Jennings Fountain* (Norman: University of Oklahoma Press, 1965). Fountain's mob law comments are quoted in Owen, 193.

Billy's wish for a pistol in his jail cell was reported in *Newman's Semi-Weekly* of Apr. 9, 1881.

Court Clerk George R. Bowman's recollections of the trial are in Helen Irwin, "When Billy the Kid Was Brought to Trial," *Frontier Times* 6 (Mar. 1929): 214. Bowman's account, like many primary sources touching on the Kid and Garrett, must be used with caution. I suspect that Bowman's quotes were embellished rather liberally by Irwin, who first published Bowman's recollections in the *Fort Worth Star Telegram* of Dec. 2, 1928.

The defense's proposed jury instructions and Judge Bristol's charge to the jury are illustrated and transcribed in Randy Russell, *Billy the Kid: The Story—The Trial*

(Lincoln, N.Mex.: The Crystal Press, 1994). The three witnesses for the Territory were Isaac Ellis, Bonifacio Baca, and Jacob B. "Billy" Mathews. Surprisingly, Simeon Newman did not report on the substance of the Kid's trial in the pages of his *Semi-Weekly*, even though he was inclined to devote much space to Kid news items. It is possible that the *Mesilla News,* a weekly, reported details of the trial, but that week's issue has not survived.

According to Lew Wallace, Billy responded to Bristol's sentence with the following: "Judge, that doesn't frighten me a bit. Billy the Kid was not born to be hung." Wallace's account was first published in a 1902 newspaper article, and how Wallace obtained this information is unclear, for he was nowhere near the trial. Billy's words, however, mirror similar comments and sentiments he is known to have made. See "Gen. Lew Wallace's New Outlaw Hero," *Fort Wayne Morning Journal-Gazette,* July 13, 1902.

Billy's letter to Caypless is as quoted in William A. Keleher, *Violence in Lincoln County, 1869–1881* (Albuquerque: University of New Mexico Press, 1957), 320–321.

Editor Newman's interviews with the Kid were never published. His newspaper ceased publication in Las Cruces with the Apr. 20, 1881, issue.

Billy's views on Governor Wallace and the promised pardon are from the *Mesilla News* of Apr. 16, 1881. Governor Wallace's dismissive comments on the Kid's plight are from the *Las Vegas Gazette,* Apr. 28, 1881.

My description of Billy and his guards as they departed Las Cruces is from *Newman's Semi-Weekly,* Apr. 20, 1881, and Robert Olinger's statement of expenses for transportation of William Bonney, Apr. 21, 1881, Lincoln County Clerk's Office, Carrizozo, New Mexico.

The description of Billy's stop at Blazer's Mill with his guards is from Paul Blazer to Eve Ball, Nov. 20, 1963, interview typescript, Box 4, Folder 1, Eve Ball Papers (MSS 3096), L. Tom Perry Special Collections Library, Harold B. Lee Library, Brigham Young University, Provo, Utah; and Almer Blazer, "The Fight at Blazer's Mill, in New Mexico," *Frontier Times* 16 (Aug. 1939): 465.

Mrs. Lesnett's visit with Billy is from Mrs. Annie E. Lesnett to Edith Crawford, Sept. 30, 1937, interview typescript, American Life Histories: Manuscripts from the Federal Writers Project, 1936–1940, Library of Congress American Memory website.

2. TRAILS WEST

For Garrett's new hero status, see the *Daily New Mexican,* Dec. 28, 1880. The gift of $100 in gold was reported in the *New Mexican* of Dec. 30, 1880.

The will of Patrick F. Jarvis, dated Dec. 13, 1852, is found in Probate File No. 904, Cobb Memorial Archives, Valley, Alabama. Jarvis, who died in December 1852, willed his wife, Margaret Jarvis, two slaves named Fanny and George. However, the will specified that at the death of Margaret Jarvis, the slave George was to go to his grandson Pat Garrett, and the slave Fanny was to go to his granddaughter Margaret Garrett. As Margaret Jarvis is believed to have died a few months after Patrick, her grandson, Pat Garrett, became a slave owner at the age of two. Jarvis also willed his daughter Elizabeth (Pat Garrett's mother) two slaves named Big Ben and Little Ben. On Pat Garrett's paternal side, his great-grandfather, Miles Garrett, was a veteran of the Revolutionary War.

For John L. Garrett's Alabama slave ownership, see the slave schedules for the 1850 U.S. Census, 19th District, Chambers County, Alabama.

Garrett's recollection of how he earned his first dollar is from the *El Paso Herald*, Aug. 24, 1905.

The Garretts, overseer John Yates Coleman, and the Garrett slaves are in the 1860 U.S. Census, 7th Ward, Claiborne Parish, Louisiana.

For John Coleman's enlistment in the Twenty-seventh Louisiana, see the Civil War Soldiers and Sailors System at www.itd.nps.gov/cwss/index.html.

The disposition of the Garrett estate is recounted in Leon Metz, *Pat Garrett: The Story of a Western Lawman* (Norman: University of Oklahoma Press, 1974), 8–9. Metz states that John and Elizabeth Garrett's children refused to live in the household of Larkin Lay and their sister Margaret. However, the 1870 U.S. Census for the 7th Ward, Claiborne Parish, Louisiana, shows all the Garrett siblings but Pat and Elizabeth Ann (who was likely married by this time) residing with the Larkins.

Emerson Hough, a friend of Garrett's, provides the date for Garrett's departure from Louisiana in *The Story of the Outlaw: A Study of the Western Desperado* (New York: The Outing Publishing Company, 1907), 293.

Garrett came to the Dallas area with John Lowry. See the short sketch of Garrett's career published in the *Daily Review*, Decatur, Illinois, Dec. 14, 1901.

The Garrett quote about being homesick is from the *El Paso Herald*, Aug. 24, 1905.

Garrett's encounter with the Uvalde County cattleman and subsequent employment as a cowboy is according to W. Skelton Glenn, "Pat Garrett as I Knew Him on the Buffalo Ranges," typescript, Box 16, Leon C. Metz Papers. The Glenn manuscript is a significant source for information on Garrett, particularly his time as a buffalo hunter. However, Glenn developed a strong animosity toward his former partner; thus, his manuscript should be used with caution. Also, it is apparent that Glenn plagiarized a small portion of Emerson Hough's *The Story of the Outlaw*.

For the killing of Joe Briscoe, I have relied heavily on the Glenn manuscript. I have made one change to the Garrett quotation that precipitates his fight with Briscoe. In the manuscript, Glenn has Garrett saying, "No one but a damn Irishman would have more sense than to try to wash anything in that water." This is, of course, not the slight that Garrett obviously intended, and I have substituted "Anyone" for "No one." See also Robert N. Mullin, "Pat Garrett—Two Forgotten Killings," *Password* 10 (Summer 1965): 57–59; and Meadows, *Pat Garrett and Billy the Kid as I Knew Them*, 102.

Garrett spoke of meeting Bat Masterson in an interview published as "He Shot Billy the Kid," *Kansas City Journal*, July 20, 1902, clipping typescript in Maurice G. Fulton Collection, University of Arizona Library Special Collections, Tucson. For Wyatt Earp's recollections of Garrett, see Stuart N. Lake, *Wyatt Earp, Frontier Marshal* (Boston: Houghton Mifflin Co., 1931), 169, 210.

For reports on the decimation of the Texas bison herds and estimates on hides received, see the *Galveston Daily News*, Mar. 12 and May 3, 1878.

For more on the Glenn-Garrett party's troubles with the Comanches, see Metz, *Pat Garrett*, 18–19.

Garrett and Glenn's abandonment of the buffalo range and arrival at Fort Sumner is described by Glenn, "Pat Garrett as I Knew Him," and Hough, *The Story of the Outlaw,* 294–295. Glenn claimed that the trip to New Mexico Territory was undertaken to locate a new hunting camp in the Pecos Valley. But as it is well documented that the bison was essentially nonexistent in the region by this time, it is hard to take his explanation seriously.

For Lucien Maxwell and his family, see Lawrence R. Murphy, *Lucien Bonaparte Maxwell: Napoleon of the Southwest* (Norman: University of Oklahoma Press, 1983).

My description of Garrett upon his arrival at Fort Sumner is from Emerson Hough, "The Imitation Bad Man," *Washington Post,* Jan. 21, 1906; and Glenn, "Pat Garrett as I Knew Him."

The Garrett quotes about getting a job and his exchange with Pete Maxwell are as quoted in Hough, *The Story of the Outlaw,* 295–296.

That Garrett and his companions had shacked up with some Hispanic women at Fort Sumner is from Frank Coe, interview with J. Evetts Haley, San Patricio, New Mexico, Aug. 14, 1927, J. Evetts Haley Collection. Coe commented that, "The buffalo hunters were the hardest set of men I believe I ever saw."

Paco Anaya, a resident of Fort Sumner beginning in 1876, remembered Garrett's arrival very differently. He states, in an account written in 1931, that Pat showed up at Maxwell's corrals in August 1878 looking "like a tramp." Garrett pitched in with the branding for two days, but he was not paid for his labors and he was never hired by Maxwell as a cowboy. Paulita Maxwell Jaramillo offers still another version, stating that Garrett went up to Pete Maxwell's house and asked for a job as a cowboy. She claimed she stood behind her brother when he greeted Garrett at the door. See A. P. "Paco" Anaya, *I Buried Billy,* ed. James H. Earle (College Station, Tex.: Creative Publishing Company, 1991), 74–75. Paulita's account, as well as her description of Garrett, is in Walter Noble Burns, *The Saga of Billy the Kid* (Garden City, N.Y.: Doubleday, Page & Co., 1926), 196.

The weekly Fort Sumner *bailes* are noted by Paulita in Burns, *The Saga of Billy the Kid,* 185.

Metz, *Pat Garrett,* 40, mentions the hog business. Burns, *The Saga of Billy the Kid,* 171, states that Garrett partnered with Beaver Smith in a store and saloon. Paco Anaya says that Garrett partnered with a Sam Lock in a "little cantina" at Fort Sumner. Anaya may be referring to Fred S. Locke, who is enumerated in the 1880 U.S. Census as a thirty-eight-year-old "Saloon Keeper" living in East Las Vegas. Anaya is the source for the story of Garrett butchering stolen cattle. See Paco Anaya's *I Buried Billy,* 76–77.

The John Meadows quote about Garrett being a "working devil" is from his interview with J. Evetts Haley, Alamogordo, New Mexico, June 13, 1936, J. Evetts Haley Collection. Meadows, an important source for information on Billy and Garrett, was a friend of both men. He served as a deputy sheriff under Garrett beginning in 1896.

The newspaper mentions of Billy's age that I am referencing appear in *Newman's Thirty-Four* of Jan. 26, 1881, and *Newman's Semi-Weekly* of Apr. 2, 1881. *Newman's Thirty-Four* stated that it got its information on Billy's age from the *White Oaks Golden Era,* adding that "it ought to know." Some authors have asserted that the November 23 birth date was assigned to the Kid because it was the same as Garrett's ghostwriter

Ash Upson's. However, I have been unable to locate any *contemporary* document that verifies that Upson's birthday was indeed November 23. The earliest reference I have for that date is Walter L. Upson, *The Upson Family in America* (New Haven, Conn.: The Tuttle, Morehouse & Taylor Co., 1940), 179. It has been argued that Upson, who boarded in the Kid's household in Silver City, remembered Billy's birthday precisely because it was the same as his own. All of which leads nowhere.

Many historians and buffs have attempted to sort out Billy's childhood; their works are cited in my bibliography. See particularly Jerry Weddle, *Antrim Is My Stepfather's Name: The Boyhood of Billy the Kid* (Tucson: Arizona Historical Society, 1993); Waldo E. Koop, "Billy the Kid: The Trail of a Kansas Legend," *The Trail Guide* 9 (Sept. 1964):1–19; Robert N. Mullin, "The Boyhood of Billy the Kid," in Frederick W. Nolan, ed., *The Billy the Kid Reader* (Norman: University of Oklahoma Press, 2007), 214–224; and Jack DeMattos, "The Search for Billy the Kid's Roots," *Real West* 21 (Nov. 1978): 12–19, 39.

Billy's brother, Joseph, is found in the 1880 U.S. Census for Silverton, San Juan County, Colorado, as a seventeen-year-old miner with a birthplace of New York. He is enumerated as Joseph Antrim, and his father's birthplace is also given as New York. His mother's is given as England. Interestingly, some former schoolmates of the McCarty brothers remembered Joseph as being the eldest. Also, newspaper accounts from the early 1880s stated that Joseph was a half brother of Henry.

For Wichita, see L. Curtis Wood, *Dynamics of Faith: Wichita, 1870–1897* (Wichita: Wichita State University, 1969); Stan Hoig, *Cowtown Wichita and the Wild, Wicked West* (Albuquerque: University of New Mexico Press, 2007); and 1870 U.S. Census for Wichita Township, Sedgwick County, Kansas. My source for the number of longhorns that crossed at Wichita during the 1870 season is the *Galveston Daily News*, July 7, 1870.

The quote regarding Denver's healthful qualities is from *The Alton Telegraph*, Alton, Illinois, Feb. 17, 1871.

The Antrim-McCarty marriage was documented in both the county marriage book and the records of the Presbyterian Church. Copies of these marriage records are in the William H. Bonney Collection (AC 017-P), Fray Angélico Chávez History Library, Palace of the Governors, Santa Fe.

The observations of the *Santa Fe Sentinel* on the rush to Silver City are from the *Galveston Daily News*, June 25, 1873. Some accounts claim that the Antrims first settled in the mining camp of Georgetown, eighteen miles northeast of Silver City. If so, it was a very brief sojourn, no more than a few weeks, if not a few days. See Weddle, *Antrim Is My Stepfather's Name*, 2

My source for wages in Silver City is *The M'Kean County Miner*, Smethport, Pennsylvania, Apr. 3, 1873.

The Louis Abraham and Harry Whitehill quotes are from Weddle, *Antrim Is My Stepfather's Name*, 6; and Mullin, "The Boyhood of Billy the Kid," 221.

Harry Whitehill stated that Henry McCarty was the "Head Man in the [minstrel] show," which would have made him the interlocutor. See Robert C. Toll, *Blacking Up: The Minstrel Show in Nineteenth-Century America* (New York: Oxford University Press, 1974).

My sources for Ash Upson are Maurice G. Fulton to Eve Ball, no date, Box 20,

Folder 21, Eve Ball Papers; Mrs. Jerry Dunaway to Eve Ball, Lovington, New Mexico, Feb. 29, 1948, interview typescript, Box 11, Folder 2, Eve Ball Papers; and James D. Shinkle, *Reminiscences of Roswell Pioneers* (Roswell, N.Mex.: Hall-Poorbaugh Press, 1965), 8–24.

Chauncey Truesdell as quoted in Weddle, *Antrim Is My Stepfather's Name*, 15.

For Billy's planned heist of the candy/furniture store, see Allie Anderson, "Billy the Kid," typescript, Box 4, Folder 2, Eve Ball Papers.

The Harvey H. Whitehill interview appeared in the *Silver City Enterprise*, Jan. 3, 1902. My description of Whitehill comes from William C. McGaw, "Billy Was Just Another Brat at Silver City," *El Paso Herald-Post*, Nov. 5, 1960.

The robbery of the Chinese laundry and Billy's subsequent jail escape were reported in the *Grant County Herald*, Silver City, Sept. 5 and 26, 1875. The operators of the laundry, Charley Sun and Sam Chong, are enumerated in the 1880 U.S. Census. Sun, thirty years old, was still residing in Silver City with his wife and two daughters; occupation, "Washing & Ironing." Chong, twenty-five years old and single, had relocated to Tucson, Arizona, where his occupation was "works in Laundry."

The quote from Sheriff Whitehill's daughter appears in Josie Bishop, "Wild Women of the West," *The American Weekly*, Dec. 15, 1946. Josie was not born until 1875, the same year as the Kid's arrest, so she is not speaking here from firsthand observation. She also claimed to have played with Billy the Kid as a child, which is patently false.

Mary Chase's recollections of her former student were related by her daughter, Patience Glennon, to Bill McGaw, *El Paso Herald-Post*, Dec. 17, 1960.

For more on Billy's activities in Arizona Territory, see Weddle, *Antrim Is My Stepfather's Name*; and Lee Cotten, "True Tales of Billy the Kid: The Kid in Arizona, 1875–1877," *The Kid* (Mar. 1990): 7–15 and (July 1990): 10–19.

The William Antrim quote ordering Billy to "get out" is from Harry Whitehill as quoted in Weddle, *Antrim Is My Stepfather's Name*, 31.

The reference to the Kid being a "lightweight" at the Hooker ranch is from Weddle, *Antrim Is My Stepfather's Name*, 35.

For information on John R. Mackie, see Frederick Nolan, "First Blood: Another Look at the Killing of 'Windy' Cahill," in Nolan, ed., *The Billy the Kid Reader*, 226–227.

The quote from Miles L. Wood about Billy and Mackie is from an undated manuscript by Wood in the Robert G. McCubbin Collection, Santa Fe, New Mexico.

It is significant that Billy was overtaken by the Camp Grant troopers near McMillen's Camp. Researcher Jerry Weddle determined that one of the miners at McMillen's Camp at this time was none other than William Antrim. Henry's stepfather was back in Silver City, New Mexico, by February 24, 1877. See Weddle, *Antrim Is My Stepfather's Name*, 36 and 64 n. 63.

The original complaint of Lewis C. Hartman, dated Feb. 16, 1877, is in the Robert G. McCubbin Collection. The complaint is the first written reference to Billy's soon-to-be-famous sobriquet.

Miles Wood's account of his arrest of Billy and Mackie at Hotel de Luna and the difficult task of keeping Billy locked up is quoted from Weddle, *Antrim Is My Stepfather's Name*, 39 and 41.

For "Windy" Cahill, see Philip J. Rasch, *Trailing Billy the Kid*, ed. Robert K. DeArment (Laramie, Wyo.: National Association for Outlaw and Lawman History, 1995), 182–193; 1870 U.S. Census for Camp Crittenden, Pima County, Arizona Territory; and Statement of Second Lieutenant William J. Ross regarding discharge of Francis Cahill, Prescott, Arizona, Nov. 2, 1874, Yavapai County Board of Supervisors (RC 113), Box 1, Folder 1, Arizona State Library, Archives & Public Records, Phoenix.

Gus Gildea is a key source for what happened between Billy and Cahill in Atkins's saloon, including the exchange of words between the two as they struggled on the floor. Gildea's recollections are found in J. Fred Denton, "Billy the Kid's Friend Tells for First Time of Thrilling Incidents," *Tucson Daily Citizen*, Mar. 28, 1931; and the *El Paso Herald-Post*, July 12, 1934.

The Garrett quote about Billy refusing to stay whipped is from *The Authentic Life of Billy, the Kid*, 9.

Cahill's deathbed deposition appeared in Tucson's *Arizona Weekly Star* of Aug. 23, 1877. It is reproduced in Cotten, "True Tales of Billy the Kid: The Kid in Arizona," *The Kid* (July 1990): 10.

Chauncey Truesdell claimed to have witnessed the last meeting of Billy and his brother, Joseph. He has Henry arriving at the Nicolai farm with two Indian companions, which seems far-fetched. See Truesdell as quoted in Weddle, *Antrim Is My Stepfather's Name*, 46–47.

Billy's former teacher related to her daughter many details about Billy's visit to her home in Georgetown, including how Billy told her of his tearful meeting with brother Joseph and their good-bye kiss. See the *El Paso Herald-Post*, Dec. 17, 1960.

3. WAR IN LINCOLN COUNTY

Billy was spotted in Cooke's Canyon by Samuel P. Carpenter, a thirty-six-year-old Silver City contractor, as reported in the *Mesilla Valley Independent*, Oct. 13, 1877.

For more on Jesse Evans, see Grady E. McCright and James H. Powell, *Jessie Evans: Lincoln County Badman* (College Station, Tex.: Creative Publishing Company, 1983). The Jesse Evans involved in the Kansas counterfeiting scheme is mentioned in Koop, "Billy the Kid: The Trail of a Kansas Legend," 16–17, which also includes the quote regarding the decision of the court.

Fountain's call to string up the Evans gang is in the *Mesilla Valley Independent*, Oct. 13, 1877. The journey of The Boys across southern New Mexico was reported in the *Mesilla Valley Independent* of Oct. 6 and 13.

The story of the stolen mare, as related by the Kid himself, is in Lily Klasner, "The Kid," in Nolan, ed., *The Billy the Kid Reader*, 237.

A description of the Seven Rivers settlement as it appeared in the early 1880s is in the *Waterloo Courier*, Waterloo, Iowa, Feb. 24, 1897.

The Chisum Range is described in the *Thirty-Four*, Las Cruces, Apr. 2, 1879.

For a brief biographical sketch of Heiskell Jones, see Nolan, *The West of Billy the Kid*, 77.

In Garrett, *The Authentic Life of Billy, the Kid*, 32–39, may be found the melodramatic account of how the Kid and a companion, Tom O'Keefe, stumbled upon a party of Apaches, the result of which was the separation of the Kid from both his partner and his horse. Whether or not this episode actually occurred is something else, but Nib Jones said that Billy told this story to his mother and that "Ash [Upson] told us the same story." Ash Upson is enumerated as a boarder in the Heiskell Jones household in the 1880 U.S. Census for the 5th Precinct, Lincoln County, New Mexico. The Nib Jones interview, as well as interviews with Nib's brothers, are in Box 13, Folder 7, and Box 14, Folders 1–3, Eve Ball Papers.

Lily Casey, who would become Lily Klasner, is quoted from her book, *My Girlhood Among Outlaws,* 174. Robert Casey's negative opinion of the Kid on that first meeting is from an interview with J. Evetts Haley, Picacho, New Mexico, June 25, 1937, J. Evetts Haley Collection. Casey also told Haley that once the Kid started working for Englishman John H. Tunstall, "he paid his way, and he was a different man altogether."

The widow Casey did not complete her cattle drive to Texas. Tunstall claimed 209 of the cattle in her herd, and about October 25 a posse under Dick Brewer stopped the Casey caravan and cut Tunstall's animals out. Her sons Robert and William were subsequently arrested and taken to the county seat of Lincoln. See Frederick Nolan, *The Lincoln County War: A Documentary History* (Norman: University of Oklahoma Press, 1992), 167–168.

Frank Coe's recollection is from the *El Paso Times,* Sept. 16, 1923. Coe had a way of remembering his old friend as larger than life. So did a lot of others.

Some histories have Billy working for John Chisum during this period. While Billy likely visited Chisum's South Springs ranch headquarters, both Lily Klasner and Florencio Chávez were emphatic in stating that Billy was never employed as a Chisum cowboy. Also, James Chisum, who joined his brother's operation on the Pecos in 1877, testified in court that "Billy the Kid didn't work for me." See Klasner, "The Kid," 245–246; Eugene Cunningham, "Fought with Billy the Kid," *Frontier Times* 9 (Mar. 1932): 243; and *Territory of New Mexico vs. Robert Casey, et al.,* Case #751, New Mexico Supreme Court Records, New Mexico State Records Center & Archives, Santa Fe (NMSRCA).

The capture of The Boys and their card playing in the Lincoln jail was reported in the *Mesilla Valley Independent,* Oct. 27, 1877. My description of the jail comes from Robert Brady, "Billy the Kid Story" (typescript), as told to Edith L. Crawford, Box 49, Folder 6, Marta Weigle Collection (AC 361), Chávez History Library; and the *Mesilla Valley Independent,* Oct. 13, 1877.

For an excellent history of the town of Lincoln, see John P. Wilson, *Merchants, Guns & Money: The Story of Lincoln County and Its Wars* (Santa Fe: Museum of New Mexico Press, 1987).

Ham Mills's murder of Balenzuela is discussed in Nolan, *The West of Billy the Kid,* 47 and 306 n. 9. Interestingly, according to the 1870 U.S. Census for Lincoln County, Mills was married to a Hispanic woman, with whom he then had one child.

For details of the Evans jailbreak, I have relied on the primary sources quoted in Nolan, *The Lincoln County War,* 171–173. In 1938, Robert Brady, the son of Sheriff Brady, told the story that Billy and "his gang" simply hunted up the jailer and forced him to turn over the keys. See Brady, "Billy the Kid Story."

My sources for Billy's incarceration in December of 1877 are Robert Casey, in his interview with Haley, June 25, 1937, cited above; Klasner, "The Kid," 234 and 241; and

Garrett, *The Authentic Life of Billy, the Kid,* 74. The jail stay is also discussed by Nolan, *The West of Billy the Kid,* 87–88.

For the Lincoln County War, which has had no lack of chroniclers, I have relied upon Frederick Nolan, *The Lincoln County War: A Documentary History* (Norman: University of Oklahoma Press, 1992); John P. Wilson, *Merchants, Guns & Money: The Story of Lincoln County and Its Wars* (Santa Fe: Museum of New Mexico Press, 1987); Maurice G. Fulton, *Maurice Garland Fulton's History of the Lincoln County War,* ed. Robert N. Mullin (Tucson: University of Arizona Press, 1968); and Robert M. Utley, *High Noon in Lincoln County: Violence on the Western Frontier* (Albuquerque: University of New Mexico Press, 1987). For my narrative, I have purposely covered only the high points of the feud as they relate to the Kid. Those interested in all the specifics and the numerous personalities involved—laborious and tiresome, for the most part—should consult the above works.

The quote referring to Murphy & Co.'s local domination is from Klasner, *My Girlhood Among Outlaws,* 98.

The J. H. Tunstall letter to his father is quoted from Wilson, *Merchants, Guns & Money,* 63.

For more on Tunstall, see Frederick Nolan, *The Life & Death of John Henry Tunstall* (Albuquerque: University of New Mexico Press, 1965).

For more on McSween, see Frederick Nolan, "The Search for Alexander McSween," *New Mexico Historical Review* 62 (July 1987): 287–301. There has been some confusion as to whether or not McSween was a native of Scotland—needlessly so. McSween's wife, Susan, is the source of the confusion, for she told later scholars that her former husband was born in Canada. McSween, however, stated in his own writings that he was a "Scotchman," and a biographical sketch published in the *Cimarron News and Press,* Aug. 8, 1878, stated plainly that McSween was "a native of Scotland." In 1948, William E. Johnson told Eve Ball about taking his mother, Camelia Olinger, to see the King Vidor–directed film *Billy the Kid,* released in 1930. Camelia had known many of the principals in the Lincoln County War, including Billy and McSween. "She said the only thing in the picture true to the facts," Johnson recalled, "was the Scotch brogue of McSween." The Johnson interview is in Box 13, Folder 3, Eve Ball Papers.

A biographical sketch of James J. Dolan appears in Nolan, *The West of Billy the Kid,* 154. Dolan's obituary, dated Mar. 4, 1898, observed that he had been "a good hater," which was an understatement. The obituary is reproduced in Lillian H. Bidal, *Pisacah: A Place of Plenty* (El Paso, Tex.: Robert E. and Evelyn McKee Foundation, 1995), 307 n. 267.

The John Middleton and Robert Widenmann accounts of Tunstall's murder are published in Nolan, *The Lincoln County War,* 198, 209–210, and 231–232. Billy gave his version of the murder in a June 8, 1878, deposition to Department of Justice special investigator Frank Warner Angel, File 44-4-8-3, RG 60, Records of the Department of Justice, National Archives and Records Administration, Washington, D.C.

That the corpse was scratched and its clothes torn is from an interview of Edith Coe Rigsby to Eve Ball, Ruidoso, New Mexico, Aug. 22, 1967, Box 16, Folder 29, Eve Ball Collection. Edith Coe Rigsby was the daughter of Frank Coe.

Billy's pledge to "get some of them before I die" is quoted from Frank Coe, interview with J. Evetts Haley, San Patricio, New Mexico, Aug. 14, 1927, J. Evetts Haley Collection.

The Frank Collinson quote is from his book, *Life in the Saddle,* ed. Mary Whatley Clarke (Norman: University of Oklahoma Press, 1963), 129.

Billy's heated exchange with Sheriff Brady is quoted from Nolan, *The West of Billy the Kid,* 109.

My account of the capture and killing of William "Buck" Morton and Frank Baker essentially follows the version in Garrett, *The Authentic Life of Billy, the Kid,* 46–49, much of which supposedly came from the Kid. Morton's letter to H. H. Marshall, dated South Spring River, Mar. 8, 1878, was published in the *Mesilla Valley Independent,* Apr. 13, 1878. See also "Regulator Victims," *Wild West* 19 (Feb. 2007): 10.

Billy's remark to George Coe that he never intended to let Morton and Baker reach Lincoln alive is from George W. Coe, *Frontier Fighter: The Autobiography of George W. Coe Who Fought and Rode with Billy the Kid,* ed. Doyce B. Nunis Jr. (Chicago: The Lakeside Press, 1984), 132.

For more on Sheriff Brady, see Donald R. Lavash, *Sheriff William Brady: Tragic Hero of the Lincoln County War* (Santa Fe, N.Mex.: Sunstone Press, 1986).

It has often been written that the Kid was wounded by Billy Mathews as he stooped over Brady's body. However, Reverend Taylor F. Ealy, who treated French's wound, wrote in his personal copy of Garrett's *The Authentic Life of Billy, the Kid,* that Billy "was not hit." Ealy's copy of Garrett is in Box 1, Folder 1, Ealy Family Papers, MSS 443 BC, Center for Southwest Research, University of New Mexico, Albuquerque.

Like most things regarding Billy the Kid, there are wildly conflicting accounts as to what actually happened at Blazer's Mill on Apr. 4, 1878. Time and again, Frank Coe told the story of how he met with Roberts outside the big house before the shooting began and tried for thirty minutes to talk him into surrendering. Coe also claimed it was Charlie Bowdre, not the Kid, who delivered the fatal gunshot wound to Roberts. Coe's account is supported by a news report on the fight in the *Mesilla Valley Independent,* Apr. 13, 1878, as well as by the June 7, 1879, testimony of David M. Easton, who was employed at Blazer's Mill and claimed to have witnessed the shoot-out. This all may be true. My narrative, however, is based on the recollections and written accounts of the Blazer family, who, like Coe and Easton, were also witnesses to the affray and had the opportunity to later speak with the dying Roberts about what had transpired, as well as with Billy when he stopped at Blazer's Mill under armed guard in April 1881. Almer Blazer did not have a high opinion of Easton and considered his testimony suspect. For the Blazer accounts, see Almer Blazer, "The Fight at Blazer's Mill, in New Mexico," *Frontier Times* 16 (August 1939): 461–466; Paul Blazer, "The Fight at Blazer's Mill: A Chapter in the Lincoln County War," *Arizona and the West* 6 (Autumn 1964): 203–210; and A. N. Blazer to M. G. Fulton, Mescalero, New Mexico, Apr. 24, 1931, and Aug. 27, 1937, Box 1, Folder 7, Maurice G. Fulton Collection.

The grand jury's statement exonerating McSween is quoted from Nolan, *The Lincoln County War,* 270.

McSween's letter to Tunstall's sister is quoted from Fulton, *Maurice G. Fulton's History of the Lincoln County War,* 205.

The quote from Reverend Ealy's pupil is from Ruth R. Ealy, *Water in a Thirsty Land* (privately published), 80.

Sheriff Peppin's note to Colonel Dudley is quoted in Nolan, *The Lincoln County War*, 315.

The man who overheard the conversation between Colonel Dudley and Jimmy Dolan was Samuel G. Beard. His testimony is published in R. M. Barron, ed., *Court of Inquiry, Lieutenant Colonel N. A. M. Dudley, Fort Stanton, New Mexico, May–June–July 1879* (Edina, Minn.: Beaver's Pond Press, Inc., 2003), 1: 77.

For more on Nathan A. M. Dudley, see E. Donald Kaye, *Nathan Augustus Monroe Dudley, 1825–1910: Rogue, Hero, or Both?* (Parker, Colo.: Outskirts Press, 2007).

McSween's note to Dudley and Dudley's response are as quoted in Nolan, *The Lincoln County War*, 325.

McSween's cry that he had lost his reason is from Taylor F. Ealy, "The Lincoln County War as I Saw It," c. 1927, Ealy Papers, University of Arizona Library, Tucson. The quote urging McSween to make a run for it, which I have attributed to the Kid, is from the same source.

For Billy Bonney's testimony as to what happened at the McSween house on the night of July 19, see Barron, ed., *Court of Inquiry, Lieutenant Colonel N. A. M. Dudley*, 1: 185–187.

4. A NEW SHERIFF

The Sallie Chisum description of Garrett is from Burns, *The Saga of Billy the Kid*, 17.

The Paulita Maxwell description of Juanita Martínez is from Burns, *The Saga of Billy the Kid*, 186.

Paco Anaya, in *I Buried Billy*, 75, gives the date of the Garrett-Martínez wedding only as November 1879. Anaya is my source for the presence of Billy and his gang at the wedding. There is some disagreement over the identity of Garrett's first wife. Leon Metz suggests that Pat's first wife was named Juanita Gutiérrez, possibly a sister of his second wife, Apolinaria Gutiérrez. However, both Paulita Maxwell and Paco Anaya identify Juanita Martínez as his first bride. And Pat Garrett's son, Jarvis, in handwritten corrections found in a copy of Metz's 1974 Garrett biography, wrote that "Mama did not have a sister named Juanita Gutierrez." (My thanks to historian Marc Simmons for supplying me with the Jarvis Garrett notes.) Unfortunately, no wedding record or certificate for Garrett's wedding to Juanita Martínez has been located.

That Billy the Kid's favorite dance tune was "Turkey in the Straw" comes from Frank Coe, who was in a good position to know, as Frank played the fiddle. See Frank Coe interview with J. Evetts Haley, Feb. 20, 1828, J. Evetts Haley Collection.

For over a hundred years, Thomas Folliard's surname has been published incorrectly as O'Folliard. Garrett is the exception, giving the boy's full name as Tom O. Folliard. There is no such surname as O'Folliard, and indeed, the 1870 U.S. Census for Zavala County, Texas, enumerates a nine-year-old "Thomas Folliard" living in the household of David Cook, an uncle. Tom's parents, Stephen and Sarah Rose, are enumerated in the 1860 U.S. Census for Uvalde County with their surname spelled "Fulliard."

For my description of Tom Folliard, I have relied upon an interview with Frank Collinson in the *Amarillo Globe-News*, Aug. 14, 1938; Frank Coe's interview with J.

Evetts Haley, San Patricio, New Mexico, Aug. 14, 1927; and Susan McSween Barber's account as published in Miguel Antonio Otero, *The Real Billy the Kid,* 117.

Bowdre's father, A. R. Bowdre, is enumerated in the 1860 U.S. Census for DeSoto County, Mississippi, with real estate valued at $51,000 and a personal estate (read slaves) at $118,000. Ten years later, the value of A. R. Bowdre's real estate was given as $35,000 and his personal estate as $4,500.

Bowdre's rampage in Lincoln is fully described in a letter published in the *Mesilla Valley Democrat,* Sept. 8, 1877.

George Coe's assessment of Bowdre and Billy is quoted from Miguel Antonio Otero, *The Real Billy the Kid,* 136.

Frank Collinson considered Bowdre the best dressed of the "Kid's men." See the *Amarillo News-Globe,* Aug. 14, 1938.

Billy's quote about remaining in New Mexico is from George W. Coe, *Frontier Fighter,* 200.

Wallace's amnesty proclamation may be found in the microfilm series Territorial Archives of New Mexico, roll 21, frame 505, NMSRCA.

My account of Chapman's murder comes from a letter written by "Max" at Fort Stanton on Feb. 23, 1879, and published in the *Thirty-Four,* Las Cruces, Mar. 5, 1879; and Edgar A. Waltz, "Retrospection," typescript copy in Lincoln County War History File #20, NMSRCA.

Wallace's comment reflecting his frustration with New Mexico is quoted from Calvin Horn, *New Mexico's Troubled Years: The Story of the Early Territorial Governors* (Albuquerque: Horn & Wallace, 1963), 200.

Ira Leonard is quoted from Nolan, *The Lincoln County War,* 387.

According to Louisa Beaubien Barrett, Juanita Garrett "only lived a few days." Paulita Maxwell said she lived three weeks. See Jerry Weddle, "The Kid at Old Fort Sumner," *The Outlaw Gazette* 5 (Dec. 1992): 8; and Burns, *The Saga of Billy the Kid,* 186.

A powerful cornerstone of Kid lore is that the Kid and Garrett were the closest of friends. Both Paulita Maxwell and George Coe said so, and it has been portrayed as fact by numerous authors and screenwriters who could not resist the potently tragic tale of best friends who find themselves on opposite sides of the law, with the result that one is forced to take the other's life. Garrett is partly to blame for this, for in his 1882 biography of Billy, he stated that, "I have known 'The Kid' personally since and during the continuance of what was known as 'The Lincoln County War,' up to the moment of his death, of which I was the unfortunate instrument, in the discharge of my official duty." But this statement of Garrett's was more an attempt to establish his authority for writing such a book; he was not claiming a close personal friendship with Billy the Kid. A more realistic version of their relationship was revealed by James E. Sligh in an obscure article published in 1908, the year of Garrett's death. Sligh had grown up in Claiborne Parish, not far from the Garrett plantation, and although the two had not known each other in Louisiana, they had made each other's acquaintance in White Oaks in 1880, where they had ample opportunity—and ample reason—to talk. Garrett told Sligh that while he knew the Kid well, they were neither friends nor enemies: "He minds his business and I attend to mine. He visits my wife's folks sometimes, but he never comes around me. I just simply don't want anything to do with him, and he knows it, and he knows that he has nothing to fear from me as long as he does not interfere with me and my affairs." See J. E. Sligh, "The Lincoln County War: A Sequel to the Story of 'Billy the Kid,'" *The Overland Monthly* 52 (Aug. 1908): 170.

Several of Billy's contemporaries remembered that he was ambidextrous. That Billy favored his right hand when shooting is from Charles Nebo "Nib" Jones to Eve Ball, May 9, 1948, Globe, Arizona, Eve Ball Papers.

Paulita Maxwell told the story of Garrett and Billy shooting at a jackrabbit to Burns, *The Saga of Billy the Kid*, 197.

Emerson Hough was amazed by Garrett's skill with a six-shooter. In a rare example of immodesty, Garrett told Hough, "I am as good a revolver shot as I ever saw. I do not boast of that, but simply say it is true so far as I know." Garrett also told Hough that he had never been beaten in a revolver match. See Hough's "The American Six-Shooter: What the Real Six-Shooter Is—What It Will Do and Will Not Do," *The Outing Magazine* (Jan. 1909): 505–506.

Garrett's assessment of the Kid's shooting skills is from the *Daily New Mexican*, July 21, 1881. The Garrett quote regarding the importance of "nerve" is from the *Davenport Republican*, Davenport, Iowa, Aug. 7, 1902.

For Billy's killing of Joe Grant, I have relied almost exclusively upon the account and quotes in Garrett, *The Authentic Life of Billy, the Kid*, 74–77. The subsequent episode at Sunnyside is from the *Las Vegas Daily Optic*, Feb. 22, 1881; and the recollections of Milnor Rudolph's grandson (also named Milnor Rudolph) in "Billy the Kid" (typescript), Marta Weigle Collection, Chávez History Library. Paco Anaya claimed that Joe Grant had been hired by John Chisum to assassinate Billy. See *I Buried Billy*, 81.

Apolinaria's birth year is uncertain; her enumerations in the various censuses seldom agree, and the birth year on her grave marker does not agree with any of the censuses. Her nickname, "Negra," is mentioned by both Paco Anaya and, amazingly enough, by Mrs. James Patrick Smith of Claiborne Parish, Louisiana. In a 1967 interview, Mrs. Smith recalled that Pat and Negra visited the parish every summer "after about the middle 1880s" to see Pat's sister, Margaret Lay. She remembered that "Pat's wife was a dark complected lady with jet black hair and eyes." See Paco Anaya, *I Buried Billy*, 77, and Mrs. James Patrick Smith to J. J. Smith, May 23, 1967, Box 18, Louisiana Folder, Leon C. Metz Papers.

The Garrett-Gutiérrez marriage is recorded in Marriage Records, 1857–1946, La Yglesia de San Jose (St. Joseph), Anton Chico, New Mexico, Archives of the Archdiocese of Santa Fe, Microfilm Roll 61-A, NMSRCA. Married on that same day, in what was possibly a double ceremony, were Garrett's friend Barney Mason and Juana Madrid. There is some debate as to whether these wedding ceremonies took place at Anton Chico or Fort Sumner. It is possible that the priest married the couples at Fort Sumner and entered the record into the marriage book upon his return to Anton Chico.

For Joseph C. Lea, see Elvis E. Fleming, *Captain Joseph C. Lea: From Confederate Guerrilla to New Mexico Patriarch* (Las Cruces: Yucca Tree Press, 2002).

For Lea's recruitment of Garrett, see George Curry, *George Curry, 1861–1947: An Autobiography*, ed. H. B. Hening (Albuquerque: University of New Mexico Press, 1958), 40–41.

A tintype (more properly, ferrotype) produces a mirror image of its subject. Previous historians and writers, unaware of this significant fact, have mistakenly concluded that Billy was left-handed. The most famous result of this error is the 1958 Paul Newman/Arthur Penn film *The Left Handed Gun.* The illustration of the tintype reproduced in this book has been corrected so that Billy appears as he would in life, with his pistol on his right hip.

Mescalero Apache Indian Percy Big Mouth is quoted from Sherry Robinson, *Apache Voices: Their Stories of Survival as told to Eve Ball* (Albuquerque: University of New Mexico Press, 2000), 159.

For Rudabaugh, see Frederick Nolan, "Dirty Dave: The Life and Times of Billy the Kid's Worst Friend," *The Kid* (Dec. 1989): 7–13; and the *Brooklyn Daily Eagle,* Brooklyn, New York, June 19, 1881.

For Tom Pickett, see Don Cline, "Tom Pickett: Friend of Billy the Kid," *True West* 44 (July 1997): 40–49; Rasch, *Trailing Billy the Kid,* 99–109; and the *Las Vegas Daily Optic,* Dec. 27 and 29, 1880.

For Billy Wilson, see Rasch, *Trailing Billy the Kid,* 58–71.

Azariah Wild's New Mexico reports are found in Reports of Special Operative Azariah F. Wild, Daily Reports of U.S. Secret Service Agents, 1875–1936, Records of the United States Secret Service, RG 87, Microfilm T915, roll 308, National Archives and Records Administration, Washington, D.C.

There are two versions of George Curry's encounter with Billy the Kid, and I have drawn upon both. See Curry, *George Curry,* 18–19; and William A. Keleher, *The Fabulous Frontier: Twelve New Mexico Items* (Santa Fe: The Rydal Press, 1945), 62.

W. G. Ritch's Thanksgiving Proclamation is in the Territorial Archives of New Mexico, roll 99, frame 139.

5. OUTLAWS AND LAWMEN

Frank Nelson Page told of his encounter with the Kid and Billy Wilson in a long letter to the *New Mexico State Tribune,* Albuquerque, circa 1926; a typescript copy is in the Maurice G. Fulton Collection. Page's wife, Albenita, a native New Mexican, also had a memorable encounter with Billy at Puerto de Luna. She said that the Kid walked into Grzelachowski's mercantile one day when it was unattended and began taking dress goods off the shelves and handing them to her and other women who were also in the store. She said that the women did not tell on Billy. See the obituary for Albenita Page in the *Albuquerque Tribune,* Aug. 12, 1958.

The Kid's involvement in the mail robberies is noted by Azariah Wild in his reports of Oct. 22 and 28, and Nov. 6, 1880. Billy's letter to Ira Leonard is discussed in Wild's reports for Oct. 6 and Oct. 9. The gang's raid on White Oaks is mentioned by Wild in his report for Nov. 22.

For the events surrounding the Kid, Wilson, and Rudabaugh's standoff with the White Oaks posse and the killing of Jimmy Carlyle, see Garrett, *The Authentic Life of Billy, the Kid,* 82–85; the account of Joe Steck as published in Keleher, *The Fabulous Frontier,* 59–62; and Billy's own account as originally published in the *Las Vegas Gazette* and reprinted in Keleher, *Violence in Lincoln County,* 288–289.

For a biographical sketch of Jimmy Carlyle, see Miles Gilbert, Leo Remiger, and

Sharon Cunningham, *Encyclopedia of Buffalo Hunters and Skinners,* vol. 1 (Union City, Tenn.: Pioneer Press, 2003), 90. Carlyle's estate inventory lists, among other things, one buffalo gun, value $10.00, and one pair mules, value $125.00. (Did the posse recover Carlyle's stolen mules at the Greathouse-Kuch ranch?) See probate file #98, Lincoln County Clerk's Office, Carrizozo, New Mexico.

Dave Rudabaugh, as quoted in the *Las Vegas Daily Optic,* Jan. 21, 1881, is the source for the number of shots fired at Carlyle and who fired them.

There is evidence that Garrett had served as a Lincoln County deputy sheriff earlier in the year. According to the minutes from the Lincoln County Commissioners' book, Garrett presented accounts against the county on May 7 and July 9 for "services rendered as Deputy Sheriff." What exactly these services were is unknown, although they appear to have been of a temporary nature. Typed transcriptions of the minutes pertaining to Garrett are in the Donald Cline Collection, Series 10419, Folder 69, NMSRCA.

Wild's comment about the deputy U.S. marshals is quoted from his report for Friday, Dec. 4, 1880.

For Barney Mason, I have relied upon Philip J. Rasch, *Warriors of Lincoln County,* ed. Robert K. DeArment (Laramie, Wyo.: National Association for Outlaw and Lawman History, 1998), 102–107; Azariah Wild's report for Nov. 20, 1880; and Mason's entries in the 1880 and 1910 U.S. censuses for New Mexico and California, respectively.

For the activities of Garrett's posse on its jaunts to the Yerby ranch and Los Portales, I have relied primarily on the reports of Azariah Wild and Garrett's own account in his *The Authentic Life of Billy, the Kid.*

Los Portales today hardly resembles the distinctive rock formation that greeted Billy the Kid and others in the late nineteenth century. For histories of Los Portales and, most importantly, photographs that depict the site as it probably appeared in Billy and Garrett's time, see the *Clovis News-Journal,* Clovis, New Mexico, May 29, 1938, and June 2, 1940.

John P. Meadows is the source for Garrett's stipulation that Charlie Bowdre arrive at their parley unarmed. See Meadows, *Pat Garrett and Billy the Kid,* 43–44.

For the Garrett-Leiva gunfight, I have supplemented Garrett's own account with newspaper articles in the *Daily New Mexican,* Dec. 17, 1880, and the *Las Vegas Daily Optic,* Aug. 18, 1881. Leiva was subsequently charged with assault with intent to kill and tried in Las Vegas in August 1881. He was found guilty but received only a small fine, which, according to the *Las Vegas Gazette* of Sept. 7, 1881, incensed Puerto de Luna area residents. Some of the "best citizens" of that section told the *Gazette* that Leiva would likely be lynched if he returned to Puerto de Luna. Over four decades later, Francisco Romero, objecting to his unflattering portrayal in Garrett's *The Authentic Life of Billy, the Kid,* sought to prevent the distribution of a 1927 reprint of Garrett's book by Macmillan. In an attempt to save face, Romero wrote an alternate version of that day's events in which he claimed to have disarmed Garrett and Mason in Grzelachowski's store after the gunfight. Not likely. Romero was successful in getting the reprint withdrawn for a short time, but Macmillan re-released the book unchanged. See Maurice G. Fulton to James H. East, Roswell, New Mexico, Sept. 15, 1928; and Statement of Francisco Romero, Box 16, Leon C. Metz Papers.

6. THE KID HUNTED

Billy's original letter to Governor Wallace of Dec. 12, 1880, is available for viewing online as part of the Indiana Historical Society's Digital Image Library (http://images.indianahistory.org). According to Garrett, Billy also wrote a letter about this same time to Joseph C. Lea at Roswell, saying that "if the officers would give him a little time, and let him alone until he could rest up his horses and get ready, he would leave the country for good; but if he was pursued, or harassed, he would inaugurate a bloody war, and fight it out to the fatal end." See *The Authentic Life of Billy, the Kid*, 101.

Governor Wallace's reward proclamation of Dec. 13 is found in the Territorial Archives of New Mexico, roll 21, frame 565. Notice of the proclamation was published in the *Daily New Mexican*, Dec. 14, 1880. The *Las Vegas Gazette*'s criticism of the reward, published in its issue of Dec. 15, 1880, is as quoted in Keleher, *Violence in Lincoln County*, 291.

There are several primary accounts that illuminate Garrett's hunt for and capture of the Kid. The best, and the one produced closest to when the events occurred, is Garrett's *The Authentic Life of Billy, the Kid*, from which I have drawn the bulk of my quoted material. Charlie Siringo, one of the Texas posse members who chose not to go with Garrett, published his version of these events in 1885 in his *A Texas Cow Boy, or, Fifteen Years on the Hurricane Deck of a Spanish Pony*. Siringo reproduced the account of posse member Lon Chambers, who Siringo claimed related it to him a short time later. Unfortunately, Siringo liked to spin a good tale even more than the Kid. Other posse members also left accounts, but they were either written or collected decades later and, like Siringo's, are not always reliable. By far the best of these is James East's interview with J. Evetts Haley, Douglas, Arizona, Sept. 27, 1927, J. Evetts Haley Collection. See also the account of Louis Bousman in James H. Earle, ed., *The Capture of Billy the Kid* (College Station, Tex.: Creative Publishing Company, 1988). The two Las Vegas newspapers, the *Gazette* and the *Daily Optic*, also contain valuable contemporary reporting on these same events. See *Billy the Kid: Las Vegas Newspaper Accounts of His Career, 1880–1881*.

Garrett's comment about Tom Folliard's scream after being shot is from Hough, *The Story of the Outlaw*, 302.

The Stinking Spring site is on private property east of the present-day community of Taiban, New Mexico. Only the foundation remains of the rock house, which was discovered in 1984. Some accounts mention that the house had a window, but the majority seems to agree that the only opening in the structure was the doorway. Contemporary writings, including Garrett, refer to the site as Stinking Spring, singular, while later accounts refer to it in the plural, Stinking Springs. I've followed the historic usage. See Allen Barker, "I Refound Stinking Springs," *True West* 36 (Feb. 1989): 14–19.

Garrett does not mention Barney Mason's threat to kill Billy after he was in custody. However, both Jim East and Louis Bousman related the incident. East told the story twice, in the 1927 interview with J. Evetts Haley (cited above) and in a May 1, 1920, letter to Charlie Siringo, reprinted in Siringo's *History of "Billy the Kid,"* 97–105. Bousman told it in his interview with Haley, Oct. 23, 1934.

Both Bousman and East recalled their unpleasant encounter with Manuela Bowdre. East, in his letter to Siringo of May 1, 1920, claimed that Bowdre's wife hit him over the head with a branding iron. In a sad follow-up to Bowdre's death, Acting Governor Ritch received a letter from Captain Joseph C. Lea on Dec. 29 pleading Bowdre's case and requesting Governor Wallace to ask the district attorney to throw out Bowdre's murder indictment (for the killing of Roberts at Blazer's Mill). Lea also enclosed a letter he had received from Bowdre in which Bowdre asked for his help. Lea's letter was written on Dec. 24, the day after Bowdre was killed by Garrett's posse. See Lea to Wallace, Roswell, New Mexico, Dec. 24, 1880, and Bowdre to Lea, Fort Sumner, New Mexico, Dec. 15, 1880, both in William H. Bonney Collection (AC 017-P), Chávez History Library; and the *Daily New Mexican*, Dec. 29, 1880.

For the intimate meeting in the Maxwell residence between Billy and Paulita, see East to Charlie Siringo, Apr. 26, 1920, as quoted in Siringo, *History of "Billy the Kid,"* 105–107; and East to Judge William H. Burgess, Douglas, Arizona, May 20, 1926, Research Files, Robert N. Mullin Collection.

East told of Billy's attempt to trick him in the Puerto de Luna store in his interview with J. Evetts Haley, Sept. 27, 1927.

7. FACING DEATH BOLDLY

Olinger's unusual full name comes from the research of Frederick Nolan, *The West of Billy the Kid* (Norman: University of Oklahoma Press, 1998), 146. Interestingly, Olinger is enumerated in the 1860 U.S. Census for Mound City Township, Linn County, Kansas, as a female (the spelling of the first name in the census is Amaradath). Olinger as the "tall sycamore" is from the *Las Vegas Daily Optic* of Feb. 22, 1881.

Ranger Gillett's brief comments on Olinger are in the James Gillett folder, Box 16, Leon C. Metz Papers. The Gus Gildea quote is from A. M. Gildea to Maurice G. Fulton, Del Rio, Texas, June 5, 1929, Box 2, Folder 2, Maurice G. Fulton Collection, University of Arizona Library Special Collections. Pat Garrett's remarks on his deceased deputy are from Emerson Hough, "The Imitation Bad Man," *Washington Post*, Jan. 21, 1906. Garrett made a similar comment about Olinger to Dr. M. G. Paden. See Paden, "Billy the Kid Story" (typescript), as told to Edith L. Crawford, Nov. 22, 1937, Box 49, Folder 6, Marta Weigle Collection (AC 361), Chávez History Library.

Billy's promise to get Olinger is from Charles Nebo "Nib" Jones to Eve Ball, May 9, 1948, Globe, Arizona, interview typescript, Box 14, Folder 2, Eve Ball Papers. Olinger's "cur" remark is in the *Daily New Mexican*, May 3, 1881. Pat Garrett's description of the hatred that existed between the Kid and Olinger is in his *Authentic Life of Billy, the Kid,* 119.

The quote praising Deputy Bell is from the *Las Vegas Daily Optic*, Jan. 21, 1881. For information on Bell's background, which is frustratingly limited, see O. W. Williams, *Pioneer Surveyor–Frontier Lawyer: The Personal Narrative of O. W. Williams, 1877–1902*, ed. S. D. Myers (El Paso: Texas Western Press, 1968), 89; and the 1880 U.S. Census for White Oaks, Lincoln County, New Mexico.

The fact that Billy's cuffs were both on one hand comes from two letters written from Lincoln immediately after the Kid's courthouse escape. The letters were published in *Supplement to the New Southwest and Herald*, Silver City, New Mexico, May 14,

1881; and the *Daily New Mexican*, May 3, 1881. My account of Billy's escape is drawn from these important letters; a news report published in the *White Oaks Golden Era* of May 5, 1881; Garrett's account in his *The Authentic Life of Billy, the Kid*, 120–123, derived in part from interviews with Gottfried Gauss; an account by Gauss that appeared in the *Lincoln County Leader*, Mar. 1, 1890; and John P. Meadows, *Pat Garrett and Billy the Kid as I Knew Them: Reminiscences of John P. Meadows*, ed. John P. Wilson (Albuquerque: University of New Mexico Press, 2004), 47–50. Meadows, a friend of Billy's, claimed he received his account of the escape directly from the Kid.

Billy's exchange with Garrett regarding the killing of Carlyle is in Garrett, *The Authentic Life of Billy, the Kid*, 119.

Billy's complaint about Olinger's bullying is from Meadows, *Pat Garrett and Billy the Kid*, 47.

The prophetic warning to Olinger is quoted from the *Daily New Mexican*, May 3, 1881.

The incident where Olinger left his pistol on the table in front of the Kid is noted in *Supplement to the New Southwest and Herald*, May 14, 1881.

Olinger's boast that he could herd his prisoner like a goat is from a previously unknown newspaper interview with Garrett titled "Plucky Patrick Garrett," newspaper clipping, Nov. 26, 1900, Pat Garrett Clippings File, Denver Public Library ("The Times" is penciled on this clipping, which may indicate the weekly *Denver Times-Sun*).

Manufactured between 1870 and 1874, not more than twenty-five hundred of the Whitney double-barrel shotguns were ever made. Olinger's shotgun is now in a private collection, the only firearm in existence that we can know with absolute certainty that Billy once used.

Billy's suggestion that Olinger might shoot himself accidentally is quoted from Meadows, *Pat Garrett and Billy the Kid*, 47.

No one really knows how the Kid overpowered and shot Bell that day. Some claim that a gun had been secreted in the outhouse by a Kid confederate (e.g., see the account of Francisco Salazar in Leslie Traylor, "Facts Regarding the Escape of Billy the Kid," *Frontier Times* 13 [July 1936]: 509; and of Harry Aguayo in the *Albuquerque Tribune*, Aug. 1, 1957). It is a theory to which I do not subscribe. Forensic testing at the courthouse using luminol was conducted in 2004, which revealed substantial blood residue at the top of the courthouse stairs, blood that I believe came from the severe blow Billy delivered to Bell's head. For a news report on the forensic investigation, see the *Santa Fe New Mexican*, Aug. 2, 2004.

The last words Billy spoke to Olinger before he killed him have several variations. My source is Garrett, *The Authentic Life of Billy, the Kid*, 121. However, I do not believe that Olinger had time to say to Gauss, "Yes, and he's killed me, too," as Garrett (and Sam Peckinpah) would have us believe.

Severo Gallegos told his story to Eve Ball in 1949. Severo's role that day has been overlooked by most historians of the Kid. Young Severo is enumerated in the 1880 U.S. Census, living in the town of Lincoln, and I am inclined to accept his story. See Severo Gallegos to Eve Ball, Apr. 5, 1949, interview typescript, Box 8, Folder 21, Eve Ball Papers. Severo gave a slightly different version of his actions in an interview with William V. Morrison on Oct. 11, 1949. See C. L. Sonnichsen and William V. Morrison, *Alias Billy the Kid* (Albuquerque: University of New Mexico Press, 1955), 45 n. 44.

My reference to Lilly and La Rue and their feeble efforts to stop the Kid is from the *Las Vegas Daily Optic,* May 3, 1881.

Billy's cursing at the dead bodies of Olinger and Bell is quoted from *Supplement to the New Southwest and Herald,* May 14, 1881.

Billy's promise to return Billy Burt's horse is from Garrett, *The Authentic Life of Billy, the Kid,* 122.

The quote referring to the Kid having acted with the "coolest deliberation" comes from the *Supplement to the New Southwest and Herald,* May 14, 1881.

Garrett's admission to some fault in the Kid's escape is from his *The Authentic Life of Billy, the Kid,* 123.

Several individuals claimed to have encountered Billy after he fled Lincoln. For Francisco Gomez's account, see Leslie Traylor, "Facts Regarding the Escape of Billy the Kid," *Frontier Times* 13 (July 1936): 510. Yginio Salazar related his meeting with the Kid in an interview with J. Evetts Haley on Aug. 17, 1927 (J. Evetts Haley Collection, Midland, Texas). Salazar is buried in the cemetery at Lincoln, New Mexico.

The Lincoln County settlement of Las Tablas was renamed Arabella in 1901. It appears on maps today as Arabela.

The quotes for Billy's meeting with John Meadows come from both Meadows's interview with Haley on June 13, 1936, and his *Pat Garrett and Billy the Kid as I Knew Them: Reminiscences of John P. Meadows,* ed. John P. Wilson (Albuquerque: University of New Mexico Press, 2004), 50–52.

Billy's friend Martin Chavez claimed that he had talked to Billy at Las Tablas after the Lincoln courthouse escape and that Billy had told him that he was going to Fort Sumner to "see the girl who is to be my wife. If I die, all right; then I will die for her." Chavez's statement is in a draft chapter intended for Burns's *The Saga of Billy the Kid.* This draft chapter clearly identifies Paulita Maxwell as Billy's sweetheart; however, on orders from his publisher, Burns revised the chapter to include Paulita's denial (the publisher, Doubleday, Page & Co., feared a lawsuit). A copy of this draft chapter is found in Box 16, Leon C. Metz Papers.

8. THE DARKENED ROOM

Billy the Kid's death warrant may be found in the microfilm series Territorial Archives of New Mexico, roll 21, frames 581–582, NMSRCA.

Convincing evidence that Wallace was undeserving of the criticism he received for his performance at the Battle of Shiloh is found in Timothy B. Smith, "Why Lew Was Late," *Civil War Times* 46 (Jan. 2008): 30–37.

The story of Wallace adding handwritten comments to the offending passages of Badeau's *Military History of Ulysses S. Grant* is from *The Bucks County Gazette,* Bristol, Pennsylvania, June 23, 1881.

Wallace's description of the Kid being serenaded while in the Lincoln jail is contained in his Mar. 31, 1879, letter to Secretary of the Interior Carl Schurz and is as quoted in Jason Strykowski, "An Unholy Bargain in a Cursed Place: Lew Wallace, William Bonney, and New Mexico Territory," *New Mexico Historical Review* 82 (Spring 2007): 246–247.

The sales figures for *Ben-Hur* are as reported in the *Daily New Mexican,* Dec. 22, 1880.

The telegraph message to Wallace is as quoted in the *Daily New Mexican,* May 1, 1881.

The *Daily New Mexican* for May 1 through May 3 contains the coverage of Billy's escape from Lincoln. For examples of the varied newspapers that carried the Kid's escape on their front pages, see the *Chicago Tribune,* May 5, 1881; *The Helena Independent,* Helena, Montana, May 18, 1881; and *The Janesville Daily Gazette,* Janesville, Wisconsin, May 5, 1881.

The quote from the anonymous Lincoln correspondent cautioning Governor Wallace appears in the *Daily New Mexican* of May 3, 1881, as does Wallace's reward notice for the Kid.

The story of Governor Wallace practicing his pistol shooting at the Palace, previously unknown, comes from the *Chicago Daily Tribune,* Mar. 13, 1892. It was related by someone who claimed to have been with Wallace in Santa Fe, although the storyteller's name is not revealed in the article.

For Garrett's feelings of guilt in the deaths of Olinger and Bell, see his *Authentic Life of Billy, The Kid,* 123.

Pat Garrett served as the executor of Bob Olinger's estate. The estate inventory, prepared by Garrett, was brief: one wallet with papers, no value; one shotgun, Whitney patent (serial #903), broken, no value; one Elgin watch (serial #979197), value one dollar; one set clothes, no value. Interestingly, there is no mention of Olinger's revolver in the inventory. According to Eve Ball, his revolver, field glasses, and gauntlets were presented to Lily Casey, with whom he is said to have been engaged. See Lily Klasner, *My Girlhood Among Outlaws,* ed. Eve Ball (Tucson: University of Arizona Press, 1972), 185 and 188. The wallet and papers Olinger had on him the day he was killed, complete with bloodstains, are on display in the Lincoln County Clerk's Office, Carrizozo, New Mexico.

Garrett's words to Hough that he knew he would have to kill the Kid are quoted from Emerson Hough, *The Story of the Outlaw: A Study of the Western Desperado* (New York: The Outing Publishing Company, 1907), 305.

Barney Mason's efforts in tracking the Kid and his uncomfortable encounter with the outlaw are chronicled in Garrett, *Authentic Life of Billy, The Kid,* 124; the *Las Vegas Gazette,* May 12 and 15, 1881; the *Las Vegas Morning Gazette,* June 16, 1881; and the *Las Vegas Daily Optic,* May 14, 1881. Although the majority of accounts agree that Billy stole Montgomery Bell's horse at Fort Sumner, Frank T. Encinias wrote that Saval Gutiérrez stole the horse for Billy's use. Encinias obtained his information on the Kid from interviews with Saval Gutiérrez, Jesus Silva, Jose Lobato, and several other Fort Sumner Hispanos. The interesting Encinias account is only available in a rare untitled and undated pamphlet.

The news report claiming that Billy was hanging around Fort Sumner because of a girlfriend was published in the *Chicago Tribune,* June 13, 1881.

For the Billy/Paulita relationship, see Frederick Nolan, "The Private Life of Billy the Kid," *True West* 47 (July 2000): 38–39. After receiving the news of Billy's Lincoln escape, Sheriff James W. Southwick wrote Garrett to inform the lawman that while

Billy was incarcerated in Mesilla, he had shown Southwick a letter from "his Girl a Miss Maxwell." Because she was "very much struck on Billy," Southwick suggested that Garrett keep a close watch on her. See James W. Southwick to E. A. Brininstool, Springfield, Illinois, Sept. 18, 1920, Box 3G468, Folder 2, E. A. Brininstool Collection, Center for American History, University of Texas at Austin.

In an interview with author Walter Noble Burns, Paulita supposedly denied that she was Billy's sweetheart. However, she told a different story to Miguel Antonio Otero in a 1926 interview, or so Otero claimed to a newspaper reporter in an article published on July 14, 1926, presumably in the *Santa Fe New Mexican*. My source is a clipping in the Charles Siringo Papers (AC 212), Fray Angélico Chávez History Library, Santa Fe.

Another Fort Sumner woman linked with Billy the Kid was Abrana García, whose son, José Patrocinio "Pat" García, was rumored to have been fathered by Billy. See Elbert A. García, *Billy the Kid's Kid: The Hispanic Connection* (Santa Rosa, N. Mex.: Los Products Press, 1999).

Garrett's comments regarding his purposeful respite in pursuing the Kid, as well as his doubts about the Kid's presence at Fort Sumner, are in his *Authentic Life of Billy the Kid*, 125.

For my description of the Kid's death and the events immediately preceding, I have relied primarily on the firsthand accounts of Garrett, his deputy, John W. Poe, and contemporary newspaper reports from the *Daily New Mexican* and the *Las Vegas Daily Optic*. Garrett's version is found in his July 15, 1881, report to the governor as published in the *Daily New Mexican*, July 19, 1881; his interview with the *Las Vegas Daily Optic*, July 18, 1881; his interview with the *Daily New Mexican*, July 21, 1881; his 1882 account as published in his *The Authentic Life of Billy, the Kid;* his interview that appeared in "Plucky Patrick Garrett," a newspaper clipping dated Nov. 26, 1900, Pat Garrett Clippings File, Denver Public Library (possibly published in the *Denver Times-Sun*); his 1902 interview originally published in the *New York World* and copied in various forms in several other newspapers, including the *Kansas City Journal*, July 20, 1902, *Galveston Daily News*, Aug. 3, 1902, and the *Davenport Daily Republican*, Davenport, Iowa, Aug. 7, 1902; and his account as quoted in Hough, *The Story of the Outlaw*, 307–311. John Poe's version appears in *An Illustrated History of New Mexico* (Chicago: Lewis Publishing Co., 1895); his 1917 letter to Charles Goodnight, published in Nolan, ed., *The Billy the Kid Reader*, 331–338; and his own *The Death of Billy the Kid* (Boston: Houghton Mifflin Co., 1933). I am skeptical of a great deal of Poe's version of events. He claims much of the responsibility for the Kid's demise, from getting Garrett to travel to Fort Sumner in the first place to then persuading Garrett to visit Maxwell on the night of July 14 (Poe does not address why he failed to seek out Maxwell himself while he was in Fort Sumner for several hours earlier in the day). I suspect that Poe, perhaps envious of the massive attention received by Garrett, purposely enhanced his role in the affair.

The importance of the U.S. mail in Garrett's efforts to locate the Kid has generally been overlooked. In his July 15 report to the governor, Garrett wrote that he "had received several communications from persons in and about Fort Sumner, that William Bonny, alias the Kid, had been there, or in that vicinity for some time." James B. Gillett, a former Texas Ranger and a friend of Garrett's, wrote in 1923 that "Pat

Garrett told me out of his own mouth that a certain merchant in Fort Sumner had written him that the Kid was there hanging around Pete Maxwells, as Kid was stuck on one of Pet[e]s half breed daughters." Garrett told the *Las Vegas Daily Optic*, in the interview cited above, that "the first definite information he received that the 'Kid' was at Fort Sumner was contained in a letter written to him by Manuel Brazil." See James B. Gillett to E. A. Brininstool, Marfa, Texas, Feb. 21, 1923, Box 3G469, E. A. Brininstool Collection.

For information on Thomas "Kip" McKinney, see Nolan, *The West of Billy the Kid*, 280; 1870 U.S. Census for Uvalde County, Texas; F. W. Grey, *Seeking Fortune in America* (London: Smith, Elder & Co., 1912), 110; and Frank M. King, *Wranglin' the Past: The Reminiscences of Frank M. King* (Pasadena, Calif.: Trail's End Publishing Co., 1946), 173. Interestingly, McKinney was a cousin of Tom Folliard, and on his deathbed, Folliard had asked Barney Mason to tell McKinney to write his grandmother back in Texas and inform her of his death. Of Garrett, Poe, and McKinney, only McKinney failed to leave a written account of the shooting of the Kid. However, James B. Gillett employed McKinney as a cowhand for "many months" at the Estado Land and Cattle Company, and Gillett wrote that McKinney "told about the same storey as Powe and Garrett" (Gillett to Brininstool, Feb. 21, 1923). A much less reliable source is one Howell Johnson, county attorney for Pecos County, Texas, who in 1933 claimed that Kip McKinney told him that McKinney and not Garrett had shot Billy (*El Paso Herald-Post*, Nov. 25, 1933). In recent years, historians and outlaw buffs have pounced upon a fanciful tale in Grey's *Seeking Fortune in America* that has Garrett and McKinney tying and gagging Billy's girlfriend (presumably Paulita) so that Garrett could then ambush the unsuspecting lover from behind a sofa. The historians and buffs infer that Grey got this account directly from McKinney, but Grey makes no such claim. Grey's other whoppers include the assertion that the Kid was a "half-breed Indian" and that Billy supposedly "originated, or at least brought to perfection, the art of whirling a gun and shooting" (p. 118). Grey apparently did know Kip McKinney, but, needless to say, his book should be used with caution.

For information on the Colt and Winchester Garrett confiscated from Billy Wilson at Stinking Spring, see Mary'n Rosson, "The Gun That Killed Billy the Kid," *Old West* 14 (Winter 1977): 6–9, 32, 36–37.

There are conflicting accounts regarding Billy's destination after leaving the peach orchard. Jesus Silva claimed Billy came to his dwelling. Paco Anaya preserved testimony from Celsa and Saval Gutiérrez wherein they said Billy came to their residence. The conversation I quote between Celsa and Billy is from Anaya, *I Buried Billy*, 125–126. The Anaya/Gutiérrez account is supported by a 1951 signed affidavit from Celsa's son, Candido, in which he said the Kid stopped in their home the night he was killed. Candido stated that he saw Billy pick up the butcher knife the outlaw was later killed with; the knife belonged to his mother. The Candido Gutiérrez affidavit is reproduced in Frederick Nolan, "The Saga of the Kid Butcher Knife," *The Outlaw Gazette* (Billy the Kid Outlaw Gang, Inc.) 10 (Nov. 1997): 7.

There has been some debate over the years as to whether or not the Kid was armed with his pistol when he was shot by Garrett. Miguel Antonio Otero claimed that Jesus Silva and Deluvina Maxwell both stated to him "most positively" that Billy had only his butcher knife when they first observed the body. However, Jesus Silva contradicted himself when he told newspaperman Jack Hull in 1938 that he saw Billy's body with a knife in one hand and a pistol in the other. Remember, after he was confident that the Kid was dead, Garrett entered the room and at some point examined the Kid's pistol to see if it had been fired. He would not then have placed the pistol back on the floor, which might explain why those who entered the room afterward saw only a butcher knife—that is, if we are to accept the claims of Deluvina and Silva on this matter, which I do not. It is ludicrous to think that the Kid would have gone anywhere without a firearm. And it is highly unlikely that the Kid would have confronted Deputy Poe if armed only with a butcher knife.

The best description of Deluvina Maxwell is found in a letter by Jack Potter written on Feb. 15, 1949, and published in Rose P. White, "Full Many a Flower . . . ," *The New Mexico Folklore Record* 4 (1949–50): 15–16. Potter knew Deluvina in the 1880s. The Paulita Maxwell quote about Deluvina is in Burns, *Saga of Billy the Kid*, 195. Deluvina was interviewed by J. Evetts Haley at Fort Sumner, June 24, 1927. Interestingly, in that interview she claimed that she did not see Billy's body until the following morning. The interview is in the collections of the Panhandle-Plains Historical Museum, Canyon, Texas.

John Poe's recollection regarding Paulita's lack of emotion is from Walter Noble Burns's rejected draft chapter for *Saga of Billy the Kid*, Box 16, Leon C. Metz Papers.

Although Garrett and others have referred to the jury that investigated the Kid's death as a "coroner's jury," there was no coroner present. A copy of the handwritten verdict of the jury, written entirely in Spanish, is in the Frank W. Parker Papers, NMSRCA. Evidence that Saval Gutiérrez and fellow jury members José Silva and Lorenzo Jaramillo were illiterate is obtained from the fact that they did not sign their names to the verdict but instead made their marks next to their names.

Hispanic old-timers of Fort Sumner who were interviewed in the 1920s and 1930s about Billy's death and its aftermath include Jesus Silva, Frank Lobato, Vicente Otero, and Anastacio Trujillo. See Otero, *The Real Billy the Kid*, 155–158, and Jack Hull, "Only One Man Living Who Saw 'Billy the Kid' in Both Life and Death," *Clovis News-Journal*, Clovis, New Mexico, July 13, 1938.

The account of the Kid's funeral comes from an article by Jack Potter, who was not an eyewitness but claimed to have obtained his information from Fort Sumner residents in 1884. Potter's account is reprinted in Nolan, *The Billy the Kid Reader*, 339–342. In another article, Potter claimed that Billy's grave marker bore the following words: "Billy the Kid (Bonney)/July 14, 1881." He added that in the left-hand corner there appeared a small inscription in a woman's handwriting (he does not explain how he identified the gender of the inscription's author): "Dormir Bien Querido," which Potter translated as "sleep well, dear one." Potter, a popular New Mexico storyteller, seldom felt constrained by the truth. On a visit to the cemetery in January 1882, a special correspondent for the *Las Vegas Daily Optic* reported that the Kid's marker contained only the stenciled words "Billy the Kid"; the *Optic* article even provided a facsimile of the inscription. See Colonel Jack Potter, "Post-Mortem on Billy the Kid," *Ranch Romances* 73 (First May Number, 1937): 131–133; and Marc Simmons, *Stalking Billy the Kid: Brief Sketches of a Short Life* (Santa Fe: Sunstone Press, 2006), 175.

9. BOTH HERO AND VILLAIN

For contemporary news reports on the Kid's death culled from various newspapers, see Harold L. Edwards, *Goodbye Billy the Kid* (College Station, Tex.: Creative Publishing Company, 1995).

Garrett's defense of Pete Maxwell is in the *Daily New Mexican* of July 21, 1881. Some historians have suggested that Pete Maxwell was the primary informant who tipped off Garrett to Billy's presence at Fort Sumner, supposedly because Maxwell objected to his sister's relationship with the outlaw. If that was the case, it is very odd that Garrett did not mention that Maxwell was his informant to the *New Mexican* reporter. What better way to exonerate Maxwell? And Garrett could have done it without bringing up Paulita.

For Garrett's attempt to collect the reward money on the Kid, see the *Daily New Mexican* of July 21, 1881, and Ritch's report on Garrett's application in Territorial Archives of New Mexico, roll 21, frames 595–596.

For the subscription efforts on behalf of Garrett, see the *Daily New Mexican,* July 21, 29, and 39; the *Las Vegas Daily Optic,* July 19, 1881; the *Chicago Tribune,* Aug. 7, 1881; and the *Rio Grande Republican,* Sept. 2, 1882.

The Globe of Atchison, Kansas, which slandered Garrett in its issue of Aug. 1, 1881, had praised the lawman just two days previous. *The Globe,* which was a faithful reader of the *Las Vegas Daily Optic* due to both cities' being on the same rail line, commented on the story of Billy's finger being requested by his "sweetheart" in its issue of Sept. 23, 1881. There is no Kate Tenney in the 1880 U.S. Census for Oakland, Alameda County. However, there is a Kate Terney, a thirty-two-year-old native of Ireland whose occupation is given as servant.

For a good description of the nickel novels about Billy the Kid that appeared in 1881, see J. C. Dykes, *Billy the Kid: The Bibliography of a Legend* (Albuquerque: University of New Mexico Press, 1952). There is a common misconception that there were scores of dime novels published that featured the exploits of Billy the Kid. Actually, Billy was not a popular dime novel subject, with less than twelve or so known to have featured the outlaw, all of which appeared after his death. Much more popular was Jesse James, who appeared in dozens of dime novels. My thanks to J. Randolph Cox, editor of *Dime Novel Round-Up,* for setting me straight on the Kid's role in these famed yellow-back potboilers.

Don Jenardo's *The True Life of Billy the Kid* was number 451 in the *Five Cent Wide Awake Library,* published by Frank Tousey, New York.

In a letter to a niece written about two months after publication of *The Authentic Life of Billy, the Kid,* Upson claimed that he had written "every word" of Garrett's book, which was likely true, as Garrett may have dictated his account to his friend. Upson's contributions to the book were acknowledged in the New Mexico press in 1885. "He wrote the 'Life of Billy the Kid,' for Pat Garrett," stated the *Albuquerque Journal* (as quoted in the *Rio Grande Republican,* Dec. 26, 1885). Interestingly, the *Rio Grande Republican* referred to Upson as the "compiler" of Garrett's book in its issue of Feb. 7, 1885. Upson's letter to his niece is reproduced in James D. Shinkle, *Reminiscences of Roswell Pioneers,* 22.

The *Rio Grande Republican* of Dec. 3, 1881, announced that Garrett had closed on the contract with the New Mexican Printing and Publishing Co. to produce his book. The first announcement that the book was completed and ready for sale appeared in the *Daily New Mexican* of Mar. 12, 1882.

In his *History of "Billy the Kid,"* 133, Charlie Siringo stated that Garrett had Billy's body dug up. Phil LeNoir, who seems to have been inspired by Siringo's account, wrote a superb poem about the episode titled "The Finger of Billy the Kid." See LeNoir's *Rhymes of the Wild & Wooly* (Santa Fe: privately printed, 1920).

For information on the different printings of Garrett's *The Authentic Life of Billy, the Kid,* I am grateful to Robert McCubbin of Santa Fe, New Mexico. McCubbin owns three variants of Garrett's book, including an *extremely* rare copy bound in red flexible leather. Apparently, a very few copies of the book were bound in leather as special presentation copies for Garrett's use. McCubbin's leather-bound copy is indeed inscribed "from the author." Bob McCubbin to Mark L. Gardner, Santa Fe, New Mexico, Dec. 21, 2007.

For the meeting between Pat Garrett and Joseph Antrim, see the *Albuquerque Review*, Aug. 2, 1882 (typescript in Leon C. Metz Papers); and *Galveston Daily News*, Dec. 15, 1881. My information on the Armijo Hotel comes from *The Albuquerque Tribune*, Feb. 10, 1958; and Marc Simmons, *Albuquerque: A Narrative History* (Albuquerque: University of New Mexico Press, 1982), 226.

Garrett's displeasure with the office of Lincoln County sheriff was reported in the *Daily New Mexican*, July 19, 1881; and the *Rio Grande Republican*, July 23, 1881.

Records pertaining to the payment of Garrett's reward are found in Territorial Archives of New Mexico, roll 5, frames 127, 765–766; Pat F. Garrett: Settlements for Services Rendered, Territorial Auditor Collection #1960-030, Box 11, Folder 2, NMSRCA; and Territorial Auditor's Daybook, p. 178, NMSRCA.

Garrett's Elgin pocket watch (object #85.3.1) is currently part of the collections of the Autry Museum of the American West, Los Angeles, California. Garrett's gold Lincoln County sheriff's badge sold at auction in San Francisco on June 16, 2008, for $100,000. The badge is currently on display in the private Ruidoso River Museum, Ruidoso, New Mexico. See "Pat Garrett's Sheriff's Badge Nets $100,000," *San Francisco Chronicle*, June 17, 2008. Notice of the walking cane appeared in the *Daily New Mexican*, Mar. 31, 1883.

The *Rio Grande Republican*, July 22, 1882, reported on Garrett's decision not to run for a second term as sheriff.

For Garrett's Territorial Council run, the controversial letters from "X" and "Texan," and Garrett's pistol whipping of Roberts, see the *Rio Grande Republican*, Sept. 2, 16, 19, and 23, Nov. 4, 11, and 18; and *El Paso Lone Star*, May 14, 1884.

James E. Sligh, Garrett's friend and the former editor and publisher of the *White Oaks Golden Era*, recorded Garrett's comments about his marriage to Polinaria and the racism the couple faced: "Some people seem to think that a man who marries a Mexican woman, and stays with her, lets himself down in the estimation of white people; but I can't help that; I married my wife because I loved her and I love her still, and I intend to stay with her to the end. If people don't like me because of my wife, they can simply let me alone." When Sligh asked Garrett what his family in Louisiana thought of the marriage, Garrett said that they looked at it "as if I had married a nigger, and you know how our Southern folks take a thing like that." See Sligh, "The Lincoln County War: A Sequel to the Story of 'Billy the Kid,'" 170–171.

On Feb. 3, 1883, Garrett and Poe entered into an agreement with John N. Copeland to purchase a little over one hundred head of cattle at $22.50 each. A copy of the agreement is in the Herman B. Weisner Papers, Ms 249, Box 4, Folder G/5, Rio Grande Historical Collections, New Mexico State University Archives, Las Cruces.

The story of the Panhandle cowboy strike and the formation and activities of Garrett's rangers is best chronicled in Frederick Nolan, *Tascosa: Its Life and Gaudy Times* (Lubbock: Texas Tech University Press, 2007).

The *El Paso Lone Star* comment on Garrett's rangers is quoted from its issue of July 2, 1884. Garrett's unit was not part of the famed Texas Rangers. His company is often referred to as the LS rangers, because the largest financial backer was the LS outfit.

Garrett's purchase of the Ki Harrison ranch in Lincoln County for $5,000 was reported in the *Lone Star* of Apr. 12, 1884.

John Meadows's quote about Garrett preventing another Lincoln County War is from Nolan, *Tascosa*, 168. Garrett's suspicion that he was hired as an assassin is from Hough, *The Story of the Outlaw*, 299.

For evidence of Garrett's relocation with his family to Las Vegas, see the *Lincoln Golden Era*, Jan. 1 and 8, 1885. A copy of Garrett's oath of office for the position of cattle inspector, San Miguel County, New Mexico, Mar. 18, 1885, is in the Leon C. Metz Papers, Box 16.

Brandon C. Kirby's background and his relationship with Garrett are documented in the *Rio Grande Republican*, Aug. 8, 1885; and the *Las Vegas Daily Optic*, Dec. 6, 12, and 15, 1890.

The downturn in the New Mexico cattle business in 1886 was mentioned by Sophie Poe, wife of John W. Poe, in a letter to W. T. Moyers, Aug. 18, 1951, Box 10B, Folder 4C, Fred M. Mazzulla Collection, #1881, Stephen H. Hart Library, Colorado Historical Society, Denver.

For Garrett's irrigation business, see Metz, *Pat Garrett*, 149–154; James D. Shinkle, *Fifty Years of Roswell History, 1867–1917* (Roswell, N.Mex.: Hall-Poorbaugh Press, 1964), 93–98; and Stephen Bogener, *Ditches Across the Desert: Irrigation in the Lower Pecos Valley* (Lubbock: Texas Tech University Press, 2003).

The description of Garrett's farm is from the *Las Vegas Daily Optic* of Mar. 27, 1889. Garrett's business endeavors and political aspirations are well documented in the *Pecos Valley Register*, published in Roswell, in various issues for 1889 and 1890.

In his run for Chaves County sheriff, Garrett had been endorsed by both the *Las Vegas Daily Optic* and Roswell's *Pecos Valley Register*. He lost to the man Poe endorsed: Campbell C. Fountain.

Garrett's letter to Polinaria discussing trade for the Uvalde ditch was written from El Paso, Texas, Sept. 2, 1889. The letter is in a private collection.

The story of how Elizabeth Garrett lost her eyesight is from an interview with Mae Marley, Roswell, New Mexico, Apr. 26, 1966, Buckner Collection of Elizabeth Garrett Materials, 1893–1992, Coll. #1992-025, NMSRCA.

Ida Garrett's letter to M. A. Upson, July 24, 1891, is in the private collection of Robert G. McCubbin.

The *Uvalde Herald* article on the increase in blooded horses in west Texas is as quoted in the *Galveston Daily News,* Oct. 29, 1891.

Garrett's purchase of the St. Louis steam engine for "experiments on irrigation by machinery" was reported in the *Roswell Record,* June 23, 1893.

Garrett's letter to Polinaria, Mar. 21, 1894, is reproduced in *The Kid* (Mar. 1990): 5–6.

On Oct. 6, 1894, Ash Upson, Garrett's odd, liquor-guzzling friend of many years, died at the Garrett home. He would have turned sixty-six years old in a month.

10. ANOTHER MANHUNT

For Albert Jennings Fountain, see A. M. Gibson, *The Life and Death of Colonel Albert Jennings Fountain* (Norman: University of Oklahoma Press, 1965); and Gordon R. Owen, *The Two Alberts: Fountain and Fall* (Las Cruces: Yucca Tree Press, 1996).

For a newspaper report on Governor Thornton's El Paso meeting with Garrett, see the *San Antonio Light,* Feb. 22, 1896.

Garrett's letter to Polinaria, Feb. 25, 1896, is as quoted in Jarvis Garrett's foreword to a reprint of his father's *The Authentic Life of Billy, the Kid* (Albuquerque: Horn & Wallace, 1964), 25.

For Charles C. Perry, see Larry D. Ball, "Lawman in Disgrace: Sheriff Charles C. Perry of Chaves County, New Mexico," *New Mexico Historical Review* 61 (Apr. 1986): 125–136.

Garrett's words about never quitting are in his letter to Polinaria, Mar. 8, 1896, Las Cruces, New Mexico. A copy of this letter is in the Donald Cline Collection, Series 10419, Folder 68, NMSRCA.

For my narrative regarding the Fountain killings and the subsequent investigation and trial of Lee and Gililland, I have relied primarily on the reports of Pinkerton operatives John C. Fraser and William B. Sayers and *El Paso Daily Herald* reports on the Lee and Gililland trial, May 27–June 16, 1899. Copies of the Pinkerton reports were provided me by historian John P. Wilson. Copies are also available in the Charles Siringo Papers, Chávez History Library, Santa Fe, and the C. L. Sonnichsen Papers, MS 141, C. L. Sonnichsen Special Collections Department, University of Texas at El Paso Library. A detailed examination of the Fountain investigation and the Lee and Gililland murder trial is Corey Recko's *Murder on the White Sands: The Disappearance of Albert and Henry Fountain* (Denton, Tex.: University of North Texas Press, 2007).

During the summer of 1896, while he was in the midst of the Fountain investigation, Garrett helped secure a presidential pardon for Billy Wilson, Billy the Kid's old partner in crime, who had been living in Texas under an assumed name. See Rasch, *Trailing Billy the Kid,* 65–67.

Fall's assistance in securing Garrett's appointment as Doña Ana County sheriff was not a magnanimous gesture. Fall was able to negotiate with the governor the appointment of a new board of county commissioners—all Democrats. The unusual steps taken to secure the sheriff's office for Garrett are explained in the *Rio Grande Republican,* Aug. 14, 1896.

My account of Garrett and Maggie Fountain at the Republican rally is from the *Rio Grande Republican,* Nov. 6, 1896.

The legendary Tularosa poker game is related by Curry, a participant, in *George Curry, 1861–1947: An Autobiography*, 106–107.

The two Apr. 3, 1898, affidavits outlining Garrett's evidence in the Fountain case are reproduced in Keleher, *The Fabulous Frontier*, 216–218.

There are several accounts of the Wildy Well gunfight, making for a bit of a mess when trying to figure out exactly what happened that day. Garrett's version of events is in his sworn testimony during the trial of Lee and Gililland, as reported in the *El Paso Daily Herald*, June 7, 1899; and his account as published in the *Rio Grande Republican*, July 15, 1898. Oliver Lee gave his version thirty-nine years later to William A. Keleher, who published it in his *The Fabulous Frontier*, 200–222. By far the most interesting account is the Aug. 18, 1898, sworn statement left by Mary Madison, which, not surprisingly, is highly critical of Garrett. Her statement is in Box 11, Folder 22, Albert B. Fall Family Papers, Ms 8, Rio Grande Historical Collections.

The report that Lee withdrew a large amount of money at El Paso appeared in the *Galveston Daily News*, July 16, 1898.

The story of Lee getting startled during a poker game at the Cox ranch is from Emmett Isaacs to Herman B. Weisner, 1962, interview typescript, Box 27, Folder 1, Eve Ball Papers.

Numerous historians and authors have enjoyed repeating the tale that Albert B. Fall came up with the idea to create Otero County in order to help Lee and Gililland out of their fix, as the boundaries of the new Otero County just encompassed the Fountain murder site, technically giving Otero legal jurisdiction over the case. Fall, however, was still on active military duty when Otero County came into existence, and the issue of Otero's legal jurisdiction never became a factor in the subsequent trial of Lee and Gililland. The truth of the matter is that Lee and Gililland saw an influential ally in Sheriff George Curry, who obviously had the ear of Governor Otero, and, too, they were weary of running from a determined Pat Garrett.

George Curry's account of his negotiations with Lee, Otero, and Judge Parker are in *George Curry, 1861–1947: An Autobiography*, 111–113.

For Eugene Manlove Rhodes, see W. H. Hutchinson, *A Bar Cross Man: The Life and Personal Writings of Eugene Manlove Rhodes* (Norman: University of Oklahoma Press, 1956). Although Rhodes was an unabashed Lee partisan, he would go on to write a noted essay defending Pat Garrett and his conduct in hunting down and killing Billy the Kid. See Rhodes, "In Defense of Pat Garrett," *Sunset* 59 (Sept. 1927): 26–27, 85–91.

There are several versions of Garrett's encounter with Lee and Gililland on the train ride to Las Cruces. See "Surrendered," *Los Angeles Times*, Mar. 14, 1899; Mrs. C. C. Chase (daughter of A. B. Fall) interview typescript, Jan. 13, 1966, Leon C. Metz Papers; Hutchinson, *A Bar Cross Man*, 64–66; W. H. Hutchinson, *Another Verdict for Oliver Lee* (Clarendon, Tex.: Clarendon Press, 1965), 2–4; and Keleher, *The Fabulous Frontier*, 225–226.

The newspaper story giving Garrett's height as seven feet appeared in the *Idaho Daily Statesman*, Boise, Idaho, May 30, 1899.

John C. Fraser's letter to Governor Thornton, written at Denver, Colorado, Apr. 4, 1896, in which he states his suspicion of Oliver Lee, is in the Pinkerton reports, cited above. In the most recent full-length treatment of the Fountain murders, *Murder on the White Sands,* author Corey Recko offers his opinion that Lee, Gililland, and McNew were guilty of waylaying and killing Albert and Henry Fountain.

II. UNWANTED STAR

For the shooting of Norman Newman at the Cox ranch, see the *Rio Grande Republican,* Oct. 13 and 27, 1899; Metz, *Pat Garrett,* 237–239; and Garrett's own account in Hough, *The Story of the Outlaw,* 10–12. The bulldog, Old Booze, belonged to Albert B. Fall, so it only seems right that the dog would come in on the side of the defense.

I derived my details on Print Rhode from a Nov. 9, 1967, interview between James Cox and Leon Metz, typescript in the Leon C. Metz Papers; a Jan. 30, 1968, interview between Willis Walter and Leon Metz, typescript in Leon C. Metz Papers; the Arizona Territorial Prison (Florence) record for A. P. Rhode, Pinal County Historical Museum, Florence, Arizona; 1870 and 1880 U.S. censuses for Lavaca County, Texas; 1900 U.S. Census for Doña Ana County, New Mexico; and 1910 U.S. Census for Yavapai County, Arizona.

The best synopsis of the Las Cruces bank robbery and its aftermath is Harold L. Edwards, "Pat Garrett and the Las Cruces Bank Robbery," *True West* 45 (Feb. 1998): 8–13. I have also consulted the reports on the robbery and subsequent trial as published in the *Rio Grande Republican.* William Wilson received a ten-year sentence for bank robbery, and Oscar Wilbur received a reduced sentence of five years. Governor Otero granted Wilbur a full pardon six months later.

Garrett's interview discussing his decision to retire as Doña Ana County sheriff, as well as the reference to his sobriquet, is from "Plucky Patrick Garrett," newspaper clipping, Nov. 26, 1900.

Much of my quoted material on Garrett's rocky tenure as El Paso collector of customs comes from Jack DeMattos's *Garrett and Roosevelt* (College Station, Tex.: Creative Publishing Company, 1988), which reproduces numerous primary sources, including telegrams, letters, newspaper reports, Treasury Department correspondence, and the correspondence between Emerson Hough and President Roosevelt. See also Leon C. Metz, "Pat Garrett, El Paso Customs Collector," *Arizona and the West* 11 (Winter 1969): 327–340.

Garrett's Dec. 9, 1901, letter to Polinaria mentioning his meeting with Lew Wallace is reproduced in *The Estate of Richard C. Marohn, M.D.,* auction catalog (San Francisco: Butterfield & Butterfield, 1996), 131. Garrett and Wallace's visit to the White House was reported in the *Galveston Daily News,* Dec. 12, 1901.

The most bizarre attack on Garrett came from his former partner in the buffalo hide business, Willis Skelton Glenn. Glenn, bitter that Garrett had recently failed to corroborate his inflated Indian depredations claim with the federal government, determined to press charges against his old partner for the killing of Joe Briscoe twenty-five years previous. Glenn consulted with the Tarrant County attorney in Fort Worth, who told him he would have to press the murder charges in west Texas. Failing to derail Garrett's appointment, Glenn seems to have decided not to follow through with this threat. See *The Atlanta Constitution,* Dec. 17, 1901.

Garrett's discussion with Roosevelt during his Dec. 15 visit to the White House is quoted from "He Shot Billy The Kid," *Kansas City Journal,* July 20, 1902, clipping typescript in Maurice G. Fulton Collection.

Garrett's original commission as collector of customs and the engraved Wirt fountain pen the president used to sign the commission are illustrated in *The Estate of Richard C. Marohn, M.D.,* 132.

The newspaper article "Made the General Pay" appeared in the *Galveston Daily News,* Oct. 18, 1902.

The *New York Evening World* piece criticizing Roosevelt for his appointments of "killers" ran in its issue of Feb. 7, 1905.

The *Washington Post* issue of Dec. 16, 1905, contained the report that Garrett looked dejected after visiting the White House.

Garrett's interview with the Fort Worth reporter was published in the *Galveston Daily News,* Dec. 24, 1905.

The Finstad case and Garrett's connection thereto was reported in the *Los Angeles Times,* Jan. 2, 5, and 13, 1906; and the *Washington Post,* Mar. 17, 1906. A copy of Garrett's letter to President Roosevelt, Jan. 21, 1906, is in Folder 25, Patrick F. Garrett Family Papers, Ms 282, Rio Grande Historical Collections.

Garrett's Chihuahua mining proposition is described in a letter to Emerson Hough, May 9, 1906, El Paso, Texas, Folder 25, Patrick F. Garrett Family Papers.

The problems encountered in trying to collect on Garrett are detailed in W. G. Waltz to T. B. Catron, El Paso, Texas, May 31, 1904, copy in Leon C. Metz Papers.

Garrett's legal difficulties with the Bank of Commerce, Albuquerque, are chronicled in Metz, *Pat Garrett,* 277–280; and Don Cline, "Pat Garrett's Tragic Lawsuit," *Old West* 25 (Summer 1989): 18–23. A manuscript version of Cline's article, with a detailed list of sources, is in the Donald Cline Collection, Folder 69.

The "Dead Beat" book from Bentley's Organ store is in the Louis B. Bentley Papers, Ms 14, Rio Grande Historical Collections.

Albert Fall's decision to share in Garrett's Las Cruces grocery bill was recounted by his daughter, Mrs. C. C. Chase, in an interview with Leon C. Metz, Jan. 13, 1966, Leon C. Metz Papers.

The exchange between Albert Fall and Pat Garrett over the $50 check is from A. B. Fall to P. F. Garrett, El Paso, Texas, Dec. 29, 1906; and P. F. Garrett to A. B. Fall, Ranch (Black Mountain ranch), Jan. 15, 1907, Box 8, Folder 1, Albert B. Fall Family Papers.

The possibility of Garrett receiving the appointment as superintendent of the territorial prison was mentioned in the *Rio Grande Republican,* Apr. 27, 1907. Garrett's letter to Polinaria requesting his Prince Albert coat for the Curry inauguration was written at El Paso on July 24, 1907. The letter is in a private collection.

Garrett's brief venture into the El Paso real estate business with the firm of Maple & Co. was reported in the *Rio Grande Republican* of Aug. 31, 1907.

For Garrett's dalliance with the mysterious Mrs. Brown, see Metz, *Pat Garrett,* 284. Emerson Hough's reference to Garrett's "indiscretion" is as quoted in DeMattos, *Garrett and Roosevelt,* 116.

My description of Wayne Brazel comes from Clara Snow to Eve Ball, Nov. 7, 1977, Ruidoso, New Mexico, interview typescript, Box 17, Folder 21, Eve Ball Papers; Mrs.

C. C. Chase interview typescript, January 13, 1966, Leon C. Metz Papers; Sterling Rhode to Herman Weisner, undated interview, Leon C. Metz Papers; and *San Antonio Light*, Mar. 5, 1908.

A copy of the lease between Brazel and Poe Garrett is in Box 27, Folder 3, Eve Ball Papers. The use of Poe Garrett's name in the lease agreement was Garrett's attempt to shelter the property from the legal proceedings against him. In a July 11, 1906, written statement made in response to the sheriff's seizure of his property, Garrett also denied that the Bear Canyon ranch property belonged to him. A copy of this letter is in the Donald Cline Collection, Folder 70.

For Garrett's attempt to void the lease with Brazel in court, see Sterling Rhode to Herman Weisner, undated interview; and *San Antonio Light*, Mar. 5, 1908.

Albert Fall mentioned Garrett's Las Cruces fistfights in his letter to Eugene Manlove Rhodes, El Paso, Texas, Feb. 2, 1910, Box 8, Folder 27, Albert B. Fall Family Papers.

Garrett's letter to George Curry begging for $50 is as quoted in Keleher, *The Fabulous Frontier*, 72–73. Curry mentions the check in his *Autobiography*, 218.

For the specifics of Garrett's negotiations with Miller and Adamson, I have relied on Adamson's testimony in the *Rio Grande Republican*, Mar. 7, 1908; *San Antonio Light*, Mar. 5, 1908; and John Milton Scanland, *Life of Pat F. Garrett and the Taming of the Border Outlaw* (1908; reprint ed., Palmer Lake, Colo.: Filter Press, 1971), 4–5.

Garrett's unusual Burgess shotgun is the subject of Mark Wright's "The Garrett/Ross Folding Burgess 12 Gauge: The Story of a Remarkable Firearm and the Two Lawmen Who Used It," *The Gun Report* (Nov. 1988): 14–17.

The arrival of Garrett and Adamson at the Walter livery stable was vividly recalled by Willis Walter in his interview with Leon Metz, Jan. 30, 1968, Lordsburg, New Mexico.

Deputy Sheriff Lucero's recollections about Garrett's death and his role in the investigation, as well as Dr. William C. Field's memories of the murder scene and his autopsy on Garrett's body, were published in *The New Mexico Sentinel*, Santa Fe, Apr. 23, 1939.

Garrett's funeral was reported in the *Rio Grande Republican*, Mar. 7, 1908; the *Las Cruces Citizen*, Mar. 7, 1908; and the *Albuquerque Morning Journal*, Mar. 10, 1908.

For Jim Miller, see J. J. Bush to Gov. Curry, El Paso, Texas, Mar. 21, 1908, Territorial Archives of New Mexico, roll 165, frames 951–952; Glenn Shirley, *Shotgun for Hire: The Story of "Deacon" Jim Miller, Killer of Pat Garrett* (Norman: University of Oklahoma Press, 1970); *The Evening News*, Ada, Oklahoma, Apr. 22, 1909; and *Galveston Daily News*, Apr. 20, 1909.

The anonymous letter accusing Print Rhode of being an accessory to the murder of Garrett is found in Territorial Archives of New Mexico, roll 54, frames 201–202. Poe Garrett also received an anonymous letter warning him that he was next in line to be killed. The writer stated that "Hanging without trial is what Brazel should get." The letter was signed "One Who Knows." See Scanland, *Life of Pat F. Garrett and the Taming of the Border Outlaw*, 11.

Cox paid off a $3,000 promissory note for Garrett on May 29, 1906. The note is illustrated in *The Estate of Richard C. Marohn, M.D.*, 143. Two letters from Cox to

Polinaria Garrett are in the Patrick F. Garrett Family Papers, and a letter from Cox
to Pat Garrett is in the Robert G. McCubbin Collection. This latter is reproduced in
McCubbin, "The 100th Anniversary of Pat Garrett's Death," *True West* 55 (Jan.–Feb.
2008): 38.

For Jeff Ake's opinion of Bill Cox and his role in Garrett's death, see James B.
O'Neil, *They Die But Once: The Story of a Tejano* (New York: Knight Publications, Inc.,
1935), 195.

James M. Hervey wrote an important account of his involvement in the investigation of Garrett's death some years prior to March 1951 and sent it to W. T. Moyers,
a Denver attorney who became obsessed with who killed Garrett. This typed manuscript is in Box 3, Folder 5, Fred M. Mazzulla Collection. Hervey expanded this
account prior to his death in 1953 and it was subsequently published as "The Assassination of Pat Garrett," *True West* (Mar.–Apr. 1961): 16–27, 40–42.

The subpoenas for the telegrams of Brazel, Rhode, and others are in *Territory of
New Mexico vs. Wayne Brazel,* Case #4112, Doña Ana County District Court Records,
Box 13320, NMSRCA.

Captain Fornoff's "discovery" was shared with both Hervey and Governor
Curry. Curry wrote later that, because of Fornoff's findings, he became convinced
that Brazel was "the victim of a conspiracy rather than the killer" (*Autobiography,* 217).
Fornoff made a written report of his investigation, but that report appears to have
been destroyed. Fred Lambert, a member of the Mounted Police under Fornoff, wrote
W. T. Moyers on Apr. 7, 1951, that Fornoff "definitely established that young Brazil
[*sic*] was paid $10,000 to do the job." Lambert may have confused the story somewhat
after forty-three years, but he remembered the main point that Garrett's killing was a
conspiracy. Lambert's letter is in Box 10B, Folder 4D, Fred M. Mazzulla Collection.
For more on the Fornoff report, see Robert N. Mullin, "The Key to the Mystery of
Pat Garrett," *The Branding Iron* (Los Angeles Corral of the Westerners) 92 (June 1969):
1–5.

For newspaper reports of the Brazel verdict, see the *El Paso Times,* May 5, 1909,
and *The Evening News,* Ada, Oklahoma, May 6, 1909. Dr. Field is as quoted in the *New
Mexico Sentinel,* Apr. 23, 1939.

Wayne Brazel's apology to Mrs. Fall is as quoted in Mrs. C. C. Chase interview
typescript, Jan. 13, 1966, Leon C. Metz Papers.

A typescript of the Oliver M. Lee Jr. interview with C. L. Sonnichsen, Sept. 14,
1954, is in Box 93, Folder 404, C. L. Sonnichsen Papers. W. T. Moyers visited Alamogordo, New Mexico, in 1955 and got a very similar story from Oliver Lee Jr. Moyers
understood that after Print Rhode (Moyers uses "Mr. X" for Rhode) shot Garrett in
the back of the head with a Winchester rifle, Brazel fired his pistol into Garrett's body.
See W. T. Moyers dictation, Dec. 1, 1955; and Moyers to Fred M. Mazzulla, Denver,
Colo., Dec. 12, 1961, Box 10B, Folder 4D, Fred M. Mazzulla Collection.

Jim Cox's statement to Herman Weisner is as quoted in a typescript of Weisner's
Mar. 18, 1986, lecture at the Thomas Branigan Memorial Library, Las Cruces, RG-
T186, Rio Grande Historical Collections.

The Albert Fall quote on Garrett's death is from his letter to Eugene Manlove
Rhodes, El Paso, Texas, Feb. 2, 1910, Box 8, Folder 27, Albert B. Fall Family Papers.

James B. Gillett is as quoted in the *Brooklyn Daily Eagle,* Brooklyn, New York, Jan. 3, 1885.

For the lynching of Jim Miller, see the *Evening News,* Ada, Oklahoma, Apr. 19, 20, 22, and 23; and the *Galveston Daily News,* Apr. 20, 1909.

Carl Adamson's trial and conviction for smuggling Chinese nationals was reported in the *Rio Grande Republican,* Dec. 19, 1908; and the *Albuquerque Journal,* Aug. 23, 1911. It has been suggested that Miller and Adamson wanted Garrett's Bear Canyon ranch as a hideout for illegal aliens whom they intended to smuggle into the United States. This is extremely far-fetched. The smuggling business consisted of supplying Chinese nationals in Mexico with bogus U.S. citizenship certificates and then getting them across the border where they could be quickly shuttled to the larger U.S. cities, places where they were more likely to blend in. The smugglers charged $50 for each certificate and $50 to get the individual across the Rio Grande. There was no need of a remote hideout in New Mexico where there were no jobs except punching cattle. See "Chinese Smuggled In," *Galveston Daily News,* Nov. 5, 1907.

Bill Cox's purchase of the Garrett Black Mountain ranch was reported in the *Rio Grande Republican,* Dec. 5, 1908. The comparison of Cox's ranch with Rhode Island is in the *Rio Grande Republican* of Oct. 21, 1910. For more on Cox, see Paxton P. Price, *Mesilla Valley Pioneers, 1823–1912* (Las Cruces: Yucca Tree Press, 1995), 226–227.

Albert Fall's recommendation of Brazel for an appointment to the New Mexico Mounted Police is in the Territorial Archives of New Mexico, roll 165, frame 417. My additional details on Brazel's later life and disappearance are from Robert N. Mullin, "The Strange Story of Wayne Brazel," *Panhandle-Plains Historical Review* 42 (1969): 23–59.

My description of Print Rhode's murder of Henry L. Murphy, his incarceration, and eventual pardon comes from the *Arizona Journal-Miner,* July 9, 10, and 12, 1910; Inquest of H. L. Murphy and A. P. Rhode Petition for Writ, Arizona State Library, Archives and Public Records, Phoenix, Arizona; and Arizona Territorial Prison (Florence) record for A. P. Rhode. Although Print Rhode has been mentioned by other writers as a possible suspect in Garrett's murder, I am the first to present significant evidence identifying him as the killer. See Robert N. Mullin, "Who Killed Pat Garrett—and Why?" *Password* (El Paso County Historical Society) 16 (1971): 46–61.

EPILOGUE

Garrett and Hough's visit to Fort Sumner is recounted in Hough's *The Story of the Outlaw,* 305–312.

Native Texan Stanley Walker's review of Burn's *Saga of Billy the Kid* appeared in the Mar. 7, 1926, issue of the *New York Times.*

The copy of Burn's *Saga* found in Bonnie and Clyde's death car now belongs to the Bienville Depot Museum, Arcadia, Louisiana.

For Copland and his ballet, *Billy the Kid,* see Aaron Copland and Vivian Perlis, *Copland, 1900 through 1942* (New York: St. Martin's, 1984).

For the dispute over the Fort Sumner cemetery, see the *Clovis News-Journal,* July 24, 1938; and the *El Paso Herald-Post,* Feb. 18, 1939.

My information on the restoration and dedication of the old Lincoln County courthouse comes from the *Albuquerque Journal,* June 14, 1937, and July 31, 1939; *El Paso Herald-Post,* Feb. 12, 1938; *The Daily Times-News,* Burlington, North Carolina, Nov. 25, 1938; and *Las Cruces Sun-News,* July 31, 1939.

For a history of the gun that killed Billy the Kid, see Mary'n Rosson, "The Gun That Killed Billy the Kid," *Old West* 14 (Winter 1977): 6–9, 32, 36–37. The Garrett affidavit quoted is reproduced in the above article, 8. The legal struggle between Polinaria Garrett and the Powers estate is chronicled in the *El Paso Herald-Post,* Nov. 10, 1933, and Mar. 7, Oct. 6, and Oct. 8, 1934; and the *Albuquerque Journal,* Jan. 31, and Apr. 25 and 29, 1933. A list of the firearms in the Tom Powers collection, from the estate inventory, is in Box 18, Leon C. Metz Papers.

Polinaria Garrett's death was reported in the *Albuquerque Journal,* Oct. 22, 1936. Her first name was given as Pauline.

For the Garrett family's lawsuit against Howard Hughes, see the *Port Arthur News,* Port Arthur, Texas, Mar. 9, 1947; *Las Vegas Daily Optic,* Mar. 8, 1947; and *Albuquerque Journal,* Mar. 8, 1947. An excellent summary of Billy the Kid films is Paul Andrew Hutton, "Silver Screen Desperado: Billy the Kid in the Movies," *New Mexico Historical Review* 82 (Spring 2007): 149–196.

The Brushy Bill Roberts story was widely covered in the press, but see the *Santa Fe New Mexican,* Nov. 30 and Dec. 1, 1950; and *El Paso Herald-Post,* Nov. 25, 1950. Brushy's death was reported in the *Las Cruces Sun-News,* Dec. 28, 1950. See also C. L. Sonnichsen and William V. Morrison, *Alias Billy the Kid* (Albuquerque: University of New Mexico Press, 1955).

For the Sullivan/Sederwall investigation, see the *New York Times,* June 5, 2003; *Santa Fe New Mexican,* Aug. 2, 2004; *Tucson Weekly,* Apr. 13, 2006; *Houston Chronicle,* Sept. 5, 2007; *Ruidoso News,* Aug. 13, 2008; *Albuquerque Journal,* Aug. 18, 2007, and Aug. 28, 2008; and Jana Bommersbach, "Digging Up Billy," *True West* 50 (Aug./Sept. 2003): 42–45. The investigation also figures in a 2004 History Channel documentary, *Investigating History: Billy the Kid,* and a 2007 French documentary, *Requiem for Billy the Kid,* directed by Anne Feinsilber.

Florencio Chavez is as quoted in Eugene Cunningham, "Fought with Billy the Kid," *Frontier Times* 9 (Mar. 1932): 247.

For the sad condition of Garrett's grave and the removal of his remains to the Masonic cemetery, see the *Las Cruces Sun-News,* Feb. 1, 1948; *Big Spring Daily Herald,* Sept. 12, 1957; and *Las Cruces Sun-News,* Oct. 23, 1957.

Sallie Chisum is as quoted in Burns, *Saga of Billy the Kid,* 18–19.

Resources

ARCHIVAL MATERIAL

Arizona State Library, Archives & Public Records, Phoenix
    Inquest of H. L. Murphy, 1910
    A. P. Rhode Petition for Writ, 1910
    Yavapai County Board of Supervisors, RC 113

The C. L. Sonnichsen Special Collections Department, University of Texas at El Paso Library
    Leon C. Metz Papers, MS 157
    C. L. Sonnichsen Papers, MS 141

Center for American History, University of Texas at Austin
    E. A. Brininstool Collection

Center for Southwest Research, University of New Mexico, Albuquerque
    Ealy Family Papers, MSS 443 BC
    John William Poe Papers, MSS 95 SC
    Marshall Bond Papers, MSS 118 SC
    Marshall Bond Photograph Collection, PICT 000-118

Cobb Memorial Archives, Valley, Alabama
    Patrick Floyd Jarvis Probate File

Denver Public Library, Denver, Colorado
    Billy the Kid Clippings File
    Pat Garrett Clippings File
    Charles Jesse Jones Letter, Apr. 1, 1917, MSS-M414

Donnelly Library, Special Collections, New Mexico Highlands University, Las Vegas
    "The Original Las Vegas, 1835–1935," by Lynn I. Perrigo, 2 vols. (typescript),
        1975

The Fray Angélico Chávez History Library, Palace of the Governors, Santa Fe
    William H. Bonney Collection, AC 017-P
    Lincoln County Collection, AC 134
    Charles Siringo Papers, AC 212
    Marta Weigle Collection, AC 361

Haley Memorial Library and History Center, Midland, Texas
    J. Evetts Haley interview with James East, Sept. 27, 1927, J. Evetts Haley
        Collection
    New Mexico Biographical Notes, Robert N. Mullin Collection

*L. Tom Perry Special Collections Library, Harold B. Lee Library, Brigham Young University,
Provo, Utah*
    Eve Ball Papers, MSS 3096

Lincoln County Clerk's Office, Carrizozo, New Mexico
    Lincoln County Records
    James W. Bell Probate File
    James Carlyle Probate File
    Robert Olinger Probate File

Lincoln Heritage Trust, Lincoln, New Mexico
    Coroner's Jury Verdict, Deaths of Robert Olinger and J. W. Bell

National Archives and Records Administration, Washington, D.C.
    Reports of Special Operative Azariah F. Wild, Daily Reports of U.S. Secret Ser-
        vice Agents, 1875–1936, Records of the United States Secret Service, RG 87,
        Microfilm T915, roll 308

New Mexico State Records Center and Archives, Santa Fe
    Billy the Kid History File
    Buckner Collection of Elizabeth Garrett Materials, 1893–1992, Coll. #1992-025
    Donald Cline Collection
    Lincoln County War History File #20
    Marriage Records, 1857–1946, La Yglesia de San Jose (St. Joseph), Anton Chico,
        New Mexico, Archives of the Archdiocese of Santa Fe, Microfilm Roll 61-A
    Frank W. Parker Papers

Territorial Archives of New Mexico (microfilm)

Territorial Auditor Collection, #1960-030

Territory of New Mexico vs. Robert Casey, et al., Case #751, New Mexico Supreme Court Records.

Territory of New Mexico vs. Wayne Brazel, Case #4112, Doña Ana County District Court Records, Box 13320

Pinal County Historical Museum, Florence, Arizona

Arizona Territorial Prison record for A. P. Rhode, #3585

Rio Grande Historical Collections, New Mexico State University Archives, Las Cruces

Louis B. Bentley Papers, Ms 14

Albert Bacon Fall Collection, Ms 8

Patrick F. Garrett Family Papers, Ms 282

Herman B. Weisner Papers, Ms 249

Stephen H. Hart Library, Colorado Historical Society, Denver

Oliver E. Aultman Collection

Dawson Scrapbooks

Fred M. Mazzulla Collection, #1881

University of Arizona Library Special Collections, Tucson

Maurice G. Fulton Collection

Ealy Papers

PRIVATE COLLECTIONS

Robert G. McCubbin, Santa Fe, New Mexico

Marc Simmons, Cerrillos, New Mexico

Robert M. Utley, Georgetown, Texas

PUBLISHED MATERIAL

Books and Articles

Alexander, Bob. *Desert Desperadoes: The Banditti of Southwestern New Mexico*. Silver City, N.Mex.: Gila Books, 2006.

———. *Sheriff Harvey Whitehill: Silver City Stalwart*. Silver City, N.Mex.: High-Lonesome Books, 2005.

Anaya, A. P. "Paco." *I Buried Billy*. Edited by James H. Earle. College Station, Tex.: Creative Publishing Company, 1991.

Anderson, George B., ed. *History of New Mexico, Its Resources and People*. Los Angeles: Pacific States Publishing Co., 1907.

An Illustrated History of New Mexico . . . . Chicago: Lewis Publishing Co., 1895.

Ball, Eve. *Ma'am Jones of the Pecos.* Tucson: University of Arizona Press, 1969.

Ball, Larry D. *Desert Lawmen: The High Sheriffs of New Mexico and Arizona, 1846–1912.* Albuquerque: University of New Mexico Press, 1992.

———. "Lawman in Disgrace: Sheriff Charles C. Perry of Chaves County, New Mexico." *New Mexico Historical Review* 61 (Apr. 1986): 125–136.

———. *The United States Marshals of New Mexico and Arizona Territories, 1846–1912.* Albuquerque: University of New Mexico Press, 1978.

Barker, Allen. "I Refound Stinking Springs." *True West* 36 (Feb. 1989): 14–19.

Barron, R. M., ed. *Court of Inquiry, Lieutenant Colonel N. A. M. Dudley, Fort Stanton, New Mexico, May-June-July 1879.* Edina, Minn.: Beaver's Pond Press, Inc., 2003.

Beckett, Patrick H., ed. *Las Cruces, New Mexico, 1881: As Seen by Her Newspapers.* Las Cruces: COAS Publishing and Research, 2003.

Bell, Bob Boze. *The Illustrated Life and Times of Billy the Kid.* Revised and expanded second edition. Phoenix, Ariz.: Tri Star–Boze Publications, 1996.

Bidal, Lillian H. *Pisacah: A Place of Plenty.* El Paso, Tex.: Robert E. and Evelyn McKee Foundation, 1995.

Billington, Monroe Lee. *New Mexico's Buffalo Soldiers, 1866–1900.* Niwot: University Press of Colorado, 1991.

Billy the Kid: Las Vegas Newspaper Accounts of His Career. Waco, Tex.: W. M. Morrison Books,1958.

Blazer, Almer. "The Fight at Blazer's Mill, in New Mexico." *Frontier Times* 16 (August 1939): 461–466.

Blazer, Paul A. "The Fight at Blazer's Mill: A Chapter in the Lincoln County War." *Arizona and the West* 6 (Autumn 1964): 203–210.

Bogener, Stephen. *Ditches Across the Desert: Irrigation in the Lower Pecos Valley.* Lubbock: Texas Tech University Press, 2003.

Bommersbach, Jana. "Digging Up Billy." *True West* 50 (Aug./Sept. 2003): 42–45.

Braddock, James E. "Relics from Pat Garrett's Ranch." *Relics* 2 (Spring 1969): 16–17.

Branch, Louis Leon. *"Los Bilitos": The Story of "Billy the Kid" and His Gang.* New York: Carlton Press, Inc., 1980.

Buffington, Ann. "Out of the Shadows: Women of Lincoln County." *True West* 47 (July 2000): 12–22.

Burns, Walter Noble. *The Saga of Billy the Kid.* Garden City, N.Y.: Doubleday, Page & Co., 1926.

Callon, Milton W. *Las Vegas, New Mexico: The Town That Wouldn't Gamble.* Las Vegas, N.Mex.: Las Vegas Publishing Co., 1962.

Campa, Arthur L. *Hispanic Culture in the Southwest.* Norman: University of Oklahoma Press, 1979.

Carter, A. G. "Neighborhood Talk About Pat Garrett. As Told to C. L. Sonnichsen." *Old West* 7 (Fall 1970): 20–22, 62–64.

Carter, Jack. "Some Facts About Wayne Brazel—From Old-Timers Who Knew Him." *Frontier Times* 46 (June–July 1972): 10–13, 40.

Casey, Robert J. *The Texas Border and Some Borderliners*. Indianapolis: The Bobbs-Merrill Company, Inc., 1950.

Chamberlain, Kathleen P. "In the Shadow of Billy the Kid: Susan McSween and the Lincoln County War." *Montana the Magazine of Western History* 55 (Winter 2005): 36–53.

Cline, Don. *Alias Billy the Kid: The Man Behind the Legend*. Santa Fe: Sunstone Press, 1986.

———. *Antrim & Billy*. College Station, Tex.: Creative Publishing Company, 1990.

———. "Pat Garrett's Tragic Lawsuit." *Old West* 25 (Summer 1989): 18–23.

———. "Tom Pickett: Friend of Billy the Kid." *True West* 44 (July 1997): 40–49.

Cobos, Rubén. *A Dictionary of New Mexico & Southern Colorado Spanish*. Santa Fe: Museum of New Mexico Press, 2003.

Coe, George W. *Frontier Fighter: The Autobiography of George W. Coe Who Fought and Rode with Billy the Kid*. Edited by Doyce B. Nunis Jr. Chicago: The Lakeside Press, 1984.

Collinson, Frank. *Life in the Saddle*. Edited by Mary Whatley Clarke. Norman: University of Oklahoma Press, 1963.

Copland, Aaron, and Vivian Perlis. *Copland, 1900 through 1942*. New York: St. Martin's, 1984.

Cotten, Lee. "True Tales of Billy the Kid: The Kid in Arizona, 1875–1877." *The Kid* (Mar. 1990): 7–15; (July 1990): 10–19.

Cramer, T. Dudley. *The Pecos Ranchers in the Lincoln County War*. Oakland, Calif.: The Branding Iron Press, 1996.

Cummings, Billy Charles Patrick. *Frontier Parish: Recovered Catholic History of Lincoln County, 1860–1884*. Lincoln, N.Mex.: Lincoln County Historical Society, 1995.

Cunningham, Eugene. "Fought with Billy the Kid." *Frontier Times* 9 (Mar. 1932): 242–247.

Curry, George. *George Curry, 1861–1947: An Autobiography*. Edited by H. B. Hening. Albuquerque: University of New Mexico Press, 1958.

DeMattos, Jack. *Garrett and Roosevelt*. College Station, Tex.: Creative Publishing Company, 1988.

———. "The Search for Billy the Kid's Roots." *Real West* 21 (Nov. 1978): 12–19, 39.

———. "The Search for Billy the Kid's Roots—Is Over!" *Real West* 23 (Jan. 1980): 26–28, 59–60.

Dykes, J. C. *Billy the Kid: The Bibliography of a Legend.* Albuquerque: University of New Mexico Press, 1952.

Ealy, Ruth R. *Water in a Thirsty Land.* Privately published, 1955.

Earle, James H., ed. *The Capture of Billy the Kid.* College Station, Tex.: Creative Publishing Company, 1988.

Edwards, Harold L. "Barney Mason: In the Shadow of Pat Garrett and Billy the Kid." *Old West* 26 (Summer 1990): 14–19.

———. "From Prince to Knave to an Early Grave: The Story of Charlie Bowdre." *National Association for Outlaw and Lawman History Quarterly* 19 (July–Sept. 1995): 2–8.

———. *Goodbye Billy the Kid.* College Station, Tex.: Creative Publishing Company, 1995.

———. "Pat Garrett and the Las Cruces Bank Robbery." *True West* 45 (Feb. 1998): 8–13.

The Estate of Richard C. Marohn, M.D. (auction catalog). San Francisco: Butterfield & Butterfield, 1996.

Fable, Edmund. *Billy the Kid, the New Mexican Outlaw; or the Bold Bandit of the West.* Denver, Colo.: The Denver Publishing Co., 1881.

Fleming, Elvis E. *Captain Joseph C. Lea: From Confederate Guerrilla to New Mexico Patriarch.* Las Cruces: Yucca Tree Press, 2002.

———. *J. B. "Billy" Mathews: Biography of a Lincoln County Deputy.* Las Cruces: Yucca Tree Press, 1999.

Fulton, Maurice G. "Apocrypha of Billy the Kid." In *Folk-Say: A Regional Miscellany.* Edited by B. A. Botkin. Norman: University of Oklahoma Press, 1930.

———. "Billy the Kid in Life and Books." *The New Mexico Folklore Record* 4 (1949–1950): 1–6.

———. *Maurice Garland Fulton's History of the Lincoln County War.* Edited by Robert N. Mullin. Tucson: University of Arizona Press, 1968.

García, Elbert A. *Billy the Kid's Kid: The Hispanic Connection.* Santa Rosa, N.Mex.: Los Products Press, 1999.

Garrett, Pat F. *The Authentic Life of Billy, the Kid, The Noted Desperado of the Southwest, Whose Deeds of Daring and Blood Made His Name a Terror in New Mexico, Arizona and Northern Mexico.* Santa Fe: New Mexican Printing and Publishing Co., 1882.

———. *The Authentic Life of Billy, the Kid.* Introduction by Jarvis P. Garrett. Albuquerque: Horn & Wallace, 1964.

Gibson, A. M. *The Life and Death of Colonel Albert Jennings Fountain.* Norman: University of Oklahoma Press, 1965.

Gilbert, Miles, Leo Remiger, and Sharon Cunningham. *Encyclopedia of Buffalo Hunters and Skinners.* Vol. 1. Union City, Tenn.: Pioneer Press, 2003.

Gonzales, Samuel Leo. *The Days of Old.* Privately printed, 1993.

Gottschalk, Marcus Charles. *Pioneer Merchants of the Las Vegas Plaza.* Las Vegas, N.Mex.: Privately printed, 2000.

Grey, F. W. *Seeking Fortune in America*. London: Smith, Elder & Co., 1912.

Grove, Pearce S., Becky J. Barnett, and Sandra J. Hansen. *New Mexico Newspapers: A Comprehensive Guide to Bibliographical Entries and Locations*. Albuquerque: University of New Mexico Press, 1975.

Guyer, James S. *Pioneer Life in West Texas*. Brownwood, Tex.: James S. Guyer, 1938.

Haley, J. Evetts. "Jim East—Trail Hand and Cowboy." *Panhandle-Plains Historical Review* 4 (1931): 39–61.

Hall, Ruth K. *A Place of Her Own: The Story of Elizabeth Garrett*. Santa Fe: Sunstone Press, 1983.

Harkey, Dee. *Mean as Hell*. Albuquerque: University of New Mexico Press, 1948.

Hervey, James Madison. "The Assassination of Pat Garrett." *True West* (Mar.–Apr. 1961): 16–27, 40–42.

Hoig, Stan. *Cowtown Wichita and the Wild, Wicked West*. Albuquerque: University of New Mexico Press, 2007.

Horn, Calvin. *New Mexico's Troubled Years: The Story of the Early Territorial Governors*. Albuquerque: Horn & Wallace, 1963.

Hough, Emerson. "The American Six-Shooter: What the Real Six-Shooter Is— What It Will Do and Will Not Do." *The Outing Magazine* (Jan. 1909): 502–510.

———. "Billy the Kid: The True Story of a Western 'Bad Man.'" *Everybody's Magazine* 5 (Sept. 1901): 303–310.

———. *The Story of the Outlaw: A Study of the Western Desperado*. New York: The Outing Publishing Company, 1907.

Hoyt, Henry F. *A Frontier Doctor*. Edited by Doyce B. Nunis Jr. Chicago: The Lakeside Press, 1979.

Hunt, Frazier. *The Tragic Days of Billy the Kid*. New York: Hastings House, 1956.

Hunter, J. Marvin. *The Trail Drivers of Texas*. 1925. Reprint, Austin: University of Texas Press, 1992.

Hutchinson, W. H. *A Bar Cross Man: The Life and Personal Writings of Eugene Manlove Rhodes*. Norman: University of Oklahoma Press, 1956.

———. *Another Verdict for Oliver Lee*. Clarendon, Tex.: Clarendon Press, 1965.

———, ed. *The Rhodes Reader: Stories of Virgins, Villains, and Varmints*. Norman: University of Oklahoma Press, 1957.

Hutton, Paul Andrew. "Silver Screen Desperado: Billy the Kid in the Movies." *New Mexico Historical Review* 82 (Spring 2007): 149–196.

Hyde, Albert E. "The Old Regime in the Southwest, The Reign of the Revolver in New Mexico." *The Century Magazine* 63 (Mar. 1902): 690–701.

Irwin, Helen. "When Billy the Kid Was Brought to Trial." *Frontier Times* 6 (Mar. 1929): 214–215.

Jacobsen, Joel. *Such Men as Billy the Kid: The Lincoln County War Reconsidered.* Lincoln: University of Nebraska Press, 1994.

Jameson, W. C. "The Controversial Inquests and Burial of Billy the Kid." *Wild West* 19 (Feb. 2007): 42–49.

Kajencki, Francis Casimir. *Poles in the 19th Century Southwest.* El Paso, Tex.: Southwest Polonia Press, 1990.

Kaye, E. Donald. *Nathan Augustus Monroe Dudley, 1825–1910: Rogue, Hero, or Both?* Parker, Colo.: Outskirts Press, 2007.

Keleher, William A. *The Fabulous Frontier: Twelve New Mexico Items.* Santa Fe: The Rydal Press, 1945.

———. *Violence in Lincoln County, 1869–1881.* Albuquerque: University of New Mexico Press, 1957.

King, Frank M. *Mavericks: The Salty Comments of an Old-Time Cowpuncher.* Pasadena, Calif.: Trail's End Publishing Co., 1947.

———. *Wranglin' the Past: The Reminiscences of Frank M. King.* Pasadena, Calif.: Trail's End Publishing Co., 1946.

Klasner, Lily. *My Girlhood Among Outlaws.* Edited by Eve Ball. Tucson: University of Arizona Press, 1972.

Koop, Waldo E. "Billy the Kid: The Trail of a Kansas Legend." *The Trail Guide* 9 (Sept. 1964): 1–19.

Lake, Stuart N. *Wyatt Earp, Frontier Marshal.* Boston: Houghton Mifflin Co., 1931.

Lavash, Donald R. *Sheriff William Brady: Tragic Hero of the Lincoln County War.* Santa Fe: Sunstone Press, 1986.

———. *Wilson & The Kid.* College Station, Tex.: Creative Publishing Company, 1990.

LeNoir, Phil. *Rhymes of the Wild & Wooly.* Santa Fe: privately printed, 1920.

Lockwood, Frank C. *Pioneer Portraits, Selected Vignettes.* Tucson: University of Arizona Press, 1968.

McCright, Grady E., and James H. Powell. *Jessie Evans: Lincoln County Badman.* College Station, Tex.: Creative Publishing Company, 1983.

———. *Disorder in Lincoln County: Frank Warner Angel's Reports.* Las Cruces: Rio Grande Historical Collections, 1981.

McCubbin, Robert G. "The Many Faces of Billy the Kid." *True West* 54 (May 2007): 60–63.

———. "The 100th Anniversary of Pat Garrett's Death." *True West* 55 (Jan.–Feb. 2008): 32–41.

McMurtry, Larry. "Our Favorite Bandit." *The New York Review of Books,* Oct. 25, 2007, 28–29.

Meadows, John P. *Pat Garrett and Billy the Kid as I Knew Them: Reminiscences of John P. Meadows*. Edited by John P. Wilson. Albuquerque: University of New Mexico Press, 2004.

Metz, Leon C. "Billy the Kid and Pat Garrett." *True West* 44 (July 1997): 12–17.

———. "My Search for Pat Garrett and Billy the Kid." *True West* 30 (Aug. 1983): 35–38, 97.

———. "Pat Garrett, El Paso Customs Collector." *Arizona and the West* 11 (Winter 1969): 327–340.

———. *Pat Garrett: The Story of a Western Lawman*. Norman: University of Oklahoma Press, 1974.

———. "Researching the Conspiracy That Led to the Last Days of Pat Garrett." *True West* 30 (Sept. 1983): 12–15.

———. "The Truth and Tall Tales of Pat Garrett." *New Mexico Magazine* 86 (Feb. 2008): 52–55.

Miller, Benjamin S. *Ranch Life in Southern Kansas and the Indian Territory as Told by a Novice*. New York: Fless & Ridge Printing Company, 1896.

Mullin, Robert N. "The Key to the Mystery of Pat Garrett." *The Branding Iron* (Los Angeles Corral of the Westerners) 92 (June 1969): 1–5.

———. "Pat Garrett—Two Forgotten Killings." *Password* (El Paso County Historical Society) 10 (Summer 1965): 57–62.

———. "The Strange Story of Wayne Brazel." *Panhandle-Plains Historical Review* 42 (1969): 23–59.

———. "Who Killed Pat Garrett—and Why?" *Password* (El Paso County Historical Society) 16 (1971): 46–61.

Murphy, Lawrence R. *Lucien Bonaparte Maxwell: Napoleon of the Southwest*. Norman: University of Oklahoma Press, 1983.

Nolan, Frederick W., ed. *The Billy the Kid Reader*. Norman: University of Oklahoma Press, 2007.

———. "Dirty Dave: The Life and Times of Billy the Kid's Worst Friend." *The Kid* (Dec. 1989): 7–13.

———. "First Blood: Another Look at the Killing of 'Windy Cahill.'" *The Outlaw Gazette* 13 (Nov. 2000): 2–4.

———. "The Horse Thief War." *Old West* (Summer 1994): 16–23.

———. "The Hunting of Billy the Kid." *Wild West* (June 2003): 38–44.

———. *The Life & Death of John Henry Tunstall*. Albuquerque: University of New Mexico Press, 1965.

———. *The Lincoln County War: A Documentary History*. Norman: University of Oklahoma Press, 1992.

————. "The Private Life of Billy the Kid." *True West* 47 (July 2000): 33–39.

————. "The Saga of the Kid Butcher Knife." *The Outlaw Gazette* (Billy the Kid Outlaw Gang, Inc.) 10 (Nov. 1997): 6–7.

————. "The Search for Alexander McSween." *New Mexico Historical Review* 62 (July 1987): 287–301.

————. "She Taught the Kid a Lesson." *True West* 53 (May 2006): 51–53.

————. *Tascosa: Its Life and Gaudy Times.* Lubbock: Texas Tech University Press, 2007.

————. *The West of Billy the Kid.* Norman: University of Oklahoma Press, 1998.

————. "Who Killed Morris Bernstein? Murder and Mystery at Blazer's Mill." *Lincoln County Historical Society Newsletter* 21 (June 1997): 4–5, 6.

O'Connor, Richard. *Pat Garrett: A Biography of the Famous Marshal and the Killer of Billy the Kid.* New York: Doubleday & Co., 1960.

O'Neil, James B. *They Die But Once: The Story of a Tejano.* New York: Knight Publications, Inc., 1935.

Otero, Miguel Antonio. *My Life on the Frontier, 1864–1882.* 1935. Reprint, Albuquerque: University of New Mexico Press, 1987.

————. *My Nine Years as Governor of the Territory of New Mexico, 1897–1906.* Albuquerque: University of New Mexico Press, 1940.

————. *The Real Billy the Kid, With New Light on the Lincoln County War.* New York: Rufus Rockwell Wilson, Inc., 1936.

O'Toole, Fintan. "The Many Stories of Billy the Kid." *The New Yorker,* Dec. 28, 1998, and Jan. 4, 1999, 86–97.

Owen, Gordon R. *The Two Alberts: Fountain and Fall.* Las Cruces: Yucca Tree Press, 1996.

Page, Jack. "Was Billy the Kid a Superhero—or a Superscoundrel?" *Smithsonian* (Feb. 1991): 137–148.

Pearce, T. M. *New Mexico Place Names: A Geographical Dictionary.* Albuquerque: University of New Mexico Press, 1965.

Perrigo, Lynn. *Gateway to Glorieta: A History of Las Vegas, New Mexico.* Boulder, Colo.: Pruett Publishing Co., 1982.

Poe, John W. *The Death of Billy the Kid.* Boston: Houghton Mifflin Co., 1933.

Poe, Sophie A. *Buckboard Days.* Edited by Eugene Cunningham. 1936. Reprint, Albuquerque: University of New Mexico Press, 1981.

Potter, Colonel Jack. "Post-Mortem on Billy the Kid." *Ranch Romances* 73 (First May Number, 1937): 131–133.

Powell, William H. *Powell's Records of Living Officers of the United States Army.* Philadelphia: L. R. Hamersly & Co., 1890.

Price, Paxton P. *Mesilla Valley Pioneers, 1823–1912.* Las Cruces: Yucca Tree Press, 1995.

Rasch, Philip J. *Gunsmoke in Lincoln County.* Edited by Robert K. DeArment. Laramie, Wyo.: National Association for Outlaw and Lawman History, 1997.

————. *Trailing Billy the Kid*. Edited by Robert K. DeArment. Laramie, Wyo.: National Association for Outlaw and Lawman History, 1995.

————. *Warriors of Lincoln County*. Edited by Robert K. DeArment. Laramie, Wyo.: National Association for Outlaw and Lawman History, 1998.

Rathburn, Daniel C. B., and David V. Alexander. *New Mexico Frontier Military Place Names*. Las Cruces: Yucca Tree Press, 2003.

Recko, Corey. *Murder on the White Sands: The Disappearance of Albert and Henry Fountain*. Denton: University of North Texas Press, 2007.

Remiger, Leo, Miles Gilbert, and Sharon Cunningham. *Encyclopedia of Buffalo Hunters and Skinners*. Vol. 2. Union City, Tenn.: Pioneer Press, 2006.

Rhodes, Eugene Manlove. "In Defense of Pat Garrett." *Sunset* 59 (Sept. 1927): 26–27, 85–91.

Rickards, Colin. *How Pat Garrett Died*. Santa Fe: Palomino Press, 1970.

Ritch, W. G. *The Legislative Blue Book of the Territory of New Mexico*. Santa Fe: Charles W. Greene, 1882.

Robinson, Charles M. "From Billy the Kid to Bank President: John William Poe." *True West* (Sept. 1992): 32–41.

Robinson, Sherry. *Apache Voices: Their Stories of Survival as Told to Eve Ball*. Albuquerque: University of New Mexico Press, 2000.

Ross, Pete. "Some Prominent New Mexicans May Have Been Accessories to the Murder of Pat Garrett." *Wild West* 14 (Dec. 2001): 52–56.

Rosson, Mary'n. "The Gun That Killed Billy the Kid." *Old West* 14 (Winter 1977): 6–9, 32, 36–37.

Russell, Randy. *Billy the Kid: The Story—The Trial*. Lincoln, N.Mex.: The Crystal Press, 1994.

Rynning, Captain Thomas H. *Gun Notches: The Life Story of a Cowboy-Soldier. As Told to Al Cohn and Joe Chisolm*. New York: Frederick A. Stokes Company, 1931.

Sánchez, Lynda A. "Romancing the Kid." *New Mexico Magazine* (Jan. 2002): 68, 72.

————. "They Loved Billy the Kid, To Them He Was 'Billito.'" *True West* 31 (Jan. 1984): 12–16.

Scanland, John Milton. *Life of Pat F. Garrett and the Taming of the Border Outlaw*. 1908. Reprint, Palmer Lake, Colo.: Filter Press, 1971.

Shinkle, James D. *Fifty Years of Roswell History, 1867–1917*. Roswell, N.Mex.: Hall-Poorbaugh Press, 1964.

————. *Fort Sumner and the Bosque Redondo Indian Reservation*. Roswell, N.Mex.: Hall-Poorbaugh Press, 1965.

————. *Reminiscences of Roswell Pioneers*. Roswell, N.Mex.: Hall-Poorbaugh Press, 1965.

Shipman, Mrs. O. L. *Letters Past and Present to My Nephews and Nieces*. Privately printed, 1946.

Shirley, Glenn. *Shotgun for Hire: The Story of "Deacon" Jim Miller, Killer of Pat Garrett.* Norman: University of Oklahoma Press, 1970.

Siringo, Charles A. *History of "Billy the Kid."* Santa Fe: Charles A. Siringo, 1920.

———. *A Texas Cow Boy, or, Fifteen Years on the Hurricane Deck of a Spanish Pony.* Chicago: M. Umbdenstock & Co., 1885.

Sligh, J. E. "Billy-The-Kid." *The Overland Monthly* 52 (July 1908): 48–51.

———. "The Lincoln County War: A Sequel to the Story of 'Billy the Kid.'" *The Overland Monthly* 52 (Aug. 1908): 168–174.

Simmons, Marc. *Albuquerque: An Interpretive History.* Albuquerque: University of New Mexico Press, 1982.

———. *Spanish Pathways: Readings in the History of Hispanic New Mexico.* Albuquerque: University of New Mexico Press, 2001.

———. *Stalking Billy the Kid: Brief Sketches of a Short Life.* Santa Fe: Sunstone Press, 2006.

Smith, Timothy B. "Why Lew Was Late." *Civil War Times* 46 (Jan. 2008): 30–37.

Sonnichsen, C. L. *Tularosa: Last of the Frontier West.* New York: The Devin-Adair Company, 1960.

———, and William V. Morrison. *Alias Billy the Kid.* Albuquerque: University of New Mexico Press, 1955.

Stratton, David H. *Tempest Over Teapot Dome: The Story of Albert B. Fall.* Norman: University of Oklahoma Press, 1998.

Stratton, Porter A. *The Territorial Press of New Mexico.* Albuquerque: University of New Mexico Press, 1969.

Strickland, Rex W., ed. "The Recollections of W. S. Glenn, Buffalo Hunter." *Panhandle-Plains Historical Review* 22 (1949): 15–64.

Strykowski, Jason. "An Unholy Bargain in a Cursed Place: Lew Wallace, William Bonney, and New Mexico Territory." *New Mexico Historical Review* 82 (Spring 2007): 237–258.

Tanner, Karen Holliday, and John D. Tanner Jr. *New Mexico Territorial Penitentiary Inmates (1884–1912), Directory of Inmates.* Fallbrook, Calif.: Runnin' Iron, 2006.

Thorp, N. Howard, and Neil M. Clark. *Pardner of the Wind.* Caldwell, Idaho: The Caxton Printers, 1945.

Tórrez, Robert J. *Myth of the Hanging Tree: Stories of Crime and Punishment in Territorial New Mexico.* Albuquerque: University of New Mexico Press, 2008.

Traylor, Leslie. "Facts Regarding the Escape of Billy the Kid." *Frontier Times* 13 (July 1936): 506–513.

Turk, David S. "Billy the Kid and the U.S. Marshals Service." *Wild West* 19 (Feb. 2007): 34–39.

Twitchell, Ralph Emerson. *The Leading Facts of New Mexican History.* 2 vols. Cedar Rapids, Iowa: The Torch Press, 1912.

Utley, Robert M. *Billy the Kid: A Short and Violent Life.* Lincoln: University of Nebraska Press, 1989.

———. *High Noon in Lincoln County: Violence on the Western Frontier.* Albuquerque: University of New Mexico Press, 1987.

Wallace, Lew. *An Autobiography.* New York: Harper & Brothers, 1906.

Wallis, Michael. *Billy the Kid: The Endless Ride.* New York: W. W. Norton, 2007.

Warrin, Donald, and Geoffrey L. Gomes. *Land as Far as the Eye Can See: Portuguese in the Old West.* Spokane, Wash.: The Arthur H. Clark Co., 2001).

Weddle, Jerry. *Antrim Is My Stepfather's Name: The Boyhood of Billy the Kid.* Tucson: Arizona Historical Society, 1993.

———. "The Kid at Old Fort Sumner." *The Outlaw Gazette* 5 (Dec. 1992): 8–9.

Weisner, Herman B. "Garrett's Death—Conspiracy or Doublecross?" *True West* 27 (Dec. 1979): 6–9, 50–52.

White, James W. *The History of Lincoln County Post Offices.* Farmington, N.Mex.: James W. White, 2007).

White, Rose P. "Full Many a Flower . . ." *The New Mexico Folklore Record* 4 (1949–1950): 15–16.

Williams, O. W. *Pioneer Surveyor–Frontier Lawyer: The Personal Narrative of O. W. Williams, 1877–1902.* Edited by S. D. Myers. El Paso: Texas Western Press, 1968.

Wilson, H. T. *Historical Sketch of Las Vegas, New Mexico.* Chicago: Historical World Publishing Co., 1880.

Wilson, John P. "Building His Own Legend: Billy the Kid and the Media." *New Mexico Historical Review* 82 (Spring 2007): 221–235.

———. *Merchants, Guns & Money: The Story of Lincoln County and Its Wars.* Santa Fe: Museum of New Mexico Press, 1987.

Wilson, R. L. *The Peacemakers: Arms and Adventure in the American West.* New York: Random House, 1992.

Wood, L. Curtis. *Dynamics of Faith: Wichita, 1870–1897.* Wichita: Wichita State University, 1969.

Wright, Mark. "The Garrett/Ross Folding Burgess 12 Gauge: The Story of a Remarkable Firearm and the Two Lawmen Who Used It." *The Gun Report* (November 1988): 14–17.

Wurlitzer, Rudolph. *Pat Garrett and Billy the Kid.* New York: Signet, 1973.

Newspapers

Alamogordo News (NM)

Albuquerque Morning Democrat

The Albuquerque Review

The Albuquerque Tribune

The Alton Telegraph (IL)

Atlanta Constitution

Amarillo News and Globe

Arizona Weekly Star (Tucson)

Big Spring Daily Herald (TX)

Boston Morning Journal

Brooklyn Daily Eagle (NY)

The Bucks County Gazette (Bristol, PA)

Capitan News (NM)

The Carlsbad Argus (NM)

Chester Daily Times (Chester, PA)

Chicago Daily Tribune

Cimarron News and Press (NM)

Daily Gazette and Bulletin
   (Williamsport, PA)

Daily New Mexican (Santa Fe)

The Daily Review (Decatur, IL)

The Daily Times-News (Burlington,
   NC)

Davenport Republican (IA)

The Deming Headlight (NM)

Denver Post

El Paso Herald-Post

El Paso Times

The Evening News (Ada, OK)

Galveston Daily News

The Globe (Atchison, KS)

Golden Era (White Oaks and
   Lincoln, NM)

Grant County Herald (Silver City)

The Helena Independent (MT)

Idaho Daily Statesman (Boise)

The Illustrated Police News, Law Courts
   and Weekly Record (Boston)

The Indiana Progress (PA)

The Janesville Daily Gazette (WI)

Las Cruces Citizen (NM)

Las Cruces Sun-News (NM)

Las Vegas Daily Optic (NM)

Las Vegas Gazette (NM)

Lincoln Independent (NM)

Los Angeles Times

Mesilla Valley Independent (NM)

Newman's Semi-Weekly (Las Cruces)

New Mexico Herald (Las Vegas)

The New Mexico Sentinel (Santa Fe)

New Mexico Tribune (Albuquerque)

New Southwest and Herald (Silver City,
   NM)

New York Times

The Ohio Democrat (New
   Philadelphia, OH)

Otero County Advertiser (Alamogordo,
   NM)

Port Arthur News (TX)

Rio Grande Republican (Las Cruces)

Rocky Mountain Presbyterian (Denver)

Roswell Register (NM)

Roswell Register-Tribune (NM)

Silver City Enterprise (NM)

Standard (Albert Lea, MN)

The Syracuse Morning Standard (NY)

Thirty-Four (Las Cruces, NM)

Tucson Daily Citizen (AZ)

Washington Post

White Oaks Eagle (NM)

Index

Page numbers in *italics* refer to illustrations.